"Albert Jay Nock's, *Mr. Jefferson,* is a superb biographical essay, beautifully written and penetrating in analysis; Mr. Nock understands Jefferson so well that one despairs of going at all beyond him, especially in a brief essay."

Richard Hofstadter
Columbia University

Mr. JEFFERSON

THE WORKS OF
ALBERT JAY NOCK

The Myth of a Guilty Nation.
Jefferson.
A Journey into Rabelais's France.
A Journal of These Days.
Our Enemy, the State.
Free Speech and Plain Language.
Henry George; An Essay.
Memoirs of a Superfluous Man.
On Doing the Right Thing, and Other Essays.
The Book of Journeyman; Essays from the New Freeman.
The Works of Francis Rabelais, 2 vols.
The Theory of Education in the United States.
* A Journal of Forgotten Days.
* Letters from Albert Jay Nock.
* Snoring as a Fine Art and Twelve Other Essays.

Mr. Nock wrote introductions to:

Forty Years of It, by Brand Whitlock.
How Diplomats Make War, by Francis Neilson.
The Selected Works of Artemus Ward, edited by Albert J. Nock.
Man Versus the State, by Herbert Spencer.
Meditations in Wall Street, by Henry Stanley Haskins.
The Freeman Book. (Selections from the Eight Volumes of
    the Freeman, 1920-24, compiled by B.W. Huebsch.)
* Published posthumously.

For information concerning availability of these works in
various editions, reprints, etc., contact:
THE NOCKIAN SOCIETY
30 S. Broadway   Irvington-On-Hudson, New York

Mr. JEFFERSON

by
Albert Jay Nock

HALLBERG PUBLISHING CORPORATION
Nonfiction Book Publishers - ISBN 0-87319
Delavan, Wisconsin 53115

ISBN Number 0-87319-024-6
Library of Congress Catalog Card Number 82-083562
Copyright © 1983 by Hallberg Publishing Corporation
for Preface and Introduction. Copyright to Nock's
text renewed in 1956 by Samuel A. and Francis J. Nock.
Manufactured in the U.S.A. First printing March 1983.
Book Cover designed by Richard L.B. Kack.

CONTENTS

PREFACE

ALBERT JAY NOCK
(1870-1945)

Albert Jay Nock came before the public in one capacity only, as a man of letters. That's the way he wanted it, believing that the rest of him was nobody's business. We do know that he was exposed to the "grand old fortifying classical curriculum" at St. Stephens, where he earned a degree in 1892. He did graduate work in theology, was ordained and served three Episcopal parishes for a decade, entered the world of journalism, and won renown as an editor and belletrist.

His autobiography, *The Memoirs of a Superfluous Man* (1943) was literary and philosophical, setting forth his views of life and society, how he came to hold them, and why. This is the kind of book that gets under a person's skin, performing catalytically to persuade the reader into becoming what he has it in him to be.

Those whom Nock has reached do not form a movement or a clique; such men as the eminent sociologist, Robert Nisbet, out in the South Pacific during World War II where he "practically memorized" the *Memoirs;* or the influential scholar, Russell Kirk, at an army camp reading Nock and corresponding with him. Nock was a frequent guest at the Buckley home during the early '40s, and it is safe to assume that the brilliant William F. Buckley, Jr. and his "National Review" owe something to these contacts. Nock inspires the reader to do his utmost for himself or herself as the only way there is for anyone to do some real service for anyone else. There's only one way to improve society, he used to say; present it with one improved unit --yourself.

Nock laid no claim to originality; he sought to give known, tried and true ideas a new twist, a different slant which breaks through current stereotypes. As a critic he stands in the great succession of men like Rabelais and Artemus Ward, who knew that *"for life to be fruitful, life must be felt as a joy; that it is by the bonds of joy, not of happiness or pleasure, not of duty or responsibility, that the called and chosen spirits are kept together in this world."*

Nock's books were not best sellers, but they keep coming back into print. The weekly journal he edited from 1920 to 1924, the "Freeman," had a small circulation, but scholars continue to draw on it and discerning souls regard it as the high watermark of American journalism. Nock wrote for the educable few who simply want to get at the plain truth of things -- the Remnant. *"You do not know, and will never know, who the Remnant are, nor where they are, nor how many there are, nor what they are doing or will do. Two things you know, and no more; first, that they exist; and second, that they will find you."*

Nock believed that he had uncovered the plain truth of things in several areas, and he set forth his elucidations in impeccable English, serene in his faith that this fully discharged his duty. The assumption back of this faith is that truth has an internal energy of its own enabling it, if we don't stand in its way, to cut its own channels and gain acceptance in minds ready for it. Trying to make truth palatable for minds not ready for it is no service to the people involved, for it clogs whatever thought processes they have.

Truth tampered with is truth lost. The hard truth is what Nock is talking about; truth with the bark on it, truth unsophisticated by even good intentions, undiluted by ulterior considerations. Are there minds ready for this kind of truth? Nock believed that every society has such minds else it would fall apart. Every society is held together by a select few -- men and women who have the force of intellect to discern the rules upon which social life is contingent, and the force of character to exemplify those rules in their own living.

The Remnant grows, and they are finding him. Since Nock's death most of his titles have come back into print, only to be sold out. Two collections of letters were published posthumously, and another *Journal*. Two books have been written about Nock, one about his "Freeman," plus several doctoral theses - not bad for a superfluous man!

And there is a Nockian Society, at 30 South Broadway, Irvington, N.Y. 10533, with members throughout the world. The letterhead reads "No officers, No dues, No meetings." He would have liked that!

Much of Nock's work defies time, which means that he will be discovered anew by each generation. Many will make his acquaintance in the new edition of this book, whose appearance is a happy portent that Nock's best writing will never for long be out of print.

Edmund A. Opitz
The Nockian Society

INTRODUCTION

When a junior in high school, somehow I acquired a secondhand copy of a book published a decade earlier: Albert Jay Nock's *Jefferson*. This copy, just now lying on the table beside my typewriter, bears the embossed stamp of the University Library, Princeton, N.J. Between 1926, when the book was published, and 1935, when Princeton's librarians discarded the copy, some eight professors or students had withdrawn the book and presumably had read it.

This was no very startling influence to be exerted at a famous university by a book intended by its author to work "quietly and persistently undermining the strongholds of superstition." Possibly I was the first reader of that copy to regard the book seriously; certainly there was no marked passages in it. I had on my shelves, before *Jefferson* came into my possession, a copy of *Selected Works of Artemus Ward* (given to me by my grandfather about 1928), with Nock's introduction to that collection; otherwise Nock's name was new to me.

Having read Nock's *Jefferson* promptly and with close attention (about the time when I was reading also Trotsky's *History of the Russian Revolution)*, I was converted into a zealous admirer of Jefferson -- and distinctly not of Lenin. My resulting curiosity about Jefferson and his age, indeed, led me to the life and thought of Jefferson's picturesque adversary and kinsman, John Randolph of Roanoke, about whom in the fullness of time I would write my own first book. In later years it would come to pass that my admiration for Thomas Jefferson would abate somewhat. But my fondness for Albert Jay Nock's "study in conduct and character" remains to this day unimpaired.

XIII

In 1933, living at Brussels, Nock fancied himself in the sere and yellow leaf -- a melancholy induced in part, doubtless, by the centralizing triumph of President Franklin Roosevelt. But actually Nock would live thirteen years longer; his best writing was yet to come; and the small boy dwelling next to the railroad yards outside Detroit, who had just got that secondhand *Jefferson*, some few years later would become Nock's correspondent and in some degree his disciple.

During my years at college and university, I picked up a number of Nock's books. After Albert Jay Nock published his last book, *Memoirs of a Superfluous Man*, I wrote to him appreciatively from the desert camp where I was then a soldier. We exchanged several letters -- vanished now -- touching on a diversity of subjects. Nock in 1945 was drawing near to what he had prematurely called (in 1932) his "path to the river"; I then had just begun to publish essays in quarterly reviews. He was very good about replying to my letters, possibly because I was a soldier who approved his opposition to Franklin Roosevelt's foreign policies. A conscience spoke to a conscience.

I recall especially our discussing Marcus Aurelius. The Emperor meditates upon the lovely ripeness of figs, just before they fall into deliquescence; and I raised the question of whether this thought is an image of Roman society at its Antonine argentine perfection, on the eve of decadence. Nock would not grant that any touch of decadence rested upon Marcus himself. Again and again in his essays he quoted the philosopher-king -- most memorably, perhaps, in his piece "The Path to the River":

> The most beautiful figure in all human history, meditating in his encampment "among the Quadi, at the Granua," told himself with hard common sense that "he who fears death either fears the loss of sensation or a different kind of sensation. But if thou shalt have no sensation, neither wilt thou feel any harm; and if thou shalt acquire another kind of sensation, thou wilt be a different kind of living being, and thou wilt not cease to live."

Like his imperial exemplar, Albert Jay Nock did not fear death. But he did dread intimate attachments in this world, somewhat resembling in that trait both Marcus Aurelius and Thomas Jefferson. Nock abruptly left his wife, departing for Europe, and never returned to her. Years later, when Nock and his friend Bernard Iddings Bell were crossing the Atlantic together, Dr. Bell hesitantly inquired, "Albert, what was your wife like?"

"She was perfect in every respect," Nock answered, "so I left her."

Nock's individualism, glowing through his portrait of Jefferson, was so thoroughgoing that he could not endure those tender personal ties which most men and women long for: so B.I. Bell told me once. Nock strode on solitary toward his latter end: "One has few companions [on the path to the river], latterly almost none, and one is content with that. One or two are willing to go the whole way with me, which troubles me a little, and I hope they will not insist. They are young, and taking this journey just for company would break the continuity of their lives, and be but a tedious business, besides."

This deliberate isolation was that of Marcus Aurelius, who enjoined himself, "Live as upon a mountain." So it was, for the most part, with Thomas Jefferson. Yet the man who sets himself apart may be loved by many: Marcus and Jefferson and Nock, gone voyaging down the river of Time, nevertheless remain much alive to thousands of us still.

Old Mr. Nock of Canaan, Connecticut, introduced me through correspondence to "a gentleman of some intellectual distinction" (Nock's description), Dr. Bernard Iddings Bell. Years later, Canon Bell and I would spend many days together, in Chicago, in London, at Scottish country houses. But before that comradeship came to pass, Albert Jay Nock had tramped all the way down to the river: he and I never met face to face, this side of eternity.

"I could not hold it as any count against the order of nature," Nock wrote in 1932, "if my own personality did not survive death." But he added that if the personalities of Socrates, Marcus Aurelius, Dante, Cervantes, Shakespeare, and Rabelais do not endure beyond the grave -- why, "the order of nature is a most inglorious fizzle." I fancy that the strong lonely personality of Albert Jay Nock is not forever effaced.

Nock was a skeptic, rather on the good-natured model of Hume --which does not mean that he was an atheist or a nihilist. His better essays are sermons, in effect; the best-known of them, "Isaiah's Job", he borrowed from a Sunday sermon by B.I. Bell. A good many people are surprised to learn that Nock once was an Episcopalian clergyman. He departed from the ministry when he was not quite forty years old, telling B.I. Bell that he had lost his faith in Christian dogmata -- if indeed, Nock added, he ever really had known any such faith.

If he had no perfect faith in the heavenly hosts, neither had Nock any sure faith in mankind. Most people, he argued, are ineducable. He believed in a republic -- not in a democracy. American society, he suggested, is like German beer: scum at the top, dregs at the bottom. Nock set a fence about his inner self; and he mentions, in *Memoirs of a Superfluous Man*, "the danger of knowing too many people."

Yet this redoubtable individualist, gone now nearly four decades, has more friends today than ever he knew when he lived here below. The communication of the dead, Eliot tells us, is tongued with fire beyond the language of the living. There exists even a Nockian Society, to keep Nock's memory green. And although most of Nock's books are out of print and difficult to come upon, for a great while they will continue to be read by a Remnant, I venture to predict. This new edition of his *Jefferson* is intended for a rising generation that may find fresh meaning in Nock's lively and percipient pages.

So permit me to suggest why his *Jefferson* -- now entitled *Mr. Jefferson*, according to Nock's usual style for the gentleman who became Third President -- remains well worth reading, more than half a century since it was written. Let me suggest also some limitations of the book. This is a study of Jefferson by a twentieth-century writer endowed with a Jeffersonian cast of thought. It possesses Jeffersonian charm, and is embellished with Jeffersonian crochets.

Nock's book has very little to say about the Declaration of Independence. That is as it should be, for the Declaration really is not conspicuously American in its ideas or its phrases, and not even characteristically Jeffersonian. As Carl Becker sufficiently explains, the Declaration was meant to persuade the court of France, and the *philosophes* of Paris, that the Americans were sufficiently un-English to deserve military assistance. Jefferson's Declaration is a successful instrument of diplomacy; it is not a work of political philosophy or an instrument of government, and Jefferson himself said little about it after 1776.

Nock's Mr. Jefferson is no ideologue, but an easygoing gentleman of many talents, amiable and kindly enough, readily approached yet "the most impenetrable of men ... impossible of knowledge." Nock's study is suffused by warm sympathy for Mr. Jefferson -- natural enough, for truly the characters of these two were not dissimilar.

Temperate, sound in morals, sound in taste, learned in more than one discipline, open-handed, ready to fill great offices at personal sacrifice and then to retire modestly to Monticello -- this was the genuine Jefferson, no doctrinaire egalitarian, no abstract intellectual.

It is a most attractive portrait. Is it the whole Thomas Jefferson? Why, there are other sides to the man. Nock touches repeatedly upon Mr. Jefferson's calmness, coolness, lack of passion; perhaps these qualities are more attractive to Nock than to the typical reader of this study; Nock himself seems a trifle put off by this impersonality. One recalls that Nock did not include Jefferson in his pantheon of personalities meant to endure beyond the jaws of physical death. This aspect of Jefferson's character reminds one of John Locke -- and of Yeats' scoff at Whiggery:

> ... but what is Whiggery?
> A levelling, rancorous, rational sort of mind
> That never looked out of the eye of a saint
> or out of drunkard's eye.

Jefferson indeed was a Whig through and through, with the virtues and the defects of the breed. Joined with this Whiggery was another facet of his character, glossed over somewhat by Nock: a bitter partisanship, not overly scrupulous, extending even to an attempt to bring out a bowdlerized edition of Hume's *History of England,* with the Tory judgments transformed to Whig judgments. Almost repellently dispassionate in most personal relationships, Jefferson could be ferociously emotional in politics.

Being politically passionate himself, Albert Jay Nock seems to take for granted Jefferson's love of faction. (Let it be remarked that Nock, despite his affection for Mr. Jefferson, is fair to Alexander Hamilton and John Adams, calling the latter "perhaps the most congenial -- one may say perhaps the most lovable -- of any [figure] made on the page of history by an American of his period.") Nock does not deliberately obscure Jefferson's deficiencies. He touches now and again upon instances of impracticality; he finds his hero inadequately grounded in economics, despite his friendship with Pierre du Pont de Nemours and other men of the dismal science; he condemns Jefferson roundly for his ruinous Embargo Act.

So this book is not mere panegyric; rather it is a successful endeavor to resurrect a great man of political virtue, that we may contrast him with the feeble public men of the twentieth century (this by inference and implication, not by direct comparison). "Read no history, only biography," says Benjamin Disraeli, in *Contarini Fleming:* for we come to apprehend the spirit of an age better through the lives of its great personages than through chronicles of events. Nock's succinct study of Jefferson is such an evocation, through a biographical essay, of a vanished time.

But also Nock, aside from this conjuring up of Mr. Jefferson and his age, had a political purpose in writing this book: an immediate and practical political purpose. Had he written about Jefferson in the 1940s rather than in the 1920s, this political purpose might have been somewhat altered.

For in the 1920s, before Franklin Roosevelt had changed the course of American society, Nock the individualist was also Nock the economic determinist and Nock the friend of Charles A. Beard. He acknowledged his heavy debt to Beard's economic interpretation of American history, with its quasi-Marxist assumptions. Moreover (though not altogether consistently) Nock in 1926 (and indeed much later) believed in Henry George's Single Tax scheme. These economic postulates strongly affect his interpretation of Jefferson's significance.

Thus Nock holds in *Jefferson* that economic class interest determines the course of politics, everywhere, always. All political figures, Jefferson included, represent particular class interests: so Nock insisted. Mr. Jefferson, in Nock's argument, represented the "producing class." The Federalists, Jefferson's natural adversaries, represented "the exploiting class -- the minority, that is, which in every society appropriates without compensation the labour-products of the majority." The ultimate issue in America's politics during the age of Jefferson and Hamilton, Nock declares, was simply "what economic interests should control the government of the United States."

Now this argument of Nock's is a heresy: that is, a truth carried to an extreme, so that it has become false. The clash of economic interests between sections of the infant United States indeed was a huge influence upon the politics of the young Republic. Generally speaking, the South (Virginia especially) found its prosperity in agriculture; the North (Massachusetts especially), in commerce, shipping, banking, and small industries. Hamilton and other Federalists sought to create or reinforce a class of men attached to the Union through the funding of the national debt and other centralizing economic measures; Jefferson and his friends preferred the rural economy, free trade, and local autonomy. In the long run, these differences led to the Civil War.

So Nock was not in error when he pointed out the economic significance of Jefferson's politics -- though he tended to exclude from consideration other elements in Jefferson's political convictions. To represent Jefferson as the conscious or unconscious champion of his own economic class, however, verges on absurdity. Thomas Jefferson was a planter on a grand scale, holding nearly eleven thousand Virginia acres and a great many slaves. Yet he and his allies abolished entail and promogeniture, ancient statutes which were props of the class of grand planters. He would have abolished slavery, had he contrived any way to effect that end without ruining both blacks and whites. Are these the measures of economic class interest?

Of course the "capitalist, industrial and trading interests" of the North sought their own advantage, as did the Southern agricultural interest. But is it reasonable to denounce as "exploiters" the founders of America's commerce and industry? One may heartily sympathize with the Southern agrarians, as I do, without falling into the error of mistaking captains of industry for agents of Lucifer. In some passages of *Jefferson*, Albert Jay Nock slips into Marxist abuse. Why is Jefferson, selling his tobacco crop, a virtuous "producer"? And why is some early New England textile manufacturer an evil "exploiter"? Was it exploitation for Jefferson's friend E.I. du Pont (also the friend of Hamilton) to build a powder-mill in Delaware? or to solicit orders for powder from the Jefferson administration? Nock's economic concepts, like those of Jefferson, seem not to have progressed beyond the doctrines of the pre-Du Pont Physiocrats.

The investor is not, *per se*, an exploiter; and the employee of a government is not, *per se*, an oppressor of the poor. But this is not the place to argue with my old friend Albert Jay Nock over questions of economics. My purpose in raising such matters here is merely to suggest that it would be imprudent to accept uncritically all the assumptions of Nock, in his *Jefferson* and in other of his writings during the 1920s, concerning historiography and economic science. Nock himself was of another mind about some of these grave matters, at the end of his life: one may compare certain passages in *Jefferson* and in *Memoirs of a Superfluous Man*. It is not that Nock changed his ground much during two decades: it was more nearly true that he changed his front, having perceived that centralized political power, rather than selfish economic interest, had become the principal menace to American freedom.

These criticisms of some of Nock's assumptions about 1926 are not intended to suggest that *Jefferson* was a tract for those times which nowadays has lost much of its significance. The high merits of *Jefferson's* urbane and persuasive style have lost nothing since 1926; Nock's insights into Jefferson's character remain keen as ever; and the book continues to be a valuable corrective to much "superstition" and "mythmaking" about Thomas Jefferson -- the principal purpose for which Nock produced this study. May all of Nock's books somehow find a publisher to bring them into the light of day once more!

Russell Kirk
Mecosta, Michigan

Dr. Kirk is editor of THE UNIVERSITY BOOKMAN; *contributor to numerous national magazines, author of the famous book,* THE CONSERVATIVE MIND *plus twenty-three other books, several hundred essays and short stories. He is a foremost critic, historian of ideas, biographer, political theorist, journalist, distinguised professor and lecturer.*

CHAPTER I

Youth

I

IN THE year 1760, Williamsburg was the capital of colonial Virginia. It was a winter rendezvous for the lowland gentry, who set the pitch for a social life that was not without interest, but which, like the plantation life of the period, has been the subject of an immense amount of romantic exaggeration. The town itself was unattractive, save to those who knew nothing better; and south of Philadelphia there was nothing much better. Williamsburg grew up on the regular pattern of American country towns, in a straggling string of buildings lining each side of a broad road which was unlighted, dusty in summer and muddy in winter, torn and churned by horse traffic, for there was no such thing as pavement in all Virginia, and no one who had ever seen any. The Capitol stood at one end of this road, and at the other stood the College of William and Mary; while midway the road expanded into a kind of public square, ornamented with a church and some public buildings.

In point of architecture, these edifices were not impressive. Indeed, the art of building was at a low level all over Virginia. "The genius of architecture," said a cultivated native, "seems to have shed its maledictions over this land." The college and hospital at Williamsburg, according to the same authority, "are rude, misshapen piles which, but that they have roofs, would be taken for brick kilns." The public buildings, however, quite stood comparison with the private dwellings that flanked them. There were about two hundred of these, mostly built of wood, on account of the belief that brick or stone construction was unhealth-

1

ful. "The private dwellings are very rarely constructed of stone or brick, much the greatest portion being of scantling and boards, plastered with lime. It is impossible to devise things more ugly, uncomfortable and, happily, more perishable. . . . The poorest people build huts of logs, laid horizontally in pens, stopping the interstices with mud." There was no plumbing, drainage, or sewerage in Williamsburg; not a furnace or a stove; not a match; nothing to read by but candles, and little to read—few books and a single newspaper, such as it was, the only one published in Virginia. There were no shops worth speaking of, and money was little used. Goods were exchanged by primitive barter, and the general standard currency was tobacco. Williamsburg had a population of about one thousand persons who, like all the colonists, were pretty strictly on their own resources. They made what they used, largely, and extemporized their own amusements, dancing, gaming, hunting, fiddling, fighting. Some of the developments that came out of this life seem odd in their perspective. The first glimpse we have of Patrick Henry, for instance, is as a kind of vagabond, a bankrupt trader in his twenties, incorrigibly lazy, hanging about Williamsburg, fiddling at dances in the Apollo Room of the Raleigh Tavern, and making himself the life and soul of any crew of loafers that his talent for storytelling might draw together.

The College of William and Mary, named for the sovereigns who had chartered it under the auspices of the Church of England, was the second institution of the higher learning set up on this continent. For the time, it was well endowed. Among its sources of revenue were twenty thousand acres of land, which it held on the odd condition that every year, on the fifth day of March, the president should wait upon the colonial governor with two copies of a complimentary address done in Latin verse. The college followed "the grand old fortifying classical curriculum"; that is to say, it offered the student Latin, Greek, mathematics, moral philosophy, and a favorable view of the Christian faith as held by the Church of England.

But the institution never did well. Its management was poor, and its instruction worse. The Bishop of London had the spiritual direction of the colony, and he could not always resist the temptation to unload upon Virginia such of his clergy as for one reason or another he thought could be best employed away from home. The same policy often governed his appointments to professorships at William and Mary. Then too, a certain Mr. Boyle, a pious but rather unimaginative Englishman, had given the college an endowment for evangelizing and educating such Indians as could be induced to go there. A great deal of energy was frittered away on this enterprise, and the general cultural level of the college was kept low by it. Parton remarks with unconscious humor that "if the college had any success with an Indian youth, he was no sooner tamed than he sickened and died." Those who held out, he adds, threw off their clothes at the first glad moment of emancipation from Williamsburg "and ran whooping into the forest."

The college shared the privileged position of the Church, however, so there was little incentive to pull up its slack. The Church of England was "established by law" in the colony; it was, as it still is in England, a branch of the civil service, like the post office, and the laws protecting its monopoly were severe. At one period, the Virginian had to go to church twice on Sunday under penalty of a fine for the first offense, flogging for the second, and death for the third. To speak lightly of any article of the Christian faith was a capital crime, and one was liable to be flogged for disparaging a clergyman. Swearing was punishable, for the second offense, by having one's tongue bored through with an awl; for the third offense, by death. Heretics were liable to be burned at the stake. These laws were no more regularly or impartially enforced than such laws ever are; but while they tended to become obsolete, they nevertheless remained as potential instruments against those whom the authorities might dislike for other reasons. The colony had no more religious liberty than civil liberty; Great Britain's policy toward it was in every respect a policy of sheer dragooning. Hence the Church got on only in a perfunctory and disreputable fashion, and progressively less serious heed was paid it.

In 1760, an oddly assorted company of four persons drew together at Williamsburg and remained in close association, helping one another make what they could of a rather dull life, for the better part of two years. These alien spirits met at dinner at least once a week; and half a century later, one of the group, after a long experience of the best social life in both hemispheres, left record that "at these dinners I have heard more good sense, more rational and philosophical conversations, than in all my life besides." The most significant member of the group is the one who has, unfortunately, left the faintest mark on history. The little that is known of him is only enough to make us wish we knew more. This was Dr. William Small, a Scotsman, professor of mathematics at William and Mary. He seems to have been a sort of Abélard *in omne re scibili*, for at one time or another he also taught moral philosophy, rhetoric, and literature and carried on some work in applied science. No one knows what circumstances brought him to the college; but once there, he seems quickly to have had enough of a dissolute, time-serving clergy, of riotous students, and of the prevailing incompetence, indolence, and wrangling. In 1762, he went back to England and became "the great Dr. Small of Birmingham." But there too he left a provokingly slight account of himself. He was a friend of the elder Darwin; there were dark hints against his orthodoxy; and he helped James Watt in developing the steam engine. Probably, as Chateaubriand said of Joubert, he was more interested in perfection than in making a name for himself; at all events, his influence seems to have been quite disproportionate to his reputation. Such a man's great fascination is that one can never be sure of one's estimate of him, that he continually raises questions about himself and stimulates conjecture—*caret quia vate sacro*

The second of the company was a lawyer named George Wythe, subsequently Chancellor of Virginia, a signer of the Declaration of Independence, and law tutor of John Marshall and Henry Clay. Self-educated, except perhaps for Latin, he was said to be the best Greek scholar in the colony. He had some of the eccentricities common to vigorous self-trained minds. In his later years, for example, he peppered his judicial decisions with Greek, to the bitter distress of copyists; and, again, disgusted with the slow progress of measures for the general abolition of slavery, he suddenly freed all his slaves at a stroke, apparently without any question whether they would fare better or worse for the change. His integrity was high and fine, and he was equally eminent in his profession and in the esteem of colonial society.

Third in the group was the governor of the colony, Francis Fauquier, a remarkable exception to the general run of British proconsular officers. He was the most accomplished person that Virginia had ever seen, a cultivated man of the world, with every distinction and charm of manner; an excellent musician and linguist, a discerning traveler who had sampled civilized society almost everywhere in Europe. A strange passion for gambling had stood in his way. The tradition is that, having gambled away all his property at a sitting, he was glad to get the appointment to Virginia to keep himself going. He spread the contagion of his failing among the Virginian landed gentry; but otherwise he was singularly scrupulous in private and public life, and his sympathies were largely with the colonists in their growing restlessness under the blind voracity of British mercantilism.

These men who found themselves marooned in the uncongenial life of Williamsburg, were well on toward middle age. Governor Fauquier was fifty-six; Mr. Wythe was thirty-four. Dr. William Small's age is not known, but there is probably some ground for thinking he would be rather over than under forty-five. The fourth member of the group was a boy of seventeen, who had entered college early in the year. He was tall and loose-jointed, with hazel-gray eyes and sandy hair, an extremely thin skin that peeled on exposure to sun or wind, stout wrists, large hands and feet. His name was Thomas Jefferson.

II

The lad was a well-to-do half-orphan, who had come down from the Virginia frontier, one hundred and fifty miles to the northwest, from the county of Albemarle, where his father, Peter Jefferson, had operated a virgin plantation, originally of one thousand acres, but presently augmented by a purchase of four hundred acres from a neighbor for what seems a moderate price, namely: "Henry Weatherbourne's biggest bowl of arrack punch." Peter Jefferson was a pioneer yeoman of Welsh descent, who married Jane Randolph, the nineteen-year-old daughter of Isham Randolph of Dungeness, in the county of Goochland. Thomas Jefferson's autobiography, written at the age of seventy-seven, gives but a scanty account of either family, remarking dryly that the Randolphs "trace their pedigree far back in England and Scotland, to which let every one ascribe the faith and merit he chooses." Peter Jefferson was a man of great strength, both of body and mind, and a correspondingly independent spirit. Uneducated, but with a turn for learning, he read whatever he could find to read; and, like Washington, he somehow managed to rub up enough mathematics and rule of thumb to qualify as a surveyor. He helped Professor Fry in making the first actual map of Virginia and in running the boundary between Virginia and North Carolina. He died at fifty, probably from overwork. Thomas, his elder son, was then fourteen, and by the British law of primogeniture then in force in the colony, would inherit the larger share of property. Before death, Peter Jefferson had formally made known two wishes for this son and heir: that he should grow up strong and healthy, and that he should have a thorough classical education. It does not appear that he ever expressed any definite desires for his eight other children.

Both wishes were granted. Health and strength came as much by good luck as good management, in those days. The frail died young; there was nothing else for them to do. But if one could weather through until well past thirty, one might fairly count on reaching old age. Of Peter Jefferson's nine children, one died at twenty-nine, one at twenty-five, one at two months, one at birth —the fate of the average family, perhaps, or a little better—but the elder son had the luck to stand up under the hardships of existence and realize his father's hopes. Throughout his life he seldom had any indisposition, beyond periodical headaches of a somewhat severe type, at long intervals. His teeth were perfect and his eyesight practically unimpaired until the day of his death; so the two major curses of old age, one of which scourged Washington incessantly, passed him by.

One of Thomas Jefferson's letters, written late in life, gives an idea of what constitutional strength was like in that heroic period, and it also throws light on the current practice of medicine. He complains of being annoyed at the moment by "a slight salivation" caused by a dose of calomel and jalap, "though it contained no more than eight or nine grains of the former." The weak, obviously, had little chance against this kind of thing. Mr. Jefferson always had a healthy man's skepticism about the various theories of medicine and spoke of them in the vein of Daniel Defoe. "I believe we may safely affirm that the inexperienced and presumptuous band of medical tyros let loose upon the world destroys more of human life in one year than all the Robin Hoods, Cartouches and Macheaths do in a century." He remarked on one occasion that he never saw three physicians talking together, without glancing up to see if there were not a turkey buzzard hovering overhead. His own theory of medicine anticipated the modern belief that "the judicious, the moral, the humane physician should stop" with the attempt merely to assist "the salutary effort which nature makes to re-establish the disordered functions." Yet, on the other hand, he was one of the first to undergo vaccination, or "inoculation for the small pox," as practiced by Dr. Shippen of Philadelphia, stopping there for that purpose in the course of a journey to New York at the age of thirty-three.[1]

One circumstance which made for health was that anything like what we would now call a sedentary life was then impracticable. It was hard to avoid enough exercise to keep fit. Peter Jefferson trained his son to be a good shot and put him in the way of being one of the best horsemen of his time. Thomas Jefferson always rode hard, even after he was unable to walk; he took a hard ride within three weeks of his death at the age of eighty-three. Yet he thought that at best "a horse gives but a kind of half-exercise," and he had his doubts whether "we have not lost more than we have gained by the use of this animal. No one has occasioned so much the degeneracy of the human body." As for driving, he said summarily that "a carriage is no better than a cradle." Telling a young protégé that of all forms of exercise

[1] In 1806, he wrote a complimentary letter to Jenner, in which he speaks of himself as "having been among the early converts." Whatever Dr. Shippen's mode of practice may have been, the general method of inoculation was a terrible business, and it must have taken a deal of resolution to go through with it. Among the Jefferson MSS. in the Library of Congress is a copy of the *Virginia Almanac* for 1770, "containing several interesting Pieces in Prose and Verse," one of which, by Dr. Thomas Dimsdale, gives the process as follows:

First, the patient should abstain from animal food, spices, and fermented liquors, "except small beer," for ten days. During this period he takes three doses, each of——

8 gr. calomel,
8 gr. compound powder of crab's claws,
⅛ gr. tartar emetic.

Then follows the inoculation, practically as now, save for any attempt at asepsis. Indeed, the instructions specify that the wound should not be covered. The second day after inoculation he takes——

3 gr. calomel,
3 gr. crab's claws,
$\frac{1}{10}$ gr. tartar emetic.

As soon as the vaccination begins to "take," he has the same dose again, "given overnight," and as a follow-up next morning, he takes——

2 oz. infusion of senna,
½ oz. manna,
2 dr. tincture of jalap.

walking is the best, he advised him always to carry a gun on his walks. "While this gives a moderate exercise to the body, it gives boldness, enterprise and independence to the mind," in contrast to "games played with ball, and others of that nature," which, he said, "are too violent for the body, and stamp no character on the mind." He was a true son of his father in believing that health is worth more than learning, in his distrust of drugs and coddling, and in his faith in hard exercise—at least two hours of it every day—as "the sovereign invigorator of the body." It is a robust doctrine, and only a robust person could live up to Mr. Jefferson's idea of it. For him, it worked well; but it would no doubt almost instantly have broken down his neighbor and bosom friend, James Madison, whose little body after all somehow managed to hold out for eighty-five years, two years longer than Mr. Jefferson's own.

Luck, again, which had so much to do with the fulfilment of Peter Jefferson's first wish, played almost as large a part with the second. There were no schools on the frontier; none of any account, indeed, in the whole colony. Clergymen sometimes took pupils; and by luck, Thomas Jefferson fell into the hands of a couple of clergymen who had some gift for teaching. Both were Scots. Passing from the Scotsman Douglas to the Scotsman Maury, and then to the Scotsman Small, at Williamsburg, he had a Scots education throughout. He says in his memoirs that his father "placed me at the English school at five years of age; and at the Latin at nine, where I continued until his death." His going to William and Mary, rather than to Harvard or Princeton, looked as if his uninterrupted good luck had failed at last. The choice was his own; he wrote a stiff little letter to his guardian suggesting it, though, boylike, he cannily shifts the responsibility to his mother's cousin:

Shadwell, January 14th, 1760.
Sir: I was at Colo. Peter Randolph's about a Fortnight ago, and my Schooling falling into Discourse, he said he thought it would be to my Advantage to go to the College, and was desirous I should go, as indeed I am myself for several Reasons. In the first place, as long as I stay at the Mountain, the loss of one-fourth of my Time is inevitable, by Company's coming here and detaining me from School. And likewise my Absence will in a great measure, put a stop to so much Company, and by that Means lessen the Expenses of the Estate in Housekeeping. And on the other Hand, by going to the College,

I shall get a more universal Acquaintance, which may hereafter be serviceable to me; and I suppose I can pursue my Studies in the Greek and Latin as well there as here, and likewise learn something of the Mathematics. I shall be glad of your opinion.

This ingratiating and persuasive letter is the first of all those recorded from Mr. Jefferson's pen. It seems to have had its way with his guardian; as well it might, if only for the delightful touch of unintended irony at the end. This guarded estimate of William and Mary was really pretty generous, for most people who could afford the expense were sending their sons to England for an education or to the schools in the North. But the boy's haphazard choice of William and Mary turned out to be eminently in his vein of good luck. Nowhere else, probably, were to be found just the influences suited to his temperament and type of mind. For a reflective person, two years in Williamsburg was in itself a pretty sound education in social philosophy. A capital that was nothing but a capital, housing nothing but politics, without any considerable trade or industry, or more than a handful of population, Williamsburg stood as a kind of stark exponent of exploitation through politics. Through its secular arm, the British state, in its devotion to the doctrine of mercantilism, ruthlessly and stupidly exploited the labor of the colonists. Through the church it exploited their intellect and spirit by the inculcation of a specious patriotism—"superstition in religion exciting superstition in politics," as John Adams said, "and both united in directing military force." Williamsburg was the focus of this process. It was not without point that Thomas Jefferson soon fell into the way of dating his youthful letters from "Devilsburg."

The situation, moreover, had its interpreters. Three alien spirits, drawn together as much by a common distrust of their circumstances as by their common interests and tastes, admitted him, by some miracle of good luck, to their company—formally, at any rate, as an equal. Like some other men of his period, notably Franklin, he seems to have been born with a certain maturity which made him at home in this association. He remained always the disciple of the cultivated man of science, the scholarly lawyer, and the experienced man of the world. Almost the only trace of fervency that one finds in his writings is when, late in life, he records his admiration for Governor Fauquier, Mr. Wythe, and Dr. Small, who "was to me as a father," and whose presence at Williamsburg "probably fixed the destinies of my life." Indeed, there is hardly a line of his activity that cannot be run back to one or another of these three men.

III

There is little to be known of Thomas Jefferson's early life. In 1770, his mother's house at Shadwell burned down, with the loss "of every paper I had in the world, and almost every book." By some chance, half a dozen of his youthful letters, most of them written at college to his friend John Page, have been preserved and also some of his pocket account books and memoranda. The first letter to Page was written from Fairfield, on Christmas Day, 1762, when Mr. Jefferson was in his twentieth year. It has value for the light it throws on the tendency of historians and novelists to exaggerate the elegance of Virginian colonial life. On his way home from Williamsburg to Shadwell, Mr. Jefferson stopped over to spend Christmas with a well-to-do friend who lived in rather sumptuous style at Fairfield. He took along his fiddle and some new minuets to do his share in the season's entertainment. Next morning he reports to Page, with no suggestion that he found it unusual or startling, that while he slept, "the cursed rats" had eaten up his pocketbook "which was in my pocket, within a foot of my head. And not contented with plenty for the present, they carried away my jemmy-worked silk garters and half-a-dozen new minuets I had just got."

He does not complain of this. He observes judicially: "Of this I should not have accused the devil (because you know rats will be rats, and hunger, without addition of his instigation, might have urged them to do this) if something worse, and from a different quarter, had not happened." It seems—again with no suggestion of its being unusual—that he had been put to sleep in the attic; for "when I went to bed I laid my watch in the usual place, and going to take her up after I arose this morning, I found her in the same place, it's true, but *quantum mutatus ab illo!* all afloat in water let in at a leak in the roof of the house, and as silent and still as the rats that had eat my pocketbook." Even this was not the worst. He had the picture of a brevet sweetheart in his watchcase, and the rain soaked picture and watch paper to pulp, so that in trying to take them out to dry them, "my cursed fingers gave them such a rent as I fear I shall never get over." Nevertheless, after two more sentences, his self-command is sufficiently rallied to permit an easy transition into the practical matter of his law studies. "And now, although the picture be defaced, there is so lively an image of her imprinted in my mind that I shall think of her too often, I fear, for my peace of mind; and too often, I am sure, to get through old Coke this winter; for God knows I have not seen him since I packed him up in my trunk at Williamsburg. Well, Page, I do wish the devil had old Coke, for I am sure I never was so tired of an old dull scoundrel in my life."

The damsel in question was Miss Rebecca Burwell, whom Mr. Jefferson, in subsequent letters to Page, celebrated after the Restoration fashion under the name of Belinda. He seems to have done this partly out of poetic fancy and partly for fear of some tampering with this weighty correspondence. A missive dated "Devilsburg, January 23, 1764," reports that one of Page's letters, "sent by the Secretary's boy," had been undelivered and expresses apprehension about one of his own, though "Sukey Potter, to whom I sent it, told me yesterday she delivered it to Mr. T. Nelson, the younger, who had delivered it to you—I hope with his own hand." This uneasiness leads him to write obscurely about his charmer and to adopt devices of a clumsy transparency, such as using masculine instead of feminine pronouns and writing the name Belinda in Greek characters, sometimes reversing them. Page, apparently, thought it enough insurance of secrecy to write in Latin, for Mr. Jefferson, speaking of his overdue letter, says, "I wish I had followed your example and wrote it in Latin, and that I had called my dear *campana in die*[1] instead of αδνιλεβ." The disciple of Dr. Small, however, resolves to be thorough-going —even in veiling the allusions to one's love affairs, one must keep a proper respect for whatever is *wissenschaftlich*. "We must fall on some scheme of communicating our thoughts to each other, which shall be totally unintelligible to every one but ourselves. I will send you some of these days Shelton's Tachygraphical Alphabet, and directions."

Rebecca Burwell did not take the young man's attentions any too seriously. No question she might have married him if she had liked, for marriage was the only occupation open to Virginian women, and they brought a correspondingly high professional skill

[1] I.e., "bell-in-day."

to bear on managing themselves into it. Her cautious suitor had some thought of making her a proposal. A month after his experience with the rain and rats at Fairfield, he asks Page, "How does R. B. do? Had I better stay here and do nothing, or go down and do less? . . . Inclination tells me to go, receive my sentence, and be no longer in suspense; but reason says, If you go and your attempt proves unsuccessful, you will be ten times more wretched than ever." Again, he thinks he may go to Petersburg in May to see some stage plays, and "if I do, I do not know but I may keep on to Williamsburg." However, he does neither; he remains at Shadwell all summer, tranquilly farming and reading law. At the end of May, the watchful Page tells him he has a rival and urges quick action, offering to serve as his attorney and negotiate an option on Miss Burwell's affections, if only he will hurry down from Shadwell and take the option up. No reply for a long month; then a letter full of high quietistic philosophy. "The rival you mention I know not whether to think formidable or not, as there has been so great an opening for him during my absence"—but still he sticks on at Shadwell.

This looks like craven diffidence, but really it is nothing of the kind. Aware that his attitude would strike Page as pretty lukewarm, he finally discloses his actual state of mind. He was fairly certain that he loved Miss Burwell, but wholly certain that he wanted to go traveling. "I shall visit particularly England, Holland, France, Spain, Italy (where I would buy me a good fiddle) and Egypt," and return home by way of Canada. The ideal thing would be to manage both enterprises; to get the trip, say a matter of only two or three years at most, and then get Miss Burwell— would Page look the situation over and see what could be done? He had an instinctive uneasiness about submitting this project in person to her keen professional appraisal. "I should be scared to death at making her so unreasonable a proposal as that of waiting until I return from Britain, unless she could first be prepared for it. I am afraid it will make my chance of succeeding considerably worse." In the face of any hazard, however, he remains the disciple of the great Dr. Small of Birmingham: "But the event at last must be this, that if she consents, I shall be happy; if she does not, I must endeavour to be as much so as possible."

Once started in the way of these exalted reflections, indeed, the young philosopher becomes animated and treats Page to a whole paragraph of impassioned determinism:

The most fortunate of us, in our journey through life, frequently meet with calamities and misfortunes which may greatly afflict us; and to fortify our minds against the attacks of these calamities and misfortunes should be one of the principal studies and endeavours of our lives. The only method of doing this is to assume a perfect resignation to the Divine will, to consider that whatever does happen must happen; and that by our uneasiness we cannot prevent the blow before it does fall, but we may add to its force after it has fallen. These considerations, and others such as these, may enable us in some measure to surmount the difficulties thrown in our way; to bear up with a tolerable degree of patience under this burthen of life; and to proceed with a pious and unshaken resignation till we arrive at our journey's end, when we may deliver up our trust into the hands of Him who gave it, and receive such reward as to Him shall seem proportioned to our merit. Such, dear Page, will be the language of the man who considers his situation in this life, and such should be the language of every man who would wish to render that situation as easy as the nature of it will admit. Few things will disturb him at all; nothing will disturb him much.

John Page earned a martyr's crown by stalking down Miss Burwell and putting the matter manfully before her. Whether he showed her the letter, with its very remarkable and splendid philosophical excursus, is not known. But even without that, Miss Burwell could easily appraise the situation by all the force of that superiority in realism which comes of a purely professional training; besides, she had another string to her bow. So it is not surprising that she demurely accepted in principle Page's proposal to maintain the diplomatic *status quo* until her swain should make his leisurely way back to Williamsburg in October and offer her a formal understanding upon all points covered by the protocol—his heartfelt devotion, the trip to Europe, the new fiddle, and marriage.

October came. "Last night, as merry as agreeable company and dancing with Belinda in the Apollo[1] could make me, I never thought the succeeding sun would have seen me so wretched as I now am. I was prepared to say a great deal" in the intervals between dances, but all it came to was "a few broken sentences ut-

[1] The Apollo Room in the Raleigh Tavern, where the colony's first retaliatory measures against Great Britain were subsequently organized.

tered in great disorder and interrupted with pauses of uncommon length." Trying again a week later, he finally managed to
compass the terrible business of a conditional proposal. "I asked
no question which would admit of a categorical answer; but I
assured αδνιλεβ that such questions would one day be asked." He
left her "satisfied that I shall make her an offer, and if she intends
to accept of it, she will disregard those made by others," and if,
on the other hand, her "present resolutions" are not favorable,
"it is out of my power to say anything to make them so, which
I have not said already."

No doubt while Miss Burwell laughed herself to sleep that
autumn night, she felt the indulgent pity which the kindly
professional feels for the amateur—the awkward amateur, who
trained every cannon in Dr. Small's whole philosophical arsenal
on the poor butterfly of boy love. All this, however, lay behind
her when next morning she put a firm professional hand to her
second string and pulled it. She almost immediately married the
none-too-dreaded, none-too-hated rival. Her slacktwisted lover
survived, as most lovers do, even when they have not the moral
support of a Small and a Fauquier; six years later he is urging
Page to reassemble a houseparty of young ladies, promising in
quite the old sprightly vein to "carry Sally Nicholas in the green
chair to Newquarter, where your periagua . . . will meet us,
automaton-like, of its own accord." He never got his Belinda; it
was long before he got a trip to Europe, and indeed *the* trip to
Europe he never got; a dozen years dragged by before he got the
new fiddle; and on the ninth of April, 1764, the name of Belinda
fades forever from his correspondence.

IV

During the last year of his Presidency, Mr. Jefferson wrote a
letter of general good advice to a grandson, in which he says:
"When I recollect that at fourteen years of age the whole care
and direction of myself was thrown on myself entirely, without
a relation or friend qualified to advise or guide me, and recollect
the various sorts of bad company with which I associated from
time to time, I am astonished I did not turn off with some of
them and become as worthless to society as they were." Here
he himself intimates rather artlessly the most interesting question
that a survey of his early years brings out. Tobacco was the staple

of Virginia's commerce; he raised it, dealt in it, and never used it. The planter's table, Mr. Jefferson's own table notably, was abundant; and he was always the most abstemious of men, practically a vegetarian, "eating little animal food, and that not as an aliment so much as a condiment for the vegetables which constitute my principal diet." Surrounded by heavy drinking, he drank little, using "the weak wines only. The ardent wines I can not drink, nor do I use ardent spirits in any form." The society that surrounded him gambled at a great rate; and he never even had a card in his house. He was one of the best horsemen in the world, kept excellent horses, enjoyed watching a horse race; and once, only, he gingerly entered one of his horses for a race and then turned his back on the racecourse forever, save as an occasional spectator. He did his share of dancing and flirting with the pretty girls at Williamsburg and Rosewell, thought fondly of Belinda, sent gallant messages to Betsy Moore and Judy Burwell, bet a pair of garters with Alice Corbin, pinch-hit as a beau for Sally Nicholas, made a wry face over serving as best man for one of his acquaintances; yet his interest in these diversions seems to have left his inner nature curiously untroubled. He had a great many house servants; yet when he rose, he always built his own fire in his bedroom. His working day, even in college, averaged fifteen hours. John Page confesses that he himself was "too sociable to study as Mr. Jefferson did, who could tear himself away from his dearest friends and fly to his studies."

A few words in a letter to a relative contain all he ever said about the authoritarianism which seems to have been responsible for these anomalies and about its relative disciplinary advantages. "I had the good fortune to become acquainted very early with some characters of very high standing, and to feel the incessant wish that I could ever become what they were. Under temptations and difficulties, I would ask myself what would Dr. Small, Mr. Wythe, Peyton Randolph, do in this situation. . . . Knowing the even and dignified line they pursued, I could never doubt for a moment which of two courses would be in character for them. Whereas, seeking the same object through a process of moral reasoning, and with the jaundiced eye of youth, I should often have erred."

CHAPTER II

Beginnings

I

THE GENERAL POVERTY of fact and record concerning Mr. Jefferson's early years is threadbare in the matter of his marriage. No one knows how he met his wife or what she was like. There is a tradition that her daughter Mary, or Maria, as she later came to be known, resembled her. As far as this tradition goes, therefore, there is ground for thinking she was a slender brunette of medium height, gentle, pretty, and amiable, and otherwise not greatly gifted. Probably she was somewhat musical, though as it was then more or less the conventional thing for a girl to thrum on a spinet for general results, if she could afford to have one, there is no certainty about this. Mr. Jefferson himself played the violin diligently for years, practicing, he says, three hours a day over a long period. When traveling, he habitually carried the type of small violin called a kit, for the sake of employing his odd moments in practice. He is represented as having a keen virtuoso taste in music; but this again is uncertain, for nearly every youth in the social life of that day was some sort of township expert on the fiddle, and there is no clear evidence that Mr. Jefferson's taste and skill were much above the average, and there is a little—a very little—to show that it was not. After the battle of Saratoga, the prisoners of General Burgoyne's army were concentrated in Virginia, some in Mr. Jefferson's neighborhood, where he treated them with great kindness and hospitality. Among these was an English captain named Bibby, who fiddled duets with Mr. Jefferson and said he was one of the best violinists he ever heard. Still, Captain Bibby's heart was warmed by circumstances; and besides, no one really knows how well qualified he was to have an opinion. On the other hand, after Mr. Jefferson had set up housekeeping at Monticello, he wrote to a European correspondent whose name is unknown, asking him to look up some amateur musicians in the laboring class and send them over; and in this letter one must remark with doubt the rather special character of the ensemble he contemplates setting up. "The bounds of an American fortune will not admit the indulgence of a domestic band of musicians, yet I have thought that a passion for music might be reconciled with that economy which we are obliged to observe. I retain among my domestic servants a gardener, a weaver, a cabinet-maker and a stone-cutter, to which I would add a *vigneron*. In a country where, like yours, music is cultivated and practised by every class of men, I suppose there might be found persons of these trades who could perform on the French horn, clarinet or hautboy, and bassoon, so that one might have a band of two French horns, two clarinets, two hautboys and a bassoon, without enlarging their domestic expense." Again, he writes some years later from Paris to his friend Hopkinson, somewhat exaggerating, it would seem, the importance of "your project with the Harmonica, and the prospect of your succeeding in the application of Keys to it. It will be the greatest present which has been made to the musical world this century, not excepting the Piano-forte."

However, tradition says that Mr. Jefferson was a good musician, and that he loved music there can be no doubt. "This is the favorite passion of my soul, and fortune has cast my lot in a country where it is in a state of deplorable barbarism." It was something, certainly, to be so clearly aware of this. He played with Governor Fauquier and "two or three other amateurs in his weekly concerts." The year before his marriage, he ordered a clavichord for Monticello, but almost immediately countermanded the order, saying, "I have since seen a Forte-piano and am charmed with it. Send me this instrument then instead of the clavichord: let the case be of fine mahogany, solid, not veneered, the compass from Double G to F in alt., a plenty of spare strings: and the workmanship of the whole very handsome and worthy the acceptance of a lady for whom I intend it." Whether this was in appreciation of his sweetheart's proficiency or to tempt her to become more proficient, or both, no one knows. Tradition says, again, that his musical accomplishments, whatever they were, put him ahead of other suitors for the much-courted lady who became his wife, and that they fixed her choice.

The marriage took place on New Year's Day, 1772; the marriage license bond, drawn up in Mr. Jefferson's own handwriting, is still in existence, calling for the payment "to our sovereign lord the King" of the sum of fifty pounds current money of Virginia, in case there should be found any "lawful cause to obstruct a marriage intended to be had and solemnized between the above-bound Thomas Jefferson and Martha Skelton, of the county of Charles City, widow." The bond shows an odd momentary lapse of attention to his wife's status, for he mechanically wrote in the usual word "spinster," then crossed it out and wrote "widow." His wife was the daughter of John Wayles, a prosperous lawyer. She was twenty-three years old, and had lived an uneventful life of two years with her first husband, Bathurst Skelton, by whom she had one child, a son who died in infancy. Her father died a year after her second marriage, and her inheritance, after the clearance of Mr. Wayles's debts, which Mr. Jefferson observes "were very considerable," came to an amount "about equal to my own patrimony, and consequently doubled the ease of our circumstances."

While at college, Mr. Jefferson thought of building a house at Williamsburg. "No castle, though, I assure you," he wrote John Page, "only a small house which shall contain a room for myself and another for you, and no more, unless Belinda should think proper to favour us with her company, in which case I will enlarge the place as much as she pleases." But when Belinda's whims disappeared from consideration, the plan disappeared too; and in 1769, just before his mother's house at Shadwell burned down, he took steps toward making a home on the top of a small mountain which formed part of his estate in Albemarle, near the present city of Charlottesville. By the time of his marriage, he had completed a small structure here, a story-and-a-half brick pavilion, as the beginning of an ambitious architectural design; and thither he took his bride in a two-horse phaeton from her home in the country of Charles City, a distance of one hundred miles over indescribable roads, in midwinter of one of the hardest seasons that Virginia had ever seen. Before leaving, he got out his pocket account book and entered every item of expense that the wedding had cost him, including the fees he gave to the two officiating clergymen and some small fees to musicians and servants.

As they went up the country, the snow deepened until finally they were obliged to abandon the phaeton and go forward on horseback. The last eight miles of the journey lay over no better than a kind of bridlepath, two feet deep in snow; and when they reached Monticello late at night, the pavilion was deserted, there was no fire in it and nothing to make one of, nothing to eat or drink save part of a bottle of wine that they rummaged from a shelf behind some books, and not a servant anywhere within call. The general historical value of Virginian family tradition may not too unfairly be suggested by the statement given out on authority of the Jeffersons' oldest daughter that "tempers too sunny to be ruffled by many ten times as serious annoyances in after life, now found but sources of diversion in these ludicrous *contretemps*, and the horrible dreariness was lit up with song and merriment and laughter."

Mrs. Jefferson somehow managed to live ten years. The Marquis de Chastellux, who visited Monticello in the year of her death, speaks of her as "a mild and amiable wife." She was presumably literate, and her husband was an indefatigable letter writer. His part in public affairs from 1772 to 1782 kept him a good deal away from home, and a considerable correspondence must have passed between them. Of this, however, nothing remains. Except for entries in some household accounts that may have been hers and an appeal addressed to the women of Virginia during the Revolution, there is probably not a line of her writing in existence. Mr. Jefferson's published letters refer to her perhaps half a dozen times and then usually to remark his anxiety over her persistent bad health. Mrs. Jefferson bore her first child a little less than ten months after her marriage, and the family register kept by Mr. Jefferson on a leaf of his prayer book is a record of the progressive inanition that ended in her death:

Martha Jefferson was born September 27, 1772, at 1 o'clock A.M.

Jane Randolph Jefferson, born April 3, 1774, at 11 o'clock A.M. She died September ——, 1775.

A son, born May 28, 1777, at 10 o'clock P.M. Died June 14, at 10 o'clock and 20 minutes A.M.

Mary Jefferson, born August 1, 1778, at 1 o'clock and 30 minutes A.M. Died April 17, 1804, between 8 and 9 P.M.

A daughter, born in Richmond, November 3, 1780, at 10 o'clock and 45 minutes P.M. Died April 15, 1781, at 10 o'clock A.M.

Lucy Elizabeth Jefferson, born May 8, 1782, at 1 o'clock A.M. Died ——, 1784.

Martha Wayles Jefferson died September 6, 1782, at 11 o'clock, 45 minutes A.M.

But if all Mr. Jefferson's family correspondence lay open to view, no doubt it would have value only for its implications. *Hide thy life*, said Epicurus; and no one ever succeeded better than Thomas Jefferson at hiding his inner springs of sentiment. He was the most approachable and the most impenetrable of men, easy and delightful of acquaintance, impossible of knowledge. In matters of opinion, principle, or public policy he was always ready to speak out, and did speak out, with a frankness sometimes astonishing; but in more intimate matters, especially in matters of affection and feeling, he never spoke out. Undoubtedly he had great regard for his father and mother, but he seldom mentions either. His memoirs say nothing of his mother, beyond giving record of her name and family; and the few words about his father are quite impersonal. His letters are silent about his mother and speak of his father only once, by way of gratitude for having had him taught Greek and Latin. "I thank on my knees him who directed my early education," he writes Dr. Priestley in 1800, "for having put into my possession this rich source of delight." Even here one feels the sense of constriction and effort in the realm of the emotions; he does not say straight out, "I thank *my father*," in his usual plain style, but resorts to a Miltonian paraphrase. There is no doubt that he had an extraordinary faculty of attaching people to himself, though no one can know how he did it, and he has the record, remarkable under the circumstances, of never having forfeited an attachment; his few breaks, notably the one with John Adams, being but temporary and healing without a mark. It is hard to see how affections as deep and strong as his undoubtedly were can flow indefinitely without revealing some at least of their channels of communication; but in his case, there is no sign of them. Undoubtedly Mr. Jefferson loved his wife with an extraordinary depth of devotion. It must have been so, for there is a clear record that when she died, he was inconsolable, and that he remained always quietly faithful to her memory, never finding room in his heart for any other woman. Probably she may have had her moments of understanding him; yet one is forced to wonder what their aggregate amounted to.

While she lived, this mild and amiable wife made her achievements, whatever they were, by indirection and the sacrifice of personality; and to earn the posthumous reward they got, they must have been considerable, though of a nature that puts them beyond any power of assessment. Her death, curiously, continued her in the role of achievement by indirection and sacrifice, for it determined her husband's return to public life. Since his marriage in 1772, Mr. Jefferson had served in the Continental Congress, drafted the Declaration of Independence, served in the Virginia Assembly, done most of the work on the committee appointed to revise the laws of Virginia, and served two terms as governor of Virginia. In 1782 he decided that he had done enough in public office to earn the right to uninterrupted enjoyment of "my family, my friends, my farm and books" thenceforth. He wrote a long letter to Monroe, protesting against the idea that the state had a right to commandeer indefinitely the political services of its members. This, he says, "would be slavery, and not that liberty which the Bill of Rights has made inviolable," and for his part, he had a clear conscience about retiring. He had his own measure; he was aware that a person can best do, and should do, the kind of thing that really interests him. "Nature intended me for the tranquil pursuits of science," he told Dupont de Nemours, "by rendering them my supreme delight." But just at the intended turn in his career, his wife died, leaving him in "the stupor of mind which had rendered me as dead to the world as was she whose loss occasioned it." His scheme of life had been determined. "I had folded myself in the arms of retirement," he wrote the Marquis de Chastellux three months later, "and rested all prospects of future happiness on domestic and literary objects. A single event wiped away all my plans, and left me a blank which I had not the spirits to fill up. In this state of mind an appointment from Congress found me, requiring me to cross the Atlantic," as one of the commissioners to negotiate peace with Great Britain.

Monticello and its memories had become insupportable to him; his mind went back to the trip to Europe that he had promised himself so long ago, in the gay days of Belinda and his correspondence with John Page—the trip that, what with the un-

congenial routine of revolutions, drafts of declarations, revising
statutes, office holding, and the like, had never come off. He accepted the appointment, but even then the trip did not come off.
Before his ship sailed, word came that the peace was already in
a way to be concluded, and Congress recalled his appointment.
But his scheme of life was now recast; he still had his seat in
Congress; and, for good or ill, he put aside his plans for employing the rest of his days in the tranquil pursuits of science, with his
family, his friends, his farm and books. What heart could be in
it, without "the cherished companion of my life, in whose affections, unabated on both sides, I had lived the last ten years in
unchequered happiness"? It was then nineteen years since that
September night when, on his way back to Williamsburg, he
wrote from Richmond to William Fleming, "Dear Will, I have
thought of the cleverest plan of life that can be imagined. You
exchange lands for Edgehill, or I mine for Fairfields, you marry
Sukey Potter, I marry Rebecca Burwell, join and get a pole chair
and a pair of keen horses, practise the law in the same courts,
and drive about to all the dances in the county together. How do
you like it?"

· II

When Mr. Jefferson graduated from the society of Fauquier,
Small, and Wythe, set up for himself, and brought his bride to
Monticello, he brought with her a profession and a trade. He was
a lawyer as well as a farmer, having been admitted to practice
after going through his paces in Mr. Wythe's office. He practiced
law but a very short time, however, only until Governor Fauquier's successor, Lord Dunmore, of unpleasant memory, closed
the Virginian courts; then he retired forever from the profession,
closing out his practice to Edmund Randolph, whom Washington subsequently made Attorney General. Being well-to-do, he
could choose his practice, and having a distaste for the life of
an advocate or jury lawyer, he became a consultant. He had little
respect for the court lawyer's attainments, having cut his eye-
teeth on them some years before, when Patrick Henry, "the
laziest man in reading I ever knew," turned up at Williamsburg
for a license to practice law on the strength of six weeks' study
and actually got it, George Wythe being the only one of four
examiners with conscience enough to refuse consent. Mr. Jeffer-

son was circumspectly fascinated by Henry as by some kind of
living curiosity; he regularly shared his quarters with him when
Henry came to Williamsburg to attend court. He was always just
to Henry's talents as a popular orator and to the service he did
in the Revolutionary cause. He says that Henry's gifts for spellbinding "were great indeed; such as I never heard from any other
man. He appeared to me to speak as Homer wrote." Yet it was
sheer spellbinding. "I have frequently shut my eyes while he
spoke, and when he was done asked myself what he had said,
without being able to recollect a word of it." Appreciating Henry
fully, however, and really liking him, Mr. Jefferson had no respect
for his professional type; and as the type increased and multiplied
after its kind, this aversion was reinforced by an acute sense of the
detriment done the profession. After retiring from practice, he
writes Mr. Wythe that he thinks the bar of the General Court
a good training ground for judges, "if it be so regulated that
science may be encouraged and may live there. But this can never
be," he goes on indignantly, "if an inundation of insects is permitted to come from the county courts and consume the harvest.
. . . Men of science then (if there were to be any) would only
be employed as auxiliary counsel in difficult cases. But can they
live by that? Certainly not. The present members of that kind
therefore must turn marauders in the county courts; and in
future none will have leisure to acquire science."

Experience, in short, bred the same squeamishness toward law
that he entertained toward medicine—"it is not to physic that
I object so much as to physicians"—even though he himself
could afford to keep aloof from "the mob of the profession," and
even though all he knew about their temptations, fortunately,
was by hearsay. As a consulting lawyer he did extremely well.
His accounts show earnings of about three thousand dollars a
year from his profession, as against something like two thousand
dollars from his trade of farming; and this was a good income
for the time. But his distaste grew steadily, and even after he
gave up practice, it kept on growing. His earlier experience in
practical politics and in government building, where he saw the
worst degeneration of legal theory and practice, their frankest
dissociation from anything resembling justice and the public
good, increased his detestation of lawyers; and it was brought
to full growth by the chicanery that he found in high triumphant
progress on his return to America in 1789, after five years of

ambassadorship in Europe. As he passed into old age, it became inveterate. In 1810, advising a namesake on the choice of an occupation, he remarks that if a physician ends his days conscious that he has saved some lives and not killed anybody through carelessness, he will have "the happy reflection of not having lived in vain; while the lawyer has only to recollect how many, by his dexterity, have been cheated out of their right and reduced to beggary." If Congressmen talk too much, "how can it be otherwise," he writes contemptuously in 1821, "in a body to which the people send one hundred and fifty lawyers, whose trade it is to question everything, yield nothing, and talk by the hour?"

While his practice lasted, nevertheless, the disciple of Small brought to it all the scholarship, industry, precision, and speed of a true "man of science," as well as the touch of distinction and elevation which he contrived to put upon everything he did. Virginia had taken over English law in the gross, largely because the colonial lawyers—at all events, the "men of science" among them—already knew it, but chiefly, perhaps, because it was the only code written in a language that American lawyers could read. When the time came for Virginia to revise her statutes in conformity with her new political relations, Mr. Jefferson was a member of the assembly. He took his seat in October, 1776. A month before this, he had resigned his seat in the Continental Congress, where he had already had some instructive experience with lawyers in their deliberative capacity. "As the old Congress always sat with closed doors," said John Jay, years afterward, "the public knew no more of what passed within than what it was deemed expedient to disclose." When Mr. Jefferson left Congress, he also declined an appointment to go to France with Franklin to negotiate a treaty of alliance and commerce. To a man who liked preferment for its own sake, this appointment was flattering enough, but it was not otherwise an interesting commission. France had to be gotten into the war on the side of America, by hook or by crook, and in a hurry, too, for the military fortunes of the Revolution were at their lowest ebb; and Mr. Jefferson may reasonably have felt himself lacking in the peculiar gifts of persuasion and bargaining required for that kind of service. His own account of the matter, however, is not to be disparaged. His wife was ill—there was no doubt about that—and even Philadelphia, let alone Paris, was too far away from home. Besides, there were plenty of fish to be fried in Virginia.

"I knew that our legislation, under the regal government, had many very vicious points which urgently required reformation, and I thought I could be of more use in forwarding that work." So, for the next five years, he abandoned national interests and stuck to Virginia, always impatiently looking forward to the time when, having done what was to be done in helping his own state to weather through the period of war and reconstruction, he might call his "tour of service" finished for good and all.

With all his distaste for lawyers and the ways of lawyers, his professional training stood him in well during his service in the Virginia Assembly. He drafted and brought in a great flock of bills of a routine character, and four which represented the groundwork of his whole legislative scheme. These he considered as "forming a system by which every fibre would be eradicated of ancient or future aristocracy, and a foundation laid for a government truly republican." They are chiefly interesting now as showing how short a way they went toward these desirable ends. One was for repealing the laws of entail; and this, he quite sincerely believed, "would prevent the accumulation and perpetuation of wealth in select families, and preserve the soil of the country from being daily more and more absorbed in mortmain." Another was for the abolition of primogeniture, substituting the equal partition of estates, which he called "the best of all agrarian laws." A third was for religious liberty, to relieve the people from taxation for the support of a state church. The old days in Williamsburg had shown Mr. Jefferson quite enough of a state-owned religious monopoly, its establishment being "truly of the religion of the rich, the dissenting sects being entirely composed of the less wealthy people." The fourth bill comprised a scheme for general popular education, which he thought would qualify the citizenry "to understand their rights, to maintain them, and to exercise with intelligence their parts in self-government."

So great an advance did these measures represent that they had a hard time passing into law, and the education bill never did pass in its entirety. Yet they were popular measures, all but the education bill, which had no warm friends worth speaking of; the others touched a popular sentiment. As a desire for free trade was the animating spirit of the Revolution in one section of the country—that is to say, among the merchants and traders of New England—so free land was the desideratum among Virginians.

They wanted to see the great royal land grants broken up; they hated this monopoly as much as the Massachusetts merchant hated the British monopoly of his trade, and for the same reason: the merchant would do better in a free competitive market, and the Virginian would do better if he could get hold of some of the monopolized land for himself. Bills like Mr. Jefferson's, therefore, which squinted in the direction of this popular desire, were well received. Actually, the Virginian never got his free land; the royal patentee was dislodged only to give place to the speculator. Still, like Patrick Henry and many others, he might turn speculator himself, which was even better—there was always the chance of that—so Mr. Jefferson's bills were good bills. They had, however, to run the gantlet of a small and compact opposition, in which a number of motives had place and as many prejudices, social, economic, and religious. Washington and Patrick Henry, for instance, were not for pure voluntaryism in religion. They were for a compromise, whereby a general tax should be imposed for the support of churches, but leaving the individual taxpayer free to designate the denomination to which his contribution should go. "Although no man's sentiments are more opposed to any kind of restraint upon religious principles than mine are," Washington wrote to George Mason, "yet I confess that I am not among the number of those who are so much alarmed at the thoughts of making people pay towards the support of that which they profess." Washington was not impressed, apparently, by the prompt degeneration of a state-owned church into a mere political agency, which was the fact that chiefly impressed Mr. Jefferson, as it had impressed John Adams; and it lay at the root of the disestablishment bill.

The Virginia legislature shilly-shallied over these measures interminably; and not only over these, but over a general ratification of the work of the committee appointed to revise the existing statutes; which work was practically all done by Mr. Jefferson and George Wythe. There was nothing startling in this revision; nothing new, for instance, on the subject of slavery. "Nothing is more certainly written in the book of fate," said Mr. Jefferson, "than that these people are to be free." But he became well aware—wearily aware—that "the public mind would not yet bear the proposition." Indeed, if the temper of the legislature was any index of the public mind, it would not until 1796 bear even the proposition to limit the death penalty to cases of murder and treason or to eliminate the *lex talionis* from the criminal code. The revisers did the best they could, but their report still expressed to a great degree what Mr. Jefferson called the "revolting principle" of retaliation; it retained such penal measures as gibbeting, executing poisoners by poison, punishing maiming by maiming, and the like; and yet the legislature paltered along over the routine portions of the revision "until after the general peace in 1785, when by the unwearied exertions of Mr. Madison, in opposition to the endless quibbles, chicaneries, perversions, vexations and delays of lawyers and demi-lawyers, most of the bills were passed by the Legislature with little alteration"—and eleven years later, in 1796, the criminal code, which was lost by one vote in 1785, was finally passed.

Mr. Jefferson's professional training came handy to him occasionally also in his subsequent long career of office holding; sometimes in drafting opinions as Secretary of State under Washington and once notably during his own Presidency, in the celebrated Batture Case, to evict Edward Livingston from possession of a flat or shoal in the Mississippi, near New Orleans, called the Batture Sainte Marie. Mr. Jefferson's papers in this case, and particularly the recapitulatory brief which he drew up for use of his counsel when Livingston brought suit against him in 1811, are the work of a great lawyer, a great "man of science," and none the less great for being disillusioned. When John Adams read it, he said, "You have brought up to the view of the young generation of lawyers in our country, tracts and regions of legal information of which they never had dreamed." Mr. Jefferson's profession owed him nothing; the time and energy put in on it were well spent. "Every political measure," he wrote, "will forever have an intimate connexion with the laws of the land; and he who knows nothing of these will always be perplexed and often foiled by adversaries having the advantage of that knowledge over him."

Under pressure of a disillusionment essentially similar, his disposition to take part in public affairs evaporated with his interest in his profession. Apart from any question of abstract faith in republicanism and the parliamentary principle, he had quite got his fill of parliamentary bodies. The Continental Congress was bad enough; its tedious pettiness, its factions and feuds, its incessant collisions of self-interest and local interest made its service profoundly distasteful. Yet, after he had drawn in his horns and

retired to his own state, there was the Virginia Assembly which
was even worse. After trying to work with it as a legislator, he
tried working for it as an executive; he served two years as governor, during 1779 and 1780, in succession to Patrick Henry. He
took office at the worst possible time. The state was defenseless,
at the mercy of the British; it was without military resources.
He was as helpless at withstanding the enemy's incursions as
Henry had been at anticipating them. He had to endure the popular complaint that is always made in such circumstances; and like
any parliamentary body in such circumstances, the assembly was
always ready to make a scapegoat of the executive. A motion for
his impeachment, however, came to nothing; the charges were
preposterous; indeed, the affair ended by the assembly offering
Mr. Jefferson a unanimous and handsome resolution of amends.
This was all very well; it was a time of great stress, and some
allowances must be made. Yet it is a humiliating and repugnant
business to put oneself at the mercy of a crew of third-rate people
who do not know their own mind and have no self-reliance. Had
there not, indeed, been a strong movement in the assembly to
throw over republican government in the crisis and set up a dic-
tator? Of this Mr. Jefferson wrote indignantly that "the very
thought alone was treason against the people; was treason against
mankind in general; as rivetting forever the chains which bow
down their necks, by giving to their oppressors a proof, which
they would have trumpetted through the universe, of the im-
becility of republican government, in times of pressing danger,
to shield them from harm."

But should one go on indefinitely exposing oneself to the
brunt of ignorance, slackness, stupidity, irresponsibility, and petty
self-interest? Replying to Monroe's remonstrances, he says that
"however I might have comforted myself under the disapproba-
tion of the well-meaning but uninformed people, yet that of their
representatives was a shock on which I had not calculated." Mr.
Jefferson had not perhaps yet learned the official character of
representatives, but he was learning fast, and his own feeling was
that he had learned enough. He was forty years old, and more
than half his life was yet before him. He had been, as he wrote
Monroe, thirteen years engaged in the public service in one way
and another; and "during that time I had so totally abandoned
all attention to my private affairs as to permit them to run into
great disorder and ruin." So much was enough. Enough of public

affairs, enough of representative parliamentary bodies, enough of lawyers! Henceforth he would live as a farmer, a student, and an organizer of civilized amenities at Monticello. "I have taken my final leave," he writes Edmund Randolph, ". . . I have returned to my farm, my family and books, from which I think nothing will ever more separate me." This letter is dated September 16th, 1781; and one year later, lacking ten days, Mrs. Jefferson died.

III

Mr. Jefferson wrote his own epitaph, in which he describes himself as "author of the Declaration of American Independence, of the statute of Virginia for religious freedom, and father of the University of Virginia." We have his own word for it that these are the three achievements by which he most wished to be remembered, although he may have regarded them more impersonally than his words suggest, as illustrative of certain principles in which he was most interested. He seems so rarely to have taken a personal view of anything that this latter interpretation bears some probability. There is in existence, however, a brief note or memorandum, unfinished, undated, but evidently written when he was well along in years, a mere scrap, which lists in part his achievements for the public good. They are run off so informally that one may perhaps discern a suggestion of the relative importance that he assigned them in his own mind. The list begins abruptly:

I have sometimes asked myself whether my country is the better for my having lived at all. I do not know that it is. I have been the instrument of doing the following things; but they would have been done by others; some of them, perhaps, a little better.

The first item on the list is this:

The Rivanna had never been used for navigation; scarcely an empty canoe had ever passed down it. Soon after I came of age, I examined its obstructions, set on foot a subscription for removing them, got an Act of Assembly passed and the thing effected, so as to be used completely and fully for carrying down all our produce.

Then follows a bare notation of the Declaration of Independence; and the several items of his work on the Virginia statutes stand without comment. After this, he mentions his importation of olive trees from France in 1789 and 1790, for experimental planting an South Carolina and Georgia, and of heavy upland rice from Africa in 1790, "which I sent to Charleston in hopes it might supersede the culture of the wet rice which renders South Carolina and Georgia so pestilential through the summer." His paramount interest then comes out in the remark that "the greatest service which can be rendered to any country is to add a useful plant to its culture, especially a bread grain; next in value to bread is oil." Politics, as Homer said of words, "may make this way or that way," but to live at all, people must eat food; and the only way that food can be provided for them is by some one "labouring the earth" to produce it.

This dry but fundamental truth seems never to have been far out of Mr. Jefferson's mind. It governed his estimate of politics, of trade and commerce, of banking and manufacturing. When first he dabbled in public affairs, in pre-Revolution days, he was aware that whatever community of interest prevailed among the colonies was purely temporary and factitious. Massachusetts and Virginia, Connecticut and Pennsylvania, had for the time being to hang together, as Franklin said, lest all hands should hang separately later in London. All must unite to make the Revolution a success, but it was clear that as soon as this occasional interest was disposed of, the collision between their permanent interests would take place; and Mr. Jefferson made up his mind early—or, rather, his mind made itself up—about the side he was on. While Secretary of State in 1793, when the battle of economic interests was well under way, he wrote to an unidentified correspondent, "When I first entered on the stage of public life (now twenty-four years ago) I came to a resolution never . . . to wear any other character than that of a farmer."

But even as Virginian farming went in those days, he was not a good practical farmer. "To keep a Virginia estate together," he wrote mournfully to Monroe in the last year of his life, when his poverty amounted to destitution, "requires in the owner both skill and attention. Skill I never had, and attention I could not have; and really, when I reflect on all circumstances, my wonder is that I should have been so long as sixty years in reaching the result to which I am now reduced." If he had kept to his great resolution of 1781—that is to say, if his wife had not died—he might have become a better farmer than he was. Still, he was right about himself; skill he never had, and it is doubtful that he could have had it. He was careful, assiduous, diligent, ingenious, and no end *wissenschaftlich*—in all respects a man after

Dr. Small's own heart—nor was he quite the type of scientific adventurer who knows everything except what to do with his knowledge. Apparently he managed well, and he managed under uncommon difficulties; yet with all allowances made, he somehow lacked the knack of making more than fair-to-middling success. The Duc de la Rochefoucauld-Liancourt, who visited him in 1796, compliments the high quality of his management, especially complimenting the excellent treatment of his slaves; but he is struck with all a thrifty Frenchman's horror at the wastefulness of the "detestable method" of exhausting the soil and abandoning it, piece by piece, to recover as best it may. He remarks dryly that Mr. Jefferson "has drawn the principles of culture either from works which treat on this subject, or from conversation," which might perhaps do for Virginia, and he hopes for the best, but which he must say is often a misleading kind of knowledge, "and at all times insufficient in a country where agriculture is well understood," as in France, for example. Perhaps the distinguished exile compared the hillside fields of Albemarle with those of the Auvergne, coddled and coaxed to the limit of fertility as long ago, probably, as when they were swept by the vigilant eye of Vercingetorix. The duke mentions with dismay that on worked-over land—land that had been exhausted and left for a while to recuperate—the farmers of Albemarle got only about four bushels of wheat to the acre; and Mr. Jefferson himself writes in 1815 to the French economist Say, that "our best farmers (such as Mr. Randolph, my son-in-law) get from ten to twenty bushels of wheat to the acre; our worst (such as myself) from six to eighteen"!

Yet some of Mr. Jefferson's anticipations in the science of agriculture are interesting. He seems, for instance, to have done something in the way of efficiency studies, though the purpose to which they were directed is not clear.

Julius Shard fills the two-wheeled barrow in 3 minutes, and carries it 30 yards in 1½ minutes more. Now this is four loads of the common barrow with one wheel. So suppose that the 4 loads put in at the same time viz. 3 minutes, 4 trips will take 4 × 1½ minutes = 6, which added to 3 minutes filling = 9 minutes to fill and carry the same earth which was filled and carried in the two-wheeled barrow in 4½. From a trial I made with the same two-wheeled barrow, I found that a man could dig and carry to the distance of 50 yds, 5 cubical yds' of earth in a day of 12 hours length. Ford's Phill did it; not overlooked [i.e.

supervised] and having to mount his loaded barrow up a bank 2 f.
high and tolerably steep.

When Mr. Jefferson ventured into this special technique, he
also took on something of the efficiency engineer's slowness to
see that the human being is not for all purposes a machine. His
farm book has this note on the rye and wheat harvest of 1795:

Were the harvest to go over again with the same force, the following arrangement should take place:
The treading-floors should be laid down before harvest. ½ a doz.
   spare scythes should be mounted, and fingers for ½ a dozen
   more ready formed, bent and mortised, and some posts should
   be provided.
1, Great George, with tools and grindstone mounted in the single
   mule cart, should be constantly employed mending cradles and
   grinding scythes. The same cart would carry about the liquor,
   moving from tree to tree as the work advanced.
18 cradlers should work constantly.
18 binders, of the women and abler boys.
 6 gatherers, to wit. 5 smallest boys and 1 large for a foreman.
 3 loaders, Moses, Shepherd and Joe, leading the carts successively
   with the drivers.
 6 stackers,
 2 cooks,
 4 carters
   ___
   58
    8 would remain to keep half the ploughs a-going.
   ___
   66
In this way the whole machine would move in exact equilibrio,
no part of the force could be lessened without retarding the whole,
nor increased without a waste of force.
This force would cut, bring in and shock 54 acres a day, and complete my harvest of 320 acres in 6 days.

As a matter of mathematics, there could be no doubt about
this. Yet when the plan was put in practice on the next harvest,
the imponderabilia, as Bismarck called them, stepped in and
wrecked his calculations. The whole machine did not move in
exact equilibrio—far from it. On July 2, we have the entry, "We
stopped our ploughs, the pickers not keeping up with the cutters."
Again: "Though 18 mowers had been fixed on and furnished with
27 scythes, yet the wheat was so heavy for the most part that

we had not more than 13 or 14 mowers cutting on an average." Finally, alas! for the calculation of a complete harvest, cut brought in, and shocked in six days, though Dr. Small himself might have put the great seal of his certification on every figure, "13 cutters × 12 days = 156, which gives near 2 acres a day for each cutter, supposing 300 acres." [1]

Remembering Poe's acute observation that the truly practical man must be a balanced combination of mathematician and poet, one often finds the sheer mathematician predominating in Mr. Jefferson's dealings with human nature on the farm; as, for instance, in the observation that "a barrel of fish costing seven dollars goes as far with the labourers as two hundred pounds of pork costing fourteen dollars." Many entries, too, seem over-curious. "Cart. H. Harrison tells me it is generally allowed that 250 lb. green pork makes 220 lb. pickled." His own experiment turned out that "100 lb. of green pork makes 88 lb. pickled do. or 75 lb. of bacon." He weighed a ham and shoulder when green: "The one weighed 24 lb. the other 17 lb. After they were made into bacon each had lost exactly a fourth." Then the really important fact is dropped in with somewhat the air of an after-thought, "They were of cornfed hogs." In considering his grain harvest, he makes note that "G. Divers supposes that every cubic yard of a stack of wheat yields generally 2 bushels of grain," and that "Jo. Watkins says he knows from actual experiment that wheat loses 2 lb. in the bushel weight from Oct. to January, which is 1 pr. cent pr. month"; also "it is thought that any ground will yield as much wheat as rye, and that wheat exhausts less than rye."

There is too little of the poet also in his minute observation that the interstices in corded wood, according to one authority, make one third of the whole volume; remarking, however, that

[1] Shortly after this time, the Southern planters generally began to make studies in industrial efficiency, and developed a highly effective technique in scientific management, although, like Molière's hero, they did not call it by that name, or, indeed, by any name. With this development came the rise of excellent agricultural journals which still repay perusal from a practical as well as an antiquarian interest. Some of their reports make depressing reading. There is, for instance, an actuarial estimate, well worked out and doubtless accurate, that the life of a laborer in the ricefields would last eight years. In reckoning depreciation of capital, therefore, the planter calculated that his investment in a slave would evaporate in that period, and he managed accordingly.

"various experiments giving from 10 parts solid for from 3½ to 8 interstices, averaged on the whole 3 parts solid to 2 void, so that the interstices are 2/5 and the solid 3/5." The predominant mathematician is not content to know that cutting firewood with a saw is faster and less wasteful than cutting it with an axe. "The loss of wood in cutting firewood with an axe is 15 pr. cent, and takes twice as long as the saw, a tree of 18 i. being crosscutted in 4 minutes, and cut with the axe in 8 minutes." Again: "The circuit of the base of Monticello is 5¼ miles; the area of the base about 890 acres. Within the limits of that base I this day tried the temperature of 15 springs, 10 on the South and 5 on the N. side of the mountain, the outward air being generally about 75° of Farenheit." He then tabulates the result of this investigation, but there is nothing remarkable about the figures, and one cannot make out from them any reason why he should have taken all this trouble to get them. Again: "Tom with his 3 small mules brings 15 bundles of nailrod = 840 lb. in his cart from Milton, which he considers is a very heavy load." "Phill's 3 mules bring 1600 lb. from Milton, a very heavy load for them. It was 25 bundles of nailrod and 200 lb. bar iron."

Yet entries like these, little practical as they may be, are not quite worthless. They may be taken as a parallel to that other category of entries which runs along with them, noting the appearance of leaves, flowers, and wild fruits and the motion of birds and insects. Late in January of one year, for example, after record of the temperature comes the entry "blue-birds are here." On March 11, "blackbirds here"; on the 17th, "almonds bloom"; on the first of April, the single word "lilac"; on the second, "whippoorwill"; on the ninth, "martins appear." In June, there is a note of "a solar eclipse, almost total"; later in the month, "aurora borealis at 10 h. pm, abᵗ 45° high on the horizon"; and still later, "a feild lark at Shadwell, the first I ever saw so far Westerly." In the autumn again, in October, there is the line, "walnut and mulberry lost leaves." Later in the month, the sobering record, "Cherry, common locust, lost leaves. First frost at Montic."; and a week afterward, "Poplars, white mulberry, wild crab, nearly stripped of leaves." The winter was near.

The Duke of Saxe-Weimar paid a visit to Monticello in the last year of Mr. Jefferson's life. He saw him in his setting of long, laborious days beginning at dawn—"the sun has not caught me in bed in fifty years"—noting carefully the wind and the weather, his eye on the leaves and flowers, his ear open to the birds' note; isolated among "plain, honest and rational neighbours, some of them well informed and men of reading, all superintending their farms, hospitable and friendly, and speaking nothing but English"; intensely curious about the most insignificant of nature's doings, getting opinions about them from the experience of fellow laborers like G. Divers and Jo. Watkins, and diligently recording what he learned. In the English version of the Duke's reminiscences, there is an odd and unusual translation of the German word *ehrwürdig*, which somehow sticks in one's mind as most appropriate. On the morning of his departure, he says, "after breakfast, which we took with the family, we bid the respectable old man farewell, and set out upon our return to Charlottesville."

IV

Mr. Jefferson's farming managed to pay its way for a time, but not by a comfortable margin. At almost any point in his history one is prepared to find him anticipating the modern lawyer-farmer, who practices law to keep the farm going. He had an immense amount of land; so much that if land had been taxed even nominally, he would have been land-poor. He owned more than a dozen properties, with a total of nearly eleven thousand acres; half of it in Albemarle County, half in Bedford and Campbell. In 1774 he became owner, by land patent, of the Natural Bridge, in Rockbridge County, a matter of about 150 acres. He acquired this out of a sheer art-collector's spirit; he was in love with the place, "the most sublime of nature's works. . . . It is impossible for the sensations arising from the sublime to be felt beyond what they are here. . . . The rapture of the spectator is really indescribable. " He had thoughts now and then "of building a little hermitage at the Natural Bridge (for it is my property) and of passing there a part of the year at least"; but his building operations were always more or less overextended, and he never got around to this one. Not one fifth of his land in Albemarle was under cultivation, and not one sixth of his property in Bedford. The property at Monticello came to a little more than one thousand acres, and it barely sufficed to keep the household going; it did not—if one can believe it—yield enough surplus to feed the guests. True, the household was large; the house servants alone numbered between thirty and forty. Guests, moreover, came not singly or occasionally, but in hordes, with horses and carriages and servants; in the last twenty years of Mr. Jefferson's life, it may be said literally and without exaggeration that they ate him out of house and home. There was a good deal of hillside farming, too, on the Monticello property. But making every possible allowance for everything, almost any kind of farming ought to enable a thousand-acre property to give a better account of itself than Monticello ever gave; for in 1794 he records that on this property "on both sides of the river we have made thirty-seven and a half bushels of wheat above what has been sowed for next year"!

He complains of "the ravages of overseers" during his protracted absences on public duty, and no doubt they were bad. With a touch of grim humor he speaks his mind about overseers and also about the Virginian implantation of Scots-Irish, in a letter to William Wirt, written in 1815 in reply to a question concerning class distinctions in early Virginian society. "Certain families had risen to splendour by wealth and the preservation of it from generation to generation under the law [of] entails; some had produced a series of men of talents, families in general had remained stationary on the grounds of their forefathers, for there was no emigration to the westward in those days. The wild Irish, who had gotten possession of the valley between the Blue Ridge and North Mountain, forming a barrier over which none ventured to leap, and would still less venture to settle among. . . . There were then aristocrats, half-breeds, pretenders; a solid independent yeomanry, looking askance at those above, yet not venturing to jostle them; and, last and lowest, a fæculum of beings called overseers, the most abject, degraded and unprincipled race, always cap in hand to the Dons who employed them, and furnishing material for the exercise of their pride, insolence and spirit of domination." In his farm book he makes note of "articles for contracts with overseers," in one of which there is the odd provision that overseers are "not allowed to keep a horse or a goose, or to keep a woman out of the crop for waiting on them." Some light on the ways of overseers, perhaps, appears in the agreement that the overseer shall "exchange clear profits with his employer at the end of the year, if the employer chuses it." The overseer, too, must "pay his share of liquor and hiring at harvest," as a measure for promoting economy in the use of both.

Bad as the ravages of overseers may have been, however, there were worse, due to the military policy of terrorism established in Virginia by Cornwallis. Mr. Jefferson's interest in the four thousand prisoners of Burgoyne's army, quartered in Virginia, had been substantial. He helped them establish themselves comfortably, made their officers at home in his house, and came publicly to their defense when the rural population, in a silly panic over a possible scarcity of food, was bringing pressure on Governor Henry to make them move out. For this he got their lasting gratitude and friendship, and with some of them, such as von Riedesel, von Geismer, and von Unger, he kept up acquaintance for a long time. His philosophy of the occasion is shown in a letter to the British Major General Phillips, acknowledging some complimentary phrases, and remarking that "the great cause which divides our countries is not to be decided by individual animosities. The harmony of private societies can not weaken national efforts. To contribute by neighbourly intercourse and attention to make others happy, is the shortest and surest way of being happy ourselves." This novel doctrine no doubt puzzled Phillips considerably, for he was a good soldier, with a soldier's mentality and a soldier's sense of the public value of "individual animosities" in time of war; but it seems, nevertheless, to have made some impression on him.

Thus it was, probably, that some of the bread which Mr. Jefferson sowed on the turbid waters of nationalist hatred came back to him at the hands of Tarleton, one of the subordinate British commanders in eastern Virginia. The unexpected strength shown by the Americans in the North and the unexpected obstinacy of their resistance caused the British to turn their attention to Georgia, the Carolinas, and Virginia in a campaign of devastation. Phillips and Arnold ravaged the Tidewater and Piedmont sections of Virginia, and Tarleton moved on Albemarle County to disperse the assembly which was in session at Charlottesville. By this time, Mr. Jefferson had succeeded Patrick Henry in the governorship. While gathering up and bagging what stray legislators he could find, Tarleton, who despite his profession seems to have been much of a man, sent a detachment to Monticello under Captain McLeod, to go through the motions of capturing Governor Jefferson.[1] The expedition really amounted to no more than this. Tarleton gave strict orders that nothing

[1] Mr. Jefferson's term had, in fact, expired two days before Tarleton's demonstration.

at Monticello should be injured. Mr. Jefferson rode away from
the house on horseback no more than five minutes before McLeod
appeared, and no serious effort was made to overtake him. Captain McLeod remained at Monticello for a day, reconnoitering in
a perfunctory fashion, and then moved off. Some of his men
chivvied the Negro house servants a little, merely by way of
entertaining themselves, but no harm was done to anyone or to
anything.

In general, however, the British did their work with great thor-
oughness. "History will never relate the horrors committed by
the British army in the Southern States of America," Mr. Jefferson wrote to Dr. Gordon. "They raged in Virginia six months
only. . . . I suppose their whole devastations during those six
months amounted to about three millions sterling." Mr. Jefferson's properties outside Albemarle fell under the hand of Cornwallis himself, who seems to have been untroubled by scruples
of any kind. "He destroyed all my growing crops of corn and tobacco. He burned all my barns containing the same articles of
the last year, having first taken what corn he wanted; he used, as
was to be expected, all my stock of cattle, sheep and hogs for the
sustenance of his army, and carried off all the horses capable of
service; of those too young for service he cut the throats; and
he burned all the fences on the plantation, so as to leave it an
absolute waste. He carried off also about thirty slaves. Had this
been to give them freedom, he would have done right; but it was
to consign them to inevitable death from the small pox and putrid
fever, then raging in his camp. . . . Wherever he went, the dwell-
ing-houses were plundered of everything which could be carried
off."

Severe as these losses were, Mr. Jefferson never alluded to them
publicly, as far as is known, until seven years afterward, when, in
answer to Dr. Gordon's inquiries, he wrote the foregoing account
of them in a characteristically objective fashion. He contented
himself with entering his "losses by the British in 1781" as a bare
business item in his farm book. From his Cumberland property,
eight slaves "fled to the enemy and died." Of twenty-seven others
from his various properties, some "caught small pox from enemy
and died"; some "joined enemy, returned and died." Some stay-
at-homes "caught the camp fever from the negroes who returned,
and died." He was faithful to the sick runaways, even to those
who were too far gone to have any further value as property,

bringing them back on mattresses and stretchers, and giving them care. "Expenses seeking and bringing back some" are put down at twenty pounds sterling, and he "paid Doctors attending sick" sixty-five pounds.

These interruptions and devastations were bad for farming. In this same year, 1781, Mr. Jefferson records that most of the crops which he had on his undamaged properties were "lost for want of labourers." With the drawbacks of war, long absence, intense preoccupation with public affairs, "the ravages of overseers," slave labor, and a series of bad seasons, all added to the fact that Mr. Jefferson, notwithstanding his science, ability, and diligence, had not much of the humbler man's natural knack with practical farming, one is not surprised that his agricultural operations went on three legs to the end. The astonishing thing, as he himself says, is that they should have managed to drag on for so long a time as sixty years before coming to their final breakdown in bankruptcy.

v

One great bar to his prosperity in early days was Mrs. Jefferson's share of a debt incurred by her father to some British creditors. This amounted, in round numbers, to four thousand pounds sterling; and various depreciations of currency and fluctuations in exchange resulted actually in his paying the debt three times over, at a sacrifice of nearly half his estate. The general matter of debts due from the colonists to British creditors was an important public question which remained unsettled until the adoption of the Constitution. It was felt by many that since these debts had been in large part brought about by deliberate manipulation in the English market, they might fairly be repudiated. Several states, in fact, had enabled their repudiation more or less directly. Mr. Jefferson was not unsympathetic toward this view, but declined to exercise it in his own interest. "What the laws of Virginia are or may be," he wrote his creditors, "will in no wise influence my conduct. Substantial justice is my object, as decided by reason, and not by authority or compulsion." The damages inflicted on him by Cornwallis more than offset the debt; still, that was a matter of public policy, while the debt was a private affair, the British creditors were private persons, and he thought that the line between private and public responsibility should be kept as clear as the line between private animosities and public issues. He finally satisfied his creditors by selling his land on virtual terms of a forced sale. His first sale for this purpose amounted to £4,200, and he afterward told his grandchildren in grim jest that he got only enough out of it in real money to pay for a new overcoat; for he sold at hard-money prices, taking in payment bonds which were subsequently redeemed in paper money worth about two cents in the dollar.

He carried on some manufacturing operations on his properties under stress of necessity, for the rural proprietors in Virginia had to make nearly everything they used. "Every article is made on his farm," wrote the Duc de la Rochefoucauld-Liancourt. "His negroes are cabinet-makers, carpenters, masons, bricklayers, smiths, etc. The young and old negresses spin for the clothing of the rest." Mr. Jefferson did not go in for clothmaking on a large scale, however, until some years after the duke's visit, when commerce with Europe was interrupted by the circumstances which led up to the war of 1812; then, vowing his independence of foreign manufacturers, he put in improved machinery which, "costing $150 only, and worked by two women and two girls, will more than furnish" the two thousand yards of linen, cotton, and woollen goods which he needed yearly. He employed slaves at shoemaking, noting in his farm book that "a side of upper leather and a side of soal make 6 pr. shoes and take ½ lb. thread, so that a hide and 1 lb. of thread shoe 6 Negroes." His cost-accounting system brings the "worth of a pair of shoes," reckoning labor at two shillings, to eight shillings sixpence. It seems a good price, though slave labor was slow and inefficient. Every line of work, indeed, felt this steady drag of inefficiency. "Johnny Hemings began the body of a Landau Jan. 12, and finished it this day, being 9 weeks + 5 days. He had not more help from Lewis than made up for his interruptions. The smith's work employed the 2 smiths perhaps ⅓ of the same time." Again: "Johnny Hem. and Lewis began a dressing-table and finished it in exactly 6 weeks of which 4 weeks was such dreadful weather that, even within doors, nothing like full work could be done."

One of the perplexities incidental to the employment of slave labor lay in finding something for the children to do. Mr. Jefferson's way was perhaps as good as any. "Children till 10 years old to serve as nurses; from 10 to 16 the boys make nails, the girls spin; at 16 go into the ground [i.e., go at farm work] or learn trades." Mr. Jefferson's nailery and his grist mill on the Rivanna were the only enterprises that he operated for profit; and here again it appears that the cheapest labor is the dearest. His cost sheet on the nailery, or "Estimate on the actual work of the autumn of 1794," with its record of nearly one fourth net wastage, is a remarkable exhibit of industrial inefficiency.

But what better could be done with these boys? They could not be effectively disciplined. They could not be discharged; they were slave children, permanently on one's hands. It was to no purpose to try to educate them beyond their slave status; and even if one killed them off, their place would be taken almost immediately by others precisely like them.

VI

While Mr. Jefferson's services to practical agriculture netted him little or nothing, they were of great benefit to the nation at large. Whenever he heard of a new device that bore upon farming, he promptly looked it up and wrote about it to his fellow farmers. In the midst of the turmoil of 1793, when as Washington's Secretary of State he saw the Administration fast going on the rocks, the country at the boiling point over the economic implications of the Constitution, and himself "worn down with labours from morning to night and day to day, knowing them as fruitless to others as they are vexatious to myself," he asks Madison whether he had "ever taken notice of Tull's horse-hoeing plow," and says it is of doubtful value. Two months later, when the French minister Genêt had "thrown down the gauntlet to the President," and one of Genêt's consuls had employed armed force against a United States marshal in the matter of the seizure of two vessels in Boston harbor; when pestilence, of which "at first 3 out of 4 died, and now about 1 out of 3," was ravaging Philadelphia, the temporary capital—he informs Madison that his threshing machine has arrived, and that "fortunately the workman who made it (a millwright) is come in the same vessel to settle in America. I have written to persuade him to go on immediately to Richmond, offering him the use of my model to exhibit, and to give him letters to get him into immediate employ in making them." Shortly after this, he writes with enthusiasm about a new seedbox which "reduces the expense of seeding from six shillings to two shillings and threepence the acre, and does the business better than is possible to be done by the human hand."

He found leisure to work out several devices of his own, but never patented one of them, "never having thought of monopolizing by patent any useful idea which happens to offer itself to me." On the contrary, whenever he devised anything useful, he always published a description of it. Of his hemp beater, for example, he says, "As soon as I can speak of its effect with certainty I shall probably describe it anonymously in the public papers, in order to forestall the prevention of its use by some interloping patentee." He was step-motherly toward patents. "Nobody wishes more than I do that ingenuity should receive a liberal encouragement," and no doubt "an inventor ought to be allowed a right to the benefit of his invention for some certain time." Yet on the other hand, "it may be observed that the nations which refuse monopolies of invention are as fruitful . . . in new and useful devices" as England, the only country which granted them. The line between use and abuse was hard to draw; and it should in any case be drawn by "men of science" rather than by lawyers and legislators, since "we might in vain turn over all the lubberly volumes of the law to find a single ray which would lighten the path of the mechanic or the mathematician." Mr. Jefferson's bill of 1791 "to Promote the Progress of the Useful Arts" represented probably the best practical compromise that could be made between the interests of the inventor and those of the public; and it is no doubt due to him that the course of American patent law has borne no harder upon the public's interests than it has.

For himself, however, he would have nothing to do with patents. He had no taste for money made out of any form of monopoly. In 1810, when the country was pursuing a policy of commercial isolation, it was a mark of high patriotism not to use imported goods. About this time, merino sheep were introduced with a view to improving the wool of domestic textiles, and the demand for them at once opened a harvest for the alert profiteer. "I have been so disgusted with the scandalous extortions lately practised in the sale of these animals, and with the ascription of patriotism and praise to the sellers, as if the thousands of dollars apiece they have not been ashamed to receive were not rewards enough, that I am disposed to consider as right whatever is the reverse of what they have done." He accordingly writes to Presi-

dent Madison, suggesting a plan for the gradual cooperative distribution of the merino stock, gratis, among all the farmers of
Virginia. "No sentiment is more acknowledged in the family of
agriculturists than that the few who can afford it should incur
the risk and expense of all new improvements, and give the benefit freely to the many of more restricted circumstances." From doing this in the case of the merinos, he says there will "more
satisfaction result to ourselves than money ever administered to
the bosom of a shaver"; and then, remembering how Madison's
inveterate cautiousness was sharpened by residence in the White
House, he adds characteristically, "There will be danger that what
is here proposed, though but an act of ordinary duty, may be
perverted into one of ostentation; but malice will always find
bad motives for good actions. Shall we therefore never do good?"

He did his best to promote the culture of the fig, mulberry,
and sugar maple, as especially suitable to a slave-holding country,
because it afforded light and appropriate labor for women and
children, who were "often employed in labours disproportioned
to their sex and age." He experimented with a peach orchard to
prove that "five acres of peach trees at twenty-one feet apart will
furnish dead wood enough to supply a fireplace all winter, and
may be kept up at the trouble of only planting about seventy
peach stones a year." Each year that he was in the White House
he kept record of the first and last appearance of every variety of
vegetable—thirty-seven in all—put on sale in the Washington
market; and he made a neat tabulation at the end, covering the
whole period of eight years. He projected a kind of cooperative
volunteer weather bureau and actually did something with the
idea, but his life was so much interrupted by long absences that
it could not be fully carried out. Observing that the type of plow
in general use could be improved, he worked out the mathemati-
cal formula, which still governs the shape of plowshares, for a
moldboard of least resistance. The French national institute of
agriculture examined one of his plows and gave him a prize for
it. This plow was still on view in Paris a few years ago and probably may be seen there even now. Timepieces were scarce among
the poorer farmers of Virginia; so in 1811, while laid up with a
run of rheumatism at Poplar Forest, "I have amused myself with
calculating the hour-lines of a horizontal dial for the latitude of
this place, which I find to be 37° 22′ 26″." He sent the formula
with directions for making the sun dial to a friend in Williams-

burg, suggesting that it be passed along, since the calculations "would serve for all the counties in the line between that place and this, for your own place, New London, and Lynchburg in this neighbourhood." He devised the leather buggytop which is still in use. When phosphoric matches came out, he was among the first to try them, and he turned himself into a kind of volunteer agency for advertising and distributing them as "a beautiful discovery and very useful, especially to heads which, like yours and mine, can not at all times be got to sleep." About this time, also, or perhaps a little later, he conferred an unintended benefit upon the bureaucracies of all civilized lands by inventing the swivel chair.

CHAPTER III

1784-1789

I

In 1784 John Adams and Benjamin Franklin were in Europe, as ministers plenipotentiary to negotiate treaties of commerce, struggling to revive the wilted credit of America and galvanize its palsied trade. On the seventh of May, the Congress resolved to add a third minister to its foreign staff. Age and infirmity were telling on Franklin; he wanted to come home, and it would be a hard matter to fill his place. John Adams could not be transferred to Paris; he was hardly the man to get on with the French, and he was doing so well in London that his removal would make, practically, two holes in the foreign service instead of one. Of the few men available—for there was no great competition among able men for this kind of position, or indeed for any position under the new government—Mr. Jefferson seemed best qualified. Madison thought he would be willing to serve; he had already shown himself willing to go abroad as one of the peace commissioners, and it seemed likely, as Madison said, that "the death of Mrs. Jefferson had probably changed the sentiments of Mr. Jefferson with regard to public life." This new appointment was less interesting than the place on the peace commission, and from the point of view of the practical politician it led nowhere; still, he might be induced to accept it.

The appointment really suited him, though for reasons not contemplated by the Congress. He was drifting into a bad way.

For a year and a half, since his wife's death, he had been melancholy and despondent, giving free rein to his natural turn for solitude. His only hold on public affairs was through his seat in Congress, where he became more than ever a silent member. Despondency aggravated his contempt for the ineptitude of this body, and contempt, in turn, reacted on his despondency. The Congress, he says, "was little numerous but very contentious. Day after day was wasted on the most unimportant questions." The behavior of "those afflicted with the morbid rage of debate" caused him to regard it as "really more questionable than may at first be thought, whether Bonaparte's dumb legislature which said nothing and did much may not be preferable to one which talks much and does nothing." Listless and depressed as he was, however, he did whatever came to his hand to do. Among other matters, he proposed the present monetary unit of the United States, the dollar, and the basis of the present coinage, namely: the ten-dollar gold piece, the silver dollar, the silver ten-cent piece, and the copper penny. He drafted an ordinance for the temporary government of the Northwestern Territory, inserting an anti-slavery clause which was struck out by the Congress on the narrow margin of one vote. The Congress also struck out part of the provisions for admission of new states. Mr. Jefferson's draft not only established the boundaries of these states, but did not leave even their names to "the consent of the governed." One was to be called Pelisipia; another "within the peninsula formed by the lakes and waters of Michigan, Huron, St. Clair and Erie, shall be called Cherronesus"; another, Metropotamia; another, Polypotamia; and so on. The Congress put its shoulder manfully under this nomenclature and heaved it out of the bill.

The appointment to France was not precisely a sinecure, yet it was not exacting. It meant prying open the French market to American rice, salt fish, salt meat, fish oil, and tobacco, on as favorable terms as possible, and getting a free entry for American products into the French West Indies. Important as it was, it was nothing that a person could work at week in and week out. Mr. Jefferson saw in it a prospect of profitable leisure, which he had his own notions about employing. His ideas are exhibited in a set of traveling notes, which he prepared later on the strength of his own experience, for Messrs. Rutledge and Shippen's semi-official tour of Europe in 1788:

General Observations

On arriving at a town, the first thing is to buy the plan of the town, and the book noting its curiosities. Walk round the ramparts when there are any, go to the top of a steeple to have a view of the town and its environs.

When you are doubting whether a thing is worth the trouble of going to see, recollect that you will never again be so near it, that you may repent the not having seen it, but can never repent having seen it. But there is an opposite extreme, too, that is, the seeing too much. A judicious selection is to be aimed at, taking care that the indolence of the moment have no influence in the decision. Take care particularly not to let the porters of churches, cabinets, etc., lead you through all the little details of their profession, which will load the memory with trifles, fatigue the attention, and waste that and your time. It is difficult to confine these people to the few objects worth seeing and remembering. They wish for your money, and suppose you give it the more willingly the more they detail to you. . . . The people you will naturally see the most of will be tavern keepers, *valets de place* and postilions. These are the hackneyed rascals of every country. Of course they must never be considered when we calculate the national character.

Objects of Attention for an American

1. Agriculture. Everything belonging to this art, and whatever has a near relation to it. Useful or agreeable animals which might be transported to America. Species of plants for the farmer's garden, according to the climate of the different States.
2. Mechanical arts, so far as they respect things necessary in America, and inconvenient to be transported thither ready-made, such as forges, stone-quarries, boats, bridges (very especially), etc., etc.
3. Lighter mechanical arts, and manufactures. Some of these will be worth a superficial view; but circumstances rendering it impossible that America should become a manufacturing country during the time of any man now living, it would be a waste of attention to examine these minutely.
4. Gardens. Peculiarly worth the attention of an American, because it is the country of all others where the noblest gardens may be made without expense. We have only to cut out the superabundant plants.
5. Architecture. Worth great attention. As we double our numbers every twenty years, we must double our houses. Besides, we build of such perishable materials that one-half of our houses must be rebuilt in every space of twenty years, so that in that time houses

are to be built for three-fourths of our inhabitants. It is, then, among the most important arts; and it is desirable to introduce taste into an art which shows so much.

6. Painting. Statuary. Too expensive for the state of wealth among us. It would be useless therefore, and preposterous, for us to make ourselves connoisseurs in those arts. They are worth seeing, but not studying.

7. Politics of each country, well worth studying so far as respects internal affairs. Examine their influence on the happiness of the people. Take every possible occasion for entering into the houses of the labourers and especially at the moment of their repast; see what they eat, how they are clothed, whether they are obliged to work too hard; whether the government or their landlord takes from them an unjust proportion of their labour; on what footing stands the property they call their own, their personal liberty, etc., etc.

8. Courts. To be seen as you would see the Tower of London or menagerie of Versailles with their lions, tigers, hyaenas, and other beasts of prey, standing in the same relation to their fellows. A slight acquaintance with them will suffice to show you that under the most imposing exterior, they are the weakest and worst part of mankind.

II

Mr. Jefferson left for Europe from the port of Boston by the merchant sailing vessel *Ceres* on the fifth of July, 1784, taking with him his oldest daughter Martha and "the new fiddle" which he had originally contemplated purchasing in Italy. In 1771 he had seen with a hankering eye a magnificent violin in possession of a shoestring relative, one of the innumerable Randolph connection, living in Williamsburg. John Randolph also looked covetously at certain books in Mr. Jefferson's library. They could not agree. Mr. Jefferson could not bring himself to part with his books, nor John Randolph the violin. They finally devised an agreement for a kind of posthumous bargain or gamble: an ironclad document from which there was neither escape nor appeal. It was attested by as many as seven witnesses and duly recorded by the clerk of the General Court:

October 11th, 1771.

It is agreed between John Randolph, esq., of the city of Williamsburg, and Thomas Jefferson of the County of Albemarle, that in case the said John shall survive the said Thomas, that the Exr's or Adm'rs of the said Thomas shall deliver to the said John 800 pounds sterling of the books of the said Thomas, to be chosen by the said John, or if not books sufficient, the deficiency to be made up in money: And in case the said Thomas should survive the said John, that the Executors of the said John shall deliver to the said Thomas the violin which the said John brought with him into Virginia, together with all his music composed for the violin, or in lieu thereof if destroyed by any accident, 60 pounds sterling worth of books of the said John, to be chosen by the said Thomas. In witness whereof the said John and Thomas have hereunto subscribed their names and affixed their seals the day and year above written.

John Randolph (L.S.)
Th. Jefferson (L.S.)

Sealed and delivered in presence of

G. Wythe,	Will. Drew,
Tho's. Everand,	Richard Starke,
P. Henry, Jr.,	Wm. Johnson,

Ja. Steptoe.

Death seemed far off, however, and the said Thomas was impatient to get his itching fingers on the fiddle. He appears not to have pressed the matter on John Randolph, but neither does he seem ever to have lost sight of it. After four years—whether by force of being temporarily hard up, or wearied by Mr. Jefferson's quiet pertinacity, or for whatever reason—John Randolph finally weakened. Mr. Jefferson's pocket account book carries the entry, under date of the seventeenth of August, "Delivered to Carter Braxton an order on the Treasurer in favour of J. Randolph, Att'y-General, for £13, the purchase-money for his violin. This dissolves our bargin recorded in the General Court, and revokes a legacy of £100 sterling to him now standing in my will, which was made in consequence of that bargain."

So, with his little daughter and his violin, Mr. Jefferson set out. His journey up from his home to Boston, where his ship lay, was a matter of nearly two months, because he wished to get acquainted with the principal interests of the eastern states, "informing myself of the state of commerce of each." Heretofore he had only a hearsay acquaintance with these matters, no more than would come in the way of any intelligent Virginian planter. He made a leisurely progress through New Jersey, New York, Connecticut, and Rhode Island, wrestling valiantly with the different state currencies as he went along. His pocket account book shows a reasonable ground for gratitude that in all his wide range of early studies mathematics was "ever my favorite one."

With "New York currency, Dollars 8/" and "Connecticut, Dollars 6/" and "Rhode Island State" currency at still another rate of sterling exchange, paying for a dinner or a night's lodging was an appalling business. He reached Boston on the eighteenth of June, deposited his heavy luggage, and then left for a side trip of two weeks in New Hampshire and Vermont.

The voyage from Boston to the English port of Cowes was uncommonly fast—twenty-one days. Mr. Jefferson made his usual thrifty use of it by studying navigation. He had nothing else to do, and one can never know by what off chance new learning will some day come handy. He calculated courses, read charts, took the sun, and kept a workmanlike log, becoming a pretty fair theoretical navigator by the end of the voyage. On landing at Cowes, he got on as far as Portsmouth, where his poor little daughter, seasick and bored, having had no special interest in navigation to sustain her against ship's fare, discomfort, and tedium, took to her bed. After looking out for her as best he could for three days, Mr. Jefferson capitulated to the distrusted profession by calling in a physician, a Dr. Meek, who charged him two guineas sterling for two visits. Toward the end of July, Patsy had picked herself up enough to face the last leg of her journey, and on the thirtieth she and her father set out on the wretched crossing from Portsmouth to Havre.

Like all green travelers, Mr. Jefferson learned by experience as he went along. Practically a vegetarian, fond of fruits and nuts, he invested heavily in these luxuries during his first few days on land, welcoming the change from the restricted diet of the ship. He bought a couple of shillings' worth of nuts and a good deal of fruit as soon as he landed in England, and he did the same at Havre. Then, in about the time it would normally take for a brisk run of tourist's summer complaint to set in, these entries in his account book abruptly cease, and he seems hardly to have eaten another nut or piece of fruit for five years.

The entries for charity run a like course. Mr. Jefferson was always so open-handed that, in Philadelphia especially, his easiness became known and he was greatly pestered by beggars. When he had no money with him, he would borrow for the purpose. An item put down in 1784, for instance, records a joint investment with Monroe in an opportunity of this kind, which probably turned up as they were walking together on the street. "March 7. Borrowed Colo. Monroe 4/2—gave in charity 4/2, remember to credit him half." But although American cities spawned a measure of distress in those days, there was hardly such a thing known as hopeless involuntary poverty. In 1782, when Mr. Jefferson had already seen a good deal of American town life, he wrote in reply to the queries of the Marquis de Barbé-Marbois, "From Savannah to Portsmouth you will seldom meet a beggar. In the larger towns, indeed, they sometimes present themselves. These are usually foreigners who have never obtained a settlement in any parish. I never yet saw a native American begging in the streets or highways." There was always the land for them to turn to, and with a little temporary tiding over they would soon be on their own feet. "We have no paupers," Mr. Jefferson wrote Thomas Cooper as late as 1814, "the old and crippled among us who possess nothing and have no families to take care of them, being too few to merit notice as a separate section of society or to affect a general estimate."

But as soon as he set foot in France, Mr. Jefferson faced the real thing in involuntary poverty. After a year, he writes despondently to an American correspondent that "of twenty millions of people supposed to be in France, I am of the opinion there are nineteen millions more wretched, more accursed in every circumstance of human existence than the most conspicuously wretched individual of the whole United States." The people had been expropriated from the land and huddled into vast exploitable masses. "The property [i.e., the land] of this country is absolutely concentrated in a very few hands, having revenues of from half a million guineas a year downward"; and the consequence was that the majority lived merely on sufferance. Involuntary poverty, one might say, was so highly integrated as to erect mendicancy into an institution. This was new to Mr. Jefferson. "I asked myself what could be the reason that so many should be permitted to beg who are willing to work, in a country where there is a very considerable proportion of uncultivated lands," and his conclusion was that "whenever there is in any country uncultivated lands and unemployed poor, it is clear that the laws of property have been so far extended as to violate natural rights. The earth is given as a common stock for man to labour and live on."

However, this was France's problem, not his and not America's —thank Heaven! He writes in a fervent strain to Monroe, "My God! how little do my countrymen know what precious blessings

they are in possession of, and which no other people on earth
enjoy. I confess I had no idea of it myself." America had no end
of land, and hence no problem of poverty. Nevertheless, he was
just now in France, and France's swarming paupers were nagging
him at every turn. What could one do? Out of habit, he did for
a while as he had always done; he gave away small amounts here
and there on the moment, without question, as he happened to
be importuned. This worked well in America; it really did some
good, and at worst it was only an occasional matter. But here it
did no good and was a matter of every hour in the day. Aside
from its doing no good, moreover, one was so often swindled. The
economic system that bred mendicancy also bred roguery, and
there were many rogues among the mendicants. They too were
very much to be pitied, no doubt, but to be taken in by them
only encouraged them, and they were an incessant pest. The
"hackneyed rascals" of France were even waiting at the wharf
at Havre; the account book takes note of the demands of a
swindling *commissionaire:* "Broker attend^g me to Commandant
6 f." The upshot was that, after a couple of weeks of indiscriminate giving, he shut down on charity, save where he knew something about the applicant, as when he records giving "the poor
woman at Têtebout 12 f."

III

He found much to please him, however, in his new surroundings; he was especially attracted by the people's natural sense, so
much in accord with his own, of social life and manners. "The
roughnesses of the human mind are so thoroughly rubbed off
with them that it seems as if one might glide through a whole
life among them without a jostle." He had little trouble, even,
with the degeneration of this quality into the official *politesse sterile et rampante,* the defensive formalism of the diplomat and
statesman. The case-hardened old Foreign Minister, Vergennes,
infirm and tired but clearheaded, could still match protective
coloration with any diplomat put up against him. The diplomatic
corps warned Mr. Jefferson that he was a formidable old fellow,
"wary and slippery in his diplomatic intercourse." All this might
be true, no doubt, when he was playing the game by the rules
"with those whom he knew to be slippery and double-faced themselves." But Mr. Jefferson had no axe to grind, in the diplomatic

sense. He was not a propagandist, as Franklin had been; he was an honest broker, not in crowns, colonies and protectorates, but in sound commodities like salt codfish, tobacco, and potash. As soon therefore as Vergennes "saw that I had no indirect views, practiced no subtleties, meddled in no intrigues, pursued no concealed object, I found him as frank, as honourable, as easy of access to reason, as any man with whom I had ever done business; and I must say the same of his successor, Montmorin, one of the most honest and worthy of human beings."

His enthusiasm was kindled at once by the contemplation of French proficiency in the arts and sciences. The music of Paris, which at that time was perhaps at the height of an unmusical people's possibilities, was so much better than anything he had ever heard that he was delighted by it as "an enjoyment the deprivation of which with us [he writes this to an American correspondent] cannot be calculated. I am almost ready to say it is the only thing which from my heart I envy them, and which in spite of all the authority of the Decalogue I do covet." He is without words to tell how much he enjoys their architecture, sculpture, and painting. In science, he discovers that their literati "are half a dozen years before us. Books, really good, acquire just reputation in that time, and so become known to us and communicate to us all their advances in knowledge." America, however, really misses nothing by being behindhand. Having few publishers and presses, American intelligence is saved the chance of suffocation under huge masses of garbage, such as are shot from the many presses of France. "Is not this delay compensated to us by our being placed out of reach of that swarm of nonsensical publications which issues daily from a thousand presses and perishes almost in issuing?"

Yet, making the most of all that was good in French life, admiring its virtues, delighting oneself in its amenities, one could not feel oneself properly compensated for the missing sense of freedom. There was no freedom in France, and therefore there was no real happiness. The immense majority was in bondage to its masters; the masters were in bondage to vices which were the natural fruit of irresponsibility, which kept them in a condition really worse and more hopeless than that of those whom they exploited. "I find the general fate of humanity here most deplorable. The truth of Voltaire's observation offers itself perpetually, that every man here must be either the hammer or the anvil."

Even the sense of taste and manners, so admirable, so interesting and prepossessing, is superficial and ineffectual in the absence of liberty. It controlled polite usages; it made imperative "all those little sacrifices of self which really render European manners amiable and relieve society from the disagreeable scenes to which rudeness often subjects it." It held the minor routine of life in a generally agreeable course. "In the pleasures of the table they are far before us," temperate, fastidious, discriminating. "I have never yet seen a man drunk in France, even among the lowest of the people." All this was much to the good, and "a savage of the mountains of America" might well look on it with the keenest envy, perceiving how profoundly the fresh and simple charms of his native society might be enhanced by even this limited play of the sense of taste and manners.

But it was not enough. Good taste did not see eye to eye with justice in viewing the social structure of France as "a true picture of that country to which they say we shall pass hereafter, and where we are to see God and his angels in splendour, and crowds of the damned trampled under their feet." Such a civilization was not only iniquitous, but essentially low. Good taste did not ennoble the pursuits of the privileged minority. "Intrigues of love occupy the younger, and those of ambition the elder part of the great." This was not only vicious, but vulgar. To a man for whom conduct was three fourths of life and good taste nine tenths of conduct, this failure in the primary sanctions of taste was peculiarly repulsive. The rough society of America was more hopeful. "I would wish my countrymen to adopt just as much of European politeness" as might sweeten and temper their wholesomeness and mold them into a nation of Fauquiers. But however far from realization that millennial dream might be, "I am savage enough to prefer the woods, the wilds and the independence of Monticello to all the brilliant pleasures of this gay capital. I shall therefore rejoin myself to my native country with new attachments and with exaggerated esteem for its advantages."

Europe, especially, was no place for young Americans; they were sure to go bad under its influence. Sending a youth to Europe for an education was utter futility. "If he goes to England, he learns drinking, horse-racing and boxing. These are the peculiarities of English education. . . . He is fascinated with the privileges of the European aristocrats, and sees with abhorrence the lovely equality which the poor enjoy with the rich in his own

country. . . . He recollects the voluptuary dress and arts of the
European women, and pities and despises the chaste affections
and simplicity of those of his own country." Summing up a long
and earnest disquisition on this topic, he declares that "the consequences of foreign education are alarming to me as an American." Thinking of the Wythes, Franklins, Rittenhouses, Adamses,
Pendletons, and Madisons of his acquaintance, urging his correspondent to cast an eye over America to see "who are the men
of most learning, of most eloquence, most beloved by their
countrymen, and most trusted and promoted by them," he assures him that they are "those who have been educated among
them, and whose manners, morals and habits are perfectly ho-
mogeneous with those of the country."

IV

Mr. Jefferson regarded with profound distrust and disfavor the
phenomenon of the political woman, which he here confronted
for the first time. After four years' experience he writes to President Washington that without the evidence of one's own eyes
one could hardly "believe in the desperate state to which things
are reduced in this country from the omnipotence of an influence
which, fortunately for the happiness of the sex itself, does not
endeavour to extend in our country beyond the domestic line."
He was continually shocked by the coarseness and vulgarity, let
alone the scandalousness, of the custom which permitted women
in search of favors not only to visit public officials, but to visit
them alone, without the presence of a third person to guard the
proprieties; and he was outraged to observe that "their solicitations
bid defiance to laws and regulations." The easygoing Franklin
had been enough of an opportunist to accept this custom and
turn it to the profit of his country. In a good cause he was not
above doing some things that neither John Adams nor Mr. Jefferson would do: Adams, as a result of a "process of moral reasoning," and Mr. Jefferson out of sheer repugnance. Mr. Jefferson was
little tempted; he was not the type that women set their cap for.
Besides, even a riggish French noblewoman could hardly throw
a glamour of romance over so prosaic an interest as the Franco-
American trade in fish oil and salt cod. Still, he could not quite
avoid these women; he owed them civility, and he punctiliously
paid the debt. He disliked Mme. de Staël, but, having been kind

to him, she was not to be snubbed; nor yet was she to be courted for her youthful charms—she was then twenty-one—or for being the daughter of Necker. He moved in her social circle with the high step and arched back of feline circumspection, and it does not appear that she ever took his attitude as a challenge to her hankering for conquest. After his return to America he wrote a kind of bread-and-butter letter to several French ladies who had made something of him in a social way; and in these, at the safe distance of three thousand miles, he risks a few ceremonious compliments. He assures Mme. de Corny, whom he really liked, that her civilities were "greatly more than I had a right to expect, and they have excited in me a warmth of esteem which it was imprudent in me to have given way to for a person whom I was one day to be separated from." In the Duchesse d'Auville's character "I saw but one error; it was that of treating me with a degree of favour I did not merit." Corking down his effervescent horror of the *bas-bleu*, he declares to the Duchesse de la Rochefoucault, with a touch of irony, that if her system of ethics and of government were generally adopted, "we should have no occasion for government at all"; and he expresses to the Comtesse d'Houdetot his rather attenuated gratitude for lionizing him in her salon and begs her to accept "the homage of those sentiments of respect and attachment with which I have the honour to be, Madame la Comtesse, your most obedient and most humble servant." This was all very well; the language of compliment and ceremony was always acceptable at its face value. It was good, one might say, for this day and train only. His reservations were well understood. Still, if French women must go in for politics, it was at least something that the younger ones coming on after Calonne's régime were beginning to go in on the right side. "All the handsome young women of Paris are for the *Tiers Etat*," he writes David Humphreys in 1789, on the outbreak of the revolution, "and this is an army more powerful in France than the 200,000 men of the King." In an emergency any stick will do to beat a dog; and a reflective American might hold his nose and survey the prospect with equanimity, since it concerned another country than his own.

But for his own countrywomen such a prospect was wholly impracticable and impossible. "Our good ladies, I trust, have been too wise to wrinkle their foreheads with politics," he writes anxiously to the dazzling and skittish queen of Philadelphia's

society, Mrs. William Bingham. "They are contented to soothe
and calm the minds of their husbands returning ruffled from
political debate." Mrs. Bingham had ventured to suggest that
even if the French upper classes were a loose lot and had no
domestic virtues worth speaking of, an American woman might
yet not find Paris utterly unbearable; indeed, she might manage
to have rather a good time there. Mr. Jefferson gravely assures
her that she is mistaken about this. "Recollect the women of
this capital, some on foot, some on horses and some in carriages,
hunting pleasure in the streets, in routs and assemblies, and for-
getting that they have left it behind them in their nurseries;
compare them with our own countrywomen occupied in the
tender and tranquil amusements of domestic life, and confess
that it is a comparison of Americans and angels." On its social
side, the Jeffersonian system took little account of the individual-
ity of women, and on its political side, it made no place for them.
Assume, Mr. Jefferson wrote, that the republican principle were
carried out in practice as far as it will go; assume such an extension of the town meeting as would settle all public business in
popular assembly, "there would yet be excluded from their
deliberations: (1) Infants, until arrived at years of discretion.
(2) Women, who, to prevent depravation of morals and am-
biguity of issue, could not mix promiscuously in the public meetings of men. (3) Slaves." Women, again, like infants and slaves,
being devoid of rights both of will and property, were not only
incompetent to an exercise of will in a popular assembly, but "of
course could delegate none to the agent in a representative assembly." Woman's only chance at getting an interest represented
would be through the attorneyship or brokerage of some male
middleman, acting for her as a "qualified citizen."

But why should it be otherwise? What individual interest could
a woman have that she should prefer to maintain for herself,
rather than trust a father or husband to maintain for her? "It is
an honourable circumstance for man that the first moment he is
at his ease, he allots the internal employments to his female
partner and takes the external on himself." Women have all the
best of it under this arrangement, because their duties are so
simple. They might be a little trying sometimes, but there is
never any trouble about understanding them. "The happiness of
your life now depends on the continuing to please a single person," Mr. Jefferson wrote his daughter Martha at the time of her

marriage. "To this all other objects must be secondary, even your love for me." To his daughter Maria, on her marriage to John Eppes, he wrote, "Nothing can preserve affections uninterrupted but a firm resolution never to differ in will. . . . How light in fact is the sacrifice of any other wish when weighed against the affections of one with whom we are to pass our whole life." It was all plain and straightforward. A woman should please the particular middleman who happened to be standing for the moment as her attorney to the world; her father first, then her husband or brother or guardian. She should bend her will to his. In return, all her relations to society would be attentively prescribed for her, and she would be adjusted to them considerately, affectionately, comfortably. No reasonable woman could ask more. "American women have the good sense to value domestic happiness above all other, and the art to cultivate it beyond all other"; they are not like the forward Frenchwomen who dangle about minister's cabinets unattended, and piddle at visionary schemes of ethics and government. If now and then a renegade type turns up, she must be sent to the right-about. In the last year of his Presidency, Mr. Jefferson writes magisterially to Gallatin, his Secretary of the Treasury, "The appointment of a woman to office is an innovation for which the public is not prepared, nor am I."

Woman's duty being so incomplex, and the grasp of it needing so little brains, the education of women was correspondingly simple; so simple, indeed, that one would not think much about it. Mr. Jefferson bent his mind to the theory and practice of education for nearly fifty years; yet at the age of seventy, he says that "a plan of female education has never been a subject of systematic contemplation with me. It has occupied my attention so far only as the education of my own daughters occasionally required." Seeing that his girls were likely to live in a sparsely settled agricultural country, he thought that for vocational reasons they ought to have a solid education "which might enable them, when become mothers, to educate their own daughters, and even to direct the course for sons, should their fathers be lost or incapable or inattentive." Such few general thoughts as ever took rise from this experience are put down in a letter to a neighbor in Virginia. He finds that a great obstacle to good education for women is their inordinate passion for novels. In those who seek this release for the pent desire for romance, "the result is a bloated imagination, sickly judgment and disgust towards all the real

businesses of life." Some novels of a historical type, however, are
well enough. "For a like reason, much poetry should not be indulged. Some is useful for forming taste and style"; Dryden and
Pope, for example, and Thomson! French is indispensable. Music
is "invaluable where a person has an ear." Drawing is an innocent
and engaging amusement, often useful, and "a qualification not
to be neglected in one who is to become a mother and an instruc-
tor." Dancing is a healthy and elegant exercise, a specific against
social awkwardness, but an accomplishment of short use, "for
the French rule is wise, that no lady dances after marriage . . .
gestation and nursing leaving little time to a married lady when
this exercise can be either safe or innocent." Women must be
taught to dress neatly at all hours, for vocational reasons. "A
lady who has been seen as a sloven or slut in the morning," he
tells Martha, "will never efface the impression she has made, with
all the dress and pageantry she can afterwards involve herself in.
. . . I hope therefore, the moment you rise from bed, your first
work will be to dress yourself in such style as that you may be
seen by any gentleman without his being able to discover a pin
amiss." Finally, always for vocational reasons, women must be
taught to wash themselves; it is the acme of impracticality for
them to go dirty, since "nothing is so disgusting to our sex as a
want of cleanliness and delicacy in yours."

Mr. Jefferson did his best by his daughters. He put Patsy in
a convent school in Paris, where he bombarded her with letters
in which the expression of a larvated love was, as usual, inhibited
into a diffident formalism by the combination of natural ret-
icence and a more or less puzzled sense of responsibility. "I rest
the happiness of my life in seeing you beloved by all the world,
which you will be sure to be if to a good heart you join those
accomplishments so peculiarly pleasing in your sex." That is about
the best he can do, except by way of suggesting occupations for
her leisure hours, and in this his fertility is endless. To be sure,
her leisure hours were not many; they never had been many, even
when she was at home. The year before she went abroad, her
father had laid out the following schedule of her time:

From 8 to 10, practice music.
From 10 to 1, dance one day, and draw another.
From 1 to 2, draw on the day you dance, and write a letter the
next day.
From 3 to 4, read French.

From 4 to 5, exercise yourself in music.
From 5 till bed-time, read English, write, etc.

In Paris he is continually anxious about her not having enough
to do and about a certain listlessness toward her duties, a kind
of boredom. He has a harpsichord sent her from London; he
tries to get her interested in the note of the nightingale, so that
when she returns to Virginia she may compare it with that of
the mockingbird; he informs her all about the literary and historical associations of certain places in Italy and the South of France;
he redoubles his solicitations toward the industrious life, urging
her to remember that "a mind always employed is always happy.
This is the true secret, the grand recipe, for felicity. The idle are
the only wretched." How could one doubt it? He himself had
never been idle for an aggregate of twelve hours in his whole life,
and in the large sense, he had always been happy; when Satan
had approached him with the proverbial wares of mischief, they
found a closed market. But while Martha did her best to realize
upon her prescribed pursuits, they seemed for some reason to
pass their dividends. She was interested in her father's stories of
the fountain of Vaucluse, the tomb of Laura and the château of
Petrarch, but her interest was sentimental rather than antiquarian;
they seemed to generate, if not "a sickly judgment and disgust
towards all the real businesses of life," at least a disturbing half-
heartedness and irresolution about facing them. She tried to do
everything in reason for the nightingales, but here again she did
not find her father's exhortations as animating as they should be.
Presently, after looking over the prospects which the future
seemed to hold in store for an amiable dreamy wench in her
teens, Patsy decided that she would probably do well to dedicate
the rest of her life to the service of God. She accordingly wrote
her father for permission to enter the holy sisterhood. Two days
afterward, he appeared at the convent and took her away, with
no intimation either by word or manner that she had expressed
any such wish; and as long as he lived he never once alluded to
her request, nor did she. Thenceforth he kept her with him,
mothering her younger sister, Maria; both returned to America
with him; both fulfilled their destiny as their father's daughters
by becoming dutiful and assiduous wives, mothers, housekeepers;
and they continued in the joy of these occupations as long as
their strength held out.

V

Throughout the period of his ambassadorship, Mr. Jefferson found little doing in the way of business. Vergennes was polite, considerate, straightforward. They discussed one article of commerce after another, but could never come to much more than nominal terms. In the matter of rice, flour, fish, and "provisions of all sorts," the French were doing quite well as they were. Their own colonies supplied them with indigo, and "they thought it better than ours." They could make a good market for American peltry and furs, but the English were holding all the northwestern American posts, and therefore the supply of these commodities was effectively shut off. The only market that really amounted to anything was for tobacco. France was then buying two million livres' worth of American tobacco every year; but most of it was bought in London, and "for what they bought in the United States, the money was still remitted to London by bills of exchange." Mr. Jefferson suggested to Vergennes that this was not good business; that "if they would permit our merchants to sell this article freely, they would bring it here and take the returns on the spot, in merchandise, not money." Vergennes had no trouble about seeing the point; he "observed that my proposition contained what doubtless was useful"; but political considerations stood in the way. In plain words, he could not admit American tobacco to the French ports without incurring a head-on collision with the Farmers-General.

The French crown had, some time before, turned over the business of tax collection to private enterprise. The private company called the Farmers-General paid the King twenty-eight million livres flat revenue on tobacco and assumed all the trouble and expense of reimbursing themselves out of the consumer. They had a similar monopoly on salt, and on certain tolls collected on agricultural products at the gates of French cities. As a rule, they collected what the traffic would bear; and hence in almost no time at all they grew up into the richest and most powerful institution in France—far too powerful for any minister to tackle with a proposition to give up one of their best monopolies. Vergennes put it gently "that it was always hazardous to alter arrangements of long standing and of such infinite combinations with the fiscal system." He himself was quite for Mr. Jefferson's proposals, but they would have to take their chances with Calonne, the Comptroller-General; and Calonne, as an honorable official, was properly scandalized at the suggestion that the good faith of the nation, pledged by implication to the Farmers-General, should in any way be tarnished. Later on, perhaps, when the Farmers-General had had time to turn around, it was not impossible that the royal understanding with them might be modified by some kind of compromise; but at present nothing could be done. Calonne knew which side his bread was buttered on. Mr. Jefferson remarked in reporting this matter to Congress that "the influence of the Farmers-General has been heretofore found sufficient to shake a minister in his office," and that if Calonne opposed the tobacco monopoly, "the joint interests of France and America would be insufficient counterpoise in his favour," and he would lose his place.

After a year and a half of this kind of shilly-shallying, Mr. Jefferson writes mournfully, "What a cruel reflection, that a rich country can not long be a free one!" Wherever his eyes rested, he saw the French producer laboring under "all the oppressions which result from the nature of the general government, and from that of their particular tenures, and of the seignorial government to which they are subject." Government, in short, was, as Voltaire said, a mere device for taking money out of one man's pocket and putting it into another's. The European governments, he writes to Rutledge, are "governments of wolves over sheep." All he saw confirmed him in the view which he had laid down at the age of thirty, in his paper on *The Rights of British America*, saying that "the whole art of government consists in the art of being honest"; and in the Declaration of Independence, saying that governments are instituted among men to secure certain inherent and inalienable rights, and that "whenever any form of government becomes destructive of these ends, it is the right of the people to alter or abolish it."

A visit to England during this year stiffened his convictions. In February, 1786, John Adams sent for him to come over to London to assist in the negotiation of treaties with Portugal and Tripoli. Here he saw a population expropriated from the land, and existing at the mercy of industrial employers, with the enormous exactions of monopoly standing as a fixed charge upon the producer, though not so heavy as in France—the French producers "pay about one-half their produce in rent; the English, in general, about a third." The British governmental system was steadfastly on the side of the land monopolists who expropriated the people and of the industrialists who exploited them; it was really their agent. "The aristocracy of England, which comprehends the nobility, the wealthy commoners, the high grades of priesthood and the officers of government, have the laws and government in their hands [and] have so managed them as to reduce the eleemosynary class, or paupers, below the means of supporting life, even by labour. [They] have forced the labouring class, whether employed in agriculture or the arts, to the maximum of labour which the construction of the human body can endure, and to the minimum of food, and of the meanest kind, which will preserve it in life and in strength sufficient to perform its functions." As for the paupers, they "are used as tools to maintain their own wretchedness, and to keep down the labouring portion by shooting them whenever the desperation produced by the cravings of their stomachs drives them into riots." Over and above these patriotic duties, the paupers also "furnish materials for armies and navies to defend their country, exercise piracy on the ocean, and carry conflagration, plunder and devastation to the shores of all those who endeavour to withstand their aggressions. Such," he concludes bitterly, "is the happiness of scientific England."

Having this view of the English and French governments, Mr. Jefferson was always prompt to differentiate their character from that of their victims. The individuals of the English nation are "as faithful to their private engagements and duties, as honourable, as worthy, as those of any nation of earth," and therefore the country "presents a singular phenomenon of an honest people whose constitution, from its nature, must render their government forever dishonest." He had already remarked a similar distinction in favour of the French people, as bearing "the most benevolent, the most gay and amiable character of which the human form is susceptible," and yet as "loaded with misery by kings, nobles and priests, and by them alone." France is "the worst-governed country on earth," and the British government "the most flagitious which has existed since the days of Philip of Macedon. . . . It is not only founded in corruption itself, but insinuates the same poison into the bowels of every other, corrupts its councils, nourishes factions, stirs up revolutions, and places its own happiness in fomenting commotions and civil wars among others, thus rendering itself truly the *hostis humani generis.*" The practical upshot of this state of things is, as he writes John Adams, that "as for France and England, with all their progress in science, the one is a den of robbers, and the other of pirates."

Still, as an honest broker with goods to sell, Mr. Jefferson was disposed to lay aside his private opinions and deal with these people if he could. After all, nations must live, and to do so they must seek their advantage where they can find it. He asked no favors of the French ministry; he represented merely the enlightened self-interest of America and was trying to elicit a response from theirs. He had no prejudices against the English government that would stand out against being polite and pleasant about matters of reciprocal advantage. He was aware, as he said late in life, that "no two nations can be so helpful to each other as friends nor so hurtful as enemies"; and, indeed, if the English government could only bring itself to "treat us with justice and equity, I should myself feel with great strength the ties which bind us together, of origin, language, laws and manners." He had come late and reluctantly into the movement for American independence, believing, as most of the colonists did, that if they could get a working measure of economic independence, political independence was not worth the cost of a quarrel. "If I could permit myself to have national partialities," he writes in 1812, "and if the conduct of England would have permitted them to be directed towards her, they would have been so." And now, in his present capacity, as a peaceable commercial representative holding out the olive branch of profitable trade, he could clearly see that "a friendly, a just and a reasonable conduct on the part of the British might make us the main pillar of their prosperity and existence." Why might not the British see it too? At all events, he would not be found at fault in the matter, now or ever, for the best of reasons. "As a political man, the English shall never find any passion in me either for or against them. Whenever their avarice of commerce will let them meet us fairly half way, I should meet them with satisfaction, because it would be for our benefit."

But he could not do a hand's turn in London; he was rebuffed everywhere. A witty saying has it that there is no such thing as good manners in England, but only the right and wrong kind of bad manners; and Mr. Jefferson was treated to a liberal display of both. He was presented to the King, as a matter of routine, and "it was impossible for anything to be more ungracious" than the sullen old maniac's attitude. As for the Foreign Minister, who was then the Marquis of Caermarthen, to whom he was officially introduced by Adams, "the distance and disinclination which he betrayed in his conversation, the vagueness and evasions of his answers to us, confirmed me in the belief of their aversion to have anything to do with us." The two ambassadors, however, delivered a memorandum of their proposals, "Mr. Adams not despairing as much as I did of its effect." They never got within the gracious presence of the Foreign Minister again, though "we afterwards, by one or more notes, requested his appointment of an interview and conference, which, without directly declining, he evaded by pretences of other pressing occupations for the moment." This went on for seven weeks, and then Mr. Jefferson gave his mission up as hopeless and left England, *insula inhospitabilis*, as Tacitus had tersely styled it two thousand years before; all he ever got out of Caermarthen being a stiff note in acknowledgment of his *pour prendre congé*, "wishing me a pleas- ant journey" back to Paris.

In the course of this experience, Mr. Jefferson became aware that the English were not merely biting off their nose to spite their face. Far otherwise; "the English think we can not prevent our countrymen from bringing our trade into their laps," he wrote his old friend John Page. "A conviction of this determines them to make no terms of commerce with us. They say they will pocket our carrying trade as well as their own." There was something in this. There is little sentiment of any kind in the course of trade, and no nationalism. "Merchants have no country," Mr. Jefferson said. "The mere spot they stand on does not constitute so strong an attachment as that from which they draw their gains." Ameri- can trade was drawn back into English channels after the Revo- lution by the irresistible attractions of price, quality, and credit facilities. The stupidity of the English government lay in their refusal to recognize this tendency handsomely and lay down an enlightened doctrine of free trade with America, as John Adams kept trying to persuade them to do. Instead, they gruffly slapped their pockets and treated Adams's proposals with a porcine in- difference that was a sure runner-up of economic war. "Ever since the accession of the present King of England," Mr. Jefferson ob- serves to Carmichael in 1787, "the court has done what common sense would have dictated not to do"; and he writes at the same time to John Adams, that "I never yet found any general rule for foretelling what the British will do, but that of examining what they ought not to do." Moreover, the British ministry had been keeping its press agents busy throughout the decade since the war in fomenting popular hatred of America. "You know well that that Government always kept a kind of standing army of news-writers, who, without any regard to truth or what should be like truth, invented and put into the papers whatever might serve the ministers. . . . No paper, therefore, comes out without a dose of paragraphs against America." Nothing could be done about it; if the British government did not know which side their bread was buttered on, they must learn by experience. An economic war would cost the United States something; it would be regrettable and silly and all that, but apparently it must come. "Nothing will bring the British to reason but physical obstruction applied to their bodily senses. We must show that we are capable of fore-going commerce with them before they will be capable of consent-ing to an equal commerce. We have all the world besides open to supply us with gewgaws, and all the world to buy our tobacco." Mr. Jefferson put it even more explicitly to Colonel Smith that "of all nations on earth, the British require to be treated with the most *hauteur*. They require to be kicked into common good manners." Even John Adams, who had some misgivings about Mr. Jefferson's despondent estimate of the situation, finally came around to the same way of thinking. After the Embargo of 1807 and the War of 1812 had rubbed a sense of reality into his fine old head, he wrote Mr. Jefferson that "Britain will never be our friend until we are her master."

VI

The European *ensemble* and the progress of Constitution building in America during the years 1786-1787 turned Mr. Jefferson's mind toward some speculations on the general theory and practice of government. The trouble with government in Europe as he saw it, was its complete centralization in the hands of the relatively few nonproducers; the symbol of this centraliza-tion was monarchy. Those who actually applied labor and capital to natural resources for the production of wealth had no voice in government. Just before Mr. Jefferson set sail for Europe, he remarked to General Washington that "the hereditary branches of modern government are the patrons of privilege and prerogative, and not of the natural rights of the people, whose oppressors they generally are"; and one of his last letters from Paris, written to Edward Carrington, contained the observation that "the natural progress of things is for liberty to yield and government to gain ground." Because this tendency is wholly natural, there was no point to getting up a great sweat of moral indignation against it. One of the most profound preferences in human nature is for satisfying one's needs and desires with the least possible exertion; for appropriating wealth produced by the labor of others, rather than producing it by one's own labor. Any Frenchman, for example, would rather worm his way into the membership of the Farmers-General and levy on the wealth produced by French labor and capital than employ his own labor and capital to produce wealth for himself. Any Englishman would rather live by appropriating the economic rent of land holdings than by working. Obviously, the stronger and more centralized the government, the safer would be the guarantee of such monopolies; in other words, the stronger the government, the weaker the producer, the less consideration need be given him and the more might be taken away from him. A deep instinct of human nature being for these reasons always in favor of strong government, nothing could be a more natural progress of things than "for liberty to yield and government to gain ground." In England and France, government had gained all the ground there was, and liberty had yielded all. That was the whole story.

For America, Mr. Jefferson was convinced that republicanism was a better system because it lent itself less easily to centralization. It gave the producer some kind of voice in the direction of affairs, and since the producer was greatly in the majority in any society, he had—if he were interested and intelligent enough to profit by it—a fair chance of keeping his interests uppermost. Republicanism was not the ideal system. The Indians, as Mr. Jefferson points out to Madison, lived in a distinct and quite highly organized type of society and got on very well without any government at all. While "it is a problem not clear in my mind that [this] condition is not the best," he believed it to be "inconsistent with any great degree of population," though he seems never to have asked himself just why this should be so. Republicanism, "wherein the will of every one has a just influence," was the best system attainable; the spirit of the times had not disclosed anything better. It "has a great deal of good in it. The mass of mankind under that enjoys a precious degree of liberty and happiness."

But republicanism is no fetish; he is perfectly clearsighted about this. Republicanism gives the producing classes their chance; but it does not protect them automatically if they are not forever alive to their chance. "If once the people become inattentive to the public affairs," he writes austerely from Paris to Edward Carrington, "you and I and Congress and Assemblies, Judges and Governors, shall all become wolves. It seems to be the law of our general nature, in spite of individual exceptions." The most that can be said for republicanism is that intrinsically "the republican is the only form of government which is not externally at open or secret war with the rights of mankind"; but most of the republics of the world, he yet reminds Madison, have degenerated into governments of force; and in his draft of the Diffusion of Knowledge Bill, eight years before, he had incorporated the warning that while "certain forms of government are better calculated than others to protect individuals in the free exercise of their natural rights, and are at the same time themselves better guarded against degeneracy, yet experience hath shown that even under the best forms, those entrusted with power have, in time, and by slow operations, perverted it into tyranny."

He was aware, again, that America was far from free to work out, in isolation and on pure theory, a system of its own. Aside from collisions of domestic interests, which were shortly to furnish him most disagreeable surprises, external circumstances counted heavily. If the United States were to exist at all, and not be swallowed piecemeal by the predacious military powers of Europe, it must become, for some purposes, a nation; it must have, for instance, a central body of authority for its foreign affairs. His efforts abroad in behalf of trade had taught him that the Articles of Confederation would not answer. As long as he could not make clear whether the legal regulation of trade was a Federal or a state function, he could get no trade. But he was sure that the purposes for which the United States should be a nation must be as few as possible, otherwise the history of European exploitation would be repeated on the grand scale. The utmost concession that it would be proper to make, as he wrote to his old preceptor, George Wythe, was that "the States should

severally preserve their sovereignty in whatever concerns themselves alone, and whatever may concern another State, or any
foreign nation, should be made a part of the Federal sovereignty."
After all, the domestic functions of an honest Federal sovereignty
were few, and their character purely administrative and nonpo-
litical—carrying the mails, coining money, regulating transportation, and the like—and for the rest, speaking generally, "the
States should be left to do whatever acts they can do as well as
the General Government." In short, the United States should be
a nation abroad, and a confederacy at home.

This arrangement, he thought, would be workable and satisfactory. The producer could not be exploited unless he were first
driven off the land, and this he could not be but by a much
greater strengthening of the central government. If this were attempted, he thought that the producer, being so vastly in the
majority, might be counted on for effective resistance, thus keeping both state and Federal governments, as he called it, "virtuous."
Referring to the proposed Constitution, he therefore writes Madison in 1787 that on principle he is for the will of the majority,
and that if a majority approve of the forthcoming Constitution,
"I shall concur in it cheerfully, in hopes they will amend it
whenever they find it works wrong. This reliance can not de-
ceive us as long as we remain virtuous; and I think we shall be
so as long as agriculture is our principal object, which will be
the case while there remains vacant lands in any part of America.
When we get piled upon one another in large cities, as in Europe,
we shall become as corrupt as in Europe." His own private view
went far beyond the idea of the state as the self-governing unit;
he was for making the smallest political unit self-governing, in
order to keep the producer alert and interested. He admitted to
John Adams in 1813 that his Diffusion of Knowledge Bill had
a joker in it for this ulterior purpose, by dividing the county into
"wards," or towns, and "confiding to them the care of their poor,
their roads, police, elections, the nomination of jurors . . . in
short, to have made them little republics with a warden at the
head of each, for all those concerns which, being under their eye,
they would manage better than the larger republics of the county
or State." But it was better to concede something and get enough,
than to insist on all and get nothing; and the establishment of
the state as the domestic self-governing unit, he thought, would
probably be enough to keep the producer's head above water.

As the French Revolution drew on, Mr. Jefferson was frankly pleased with the prospect. He saw in it the chance of emancipation, not only for the French producer, but for the producing interests everywhere in Europe. The successful reformation of government in France would ensure "a general reformation through Europe, and the resurrection to a new life of their people, now ground to dust by the abuses of the governing powers." Where his class interest was concerned, he was always a stanch friend of the revolutionary principle, and he made no bones of saying so. Revolutions served a double purpose. They kept the government's ear open to its master's voice, and they also sharpened popular attention to what the government was doing. On this account he was not inclined to be overparticular about the merits of a revolutionary cause; the attitude traditionally ascribed to the southern Irish, of being more or less against the government under any and all circumstances, was one that he thought, on the whole, rather salutary. When he got news of Shays's Rebellion in Massachusetts and New Hampshire, late in 1786, he picked, out of all unlikely people in New England, the president of Yale College and the redoubtable and forthright Mrs. John Adams as candidates for a good round piece of his mind. "I like a little rebellion now and then," he wrote Mrs. Adams, ". . . The spirit of resistance to government is so valuable on certain occasions that I wish it to be always kept alive. It will often be exercised when wrong, but better so than not to be exercised at all." Yale College had just given Mr. Jefferson an honorary degree, and in acknowledging the compliment, the newly made Doctor of Laws took occasion to remark that the commotions in America "are a proof that the people have liberty enough, and I could not wish them less than they have. If the happiness of the mass of the people can be secured at the expense of a little tempest now and then, or even of a little blood, it will be a precious purchase. *Malo libertatem periculosam quam quietem servitutem.*"

Shays's Rebellion, however, had more than an academic interest for him. "These people are not entirely without excuse," he wrote Carmichael. Theirs seemed to him an uprising against an

unfair pressure of debt and taxation, applied by collusion among
a minority of exploiting interests—the rich merchant-enterprisers
or "factors" of Boston, whom he almost begrudged the right to
live; the judges and lawyers, whom he would not trust as far as
he would a dog with his dinner; and the horde of speculators,
bankers, "stock-jobbers and king-jobbers," whom he regarded as
mere vermin. He suspected that the agonized invocation of law
and order that went up against Shays's demonstration was organized by these interests, for the people were on the other side—so
much so, it turned out, that although the ringleaders were con-
demned, they were never punished. He thought that the prompt
turning of this incident to account as the basis of demand for
a stronger and more stable central government represented what
he later called "the interested clamours and sophistry of speculating, shaving and banking institutions." The Federal Congress
had not dared come to the assistance of Massachusetts in putting
down the rebellion, but it did, later in the year, make provision
for a Federal army, under plea of danger from the Indians; and
in its secret journals it made the astonishing entry of its confidence in "the most liberal exertions of the money-holders in
the State of Massachusetts and the other States in filling the loans
authorized by the resolve of this date," to pay the troops! While
Washington was writing in bewilderment from Mount Vernon
of his acute distress at "the disorders that have arisen in these
States," and of his fear that "there are combustibles in every
State which a spark might set fire to"; while General Knox was
announcing his discovery that Americans were "men possessing
all the turbulent passions belonging to that animal, and that we
must have a government proper and adequate for him"—Mr.
Jefferson, in Paris, with a revolution of the first magnitude on the
point of breaking about his ears, was scanning the latest accounts
of Shays's uprising and writing earnestly to W. S. Smith, "God
forbid we should ever be twenty years without such a rebellion.
The people can not be all and always well informed. The part
which is wrong will be discontented in proportion to the importance of the facts they misconceive. If they remain quiet
under such misconceptions, it is a lethargy, the forerunner of
death to the public liberty."

The leaders of the French Revolution in its first phase, being new at the business, were inclined to profit by Mr. Jefferson's experience. "Being from a country which had successfully passed through a similar reformation, they were disposed to my acquaintance, and had some confidence in me." The committee of the Assembly, appointed to draft a Constitution, asked him to meet with them and assist them. He declined to do this, but, chiefly through his old and good friend Lafayette, he managed to contribute some first-rate advice without getting himself into trouble; although on one occasion, friendship maneuvered him into the appearance, at least, of a pretty serious diplomatic indiscretion, and if he had not had as sensible and sympathetic a person as the French Foreign Minister to deal with, he might have found his position invidious. Lafayette invited himself and a half a dozen friends to dine at Mr. Jefferson's house one evening, and when dinner was over, the company resolved itself into a spirited caucus, finally producing, after six hours' discussion, the concordat upon which the Republicans and moderate Royalists in the Assembly subsequently united. It was the measure which "decided the fate of the Constitution." Although Mr. Jefferson was but "a silent witness" to this notable performance, it was hardly the kind of thing to be going on in the residence of the American Minister. He accordingly lost no time in looking up Montmorin next morning and making what amends he could for his apparent breach of etiquette, telling him "with truth and candour how it had happened that my house had been made the scene of conferences of such a character." But Montmorin, who saw well enough which way the wind was blowing, had no prejudices; indeed, "he earnestly wished I would habitually assist at such conferences, being sure I should be useful in moderating the warmer spirits and promoting a wholesome and practicable reformation only."

Montmorin's trust was based on sound evidence of Mr. Jefferson's attitude and disposition. He had his own sources of information about him and knew him to be neither a doctrinaire revolutionist nor a doctrinaire Republican, but the spokesman of an out-and-out class interest, with which Montmorin himself had a certain amount of cautious sympathy. Revolution was not

an end in itself, but the means to an end; its end was the economic emancipation of the producing class, and the less trouble
and disturbance about approaching this end, the less likelihood
that the end would be obscured and the line of approach de-
flected. Mr. Jefferson saw the chance that usually shines out of
such circumstances for one golden moment and then, if unim-
proved, disappears forever—the chance of what his great contemporary, the Duke of Wellington, called "a revolution by due
course of law." The government was ready to yield, as it afterward did yield, quite enough for the Revolution to go on with
and consolidate its gains in peace—the King's speech at the City
Hall, his acceptance of a popular escort headed by the Bourgeois
Guards under Lafayette, his assumption of the popular cockade,
were "such an *amende honorable* as no sovereign ever made and
no people ever received." Perceiving at the outset that the government was in a state of wholesome fear, particularly because of the
lukewarmness of many of the younger aristocrats and disaffection
in the army. Mr. Jefferson, "painfully anxious lest despotism,
after an unaccepted offer to bind its own hands, should seize you
again with tenfold fury," earnestly besought the revolutionists to
give play to the spirit of compromise. Everything gained in this
way would be a clear gain, while everything gained by admitting
the spirit of violence and passion must in the long run have the
extravagances of violence and passion charged off against it. "I
urged most strenuously an immediate compromise; to secure what
the Government was now ready to yield, and trust to future occasions for what might still be wanting." He drew up the terms
of what he thought a proper compromise, and gave the draft to
Lafayette and St. Etienne; but the revolutionary leaders rejected
it as too moderate and took no action, thus permitting the one
opportunity for peaceful adjustment to slip away.

"Events have proved their lamentable error," Mr. Jefferson
wrote thirty years later, after the Revolution had degenerated
through the course of its own enormities and made way for those
of Napoleon. The revolutionists could not foresee "the melancholy sequel of their well-meant perseverance; that their physical
force would be usurped by a first tyrant to trample on the independence and even the existence of other nations." Worst of all,
they could not foresee the ensuing defensive freemasonry of the
Russian Emperor Alexander's league of nations called the Holy
Alliance, set up to make international common cause among the

exploiting classes and unite them against the revoluntary spirit, wherever found. They could not foresee that their error "would afford a fatal example for the atrocious conspiracy of kings against their people; would generate their unholy and homicide alliance to make common cause among themselves, and to crush by the power of the whole the efforts of any part to moderate their abuses and oppressions."

Mr. Jefferson believed that the republican spirit also, like the revolutionary spirit, was going hand over head. Republicanism, he thought, in the words of an acute critic, tried to do too much and did it. He was uncompromisingly for republicanism in America, as affording the producer the best fulcrum or purchase for maintaining his political ascendancy. But France, unlike America which had no great transition to make and no binding force of political tradition to overcome, was not in shape to employ it and would make a mess of it. Mr. Jefferson saw nothing more certain than that France would finally become republican, if let alone, and in none too long time for safety. "This whole chapter in the history of man is new"; if the American experiment succeeded, which one could hardly doubt, republicanism in France, as in all the world, would catch the contagion quickly enough. The thing to be avoided meanwhile was the hazard of win-all, lose-all. "The King was now become a passive machine in the hands of the National Assembly, and had he been left to himself, he would have willingly acquiesced in whatever they should devise as best for the nation." The wisest move would be to constitutionalize the monarchy and leave Louis XVI at the head of it, "with powers so large as to enable him to do all the good of his station, and so limited as to restrain him from its abuse." Remembering the great reforms projected by Turgot in the early years of the king's reign and ended only by the opposition of the nobles and clergy, whose claws were now effectively clipped, Mr. Jefferson believed that the King would faithfully administer a sound constitutional policy, and "more than this I do not believe he ever wished." Something should certainly be done about the wretched, dissipated, slippery, half-witted little queen. "I have ever believed that had there been no queen, there would have been no Revolution"; but with all his wrath at her follies, Mr. Jefferson was not for bringing her under the law of treason. "I should have shut up the queen in a convent, putting harm out of her power, and placed the King in his sta-

tion, investing him with limited powers which I verily believe
he would have honestly exercised according to the measure of
his understanding. In this way no void would have been created,
courting the usurpation of a military adventurer, nor occasion
given for those enormities which demoralized the nations of the
world." It was in the *void* that he saw danger.

Still, one could appreciate the popular point of view; one
could even respect the spirit of the popular judgment. The nation
had suffered horribly at the hands of these people, and the
thought of vengeance was not unnatural. "Of those who judged
the King, many thought him wilfully criminal." Again, if the
King lived and if the nation kept up an ever-thinning shade of
monarchy, would there not be continual dynastic plottings and
graspings after its lost substance? Again, if the nation kept the
trappings of monarchy and at the same time made an end of
the economic exploitation of which monarchy was the symbol,
would it not live "in perpetual conflict with the horde of kings
who would war against a generation which might come home
to themselves"? Had not the Allied Powers indeed already put
a counterrevolutionary army into France, under the Duke of
Brunswick? Finally, might it not be well to have the new political
formulas applied as widely as possible and tried out as quickly
as possible in behalf of clearing their theory?

Chance made Mr. Jefferson an eyewitness of the first bloodshed
of the French Revolution. Just as a casual mob made ready to
stone a handful of cavalry drawn up in the Place Louis Quinze,
his carriage came by. They could hardly have known who he was,
but he was a stranger and that was enough. This fracas was their
own affair; it was nothing for a stranger to be mixed up in. There
was a deep unconscious significance in the action of the mob,
which, with stones in their uplifted hands, paused a moment to
let the great libertarian pass through their midst in safety. "But
the moment after I had passed, the people attacked the cavalry
with stones. . . . This was the signal for universal insurrection. . . ."

CHAPTER IV

1784-1789 (*Continued*)

I

ALTHOUGH business on the whole was dull, the American representative finally got a few concessions on minor lines of trade,
such as fish oil, potash, ship timber, and hides. He could do
little about tobacco. His efforts to loosen the tobacco monopoly,
indeed, were not wholly well thought of even at home. Robert
Morris of Philadelphia had got an exclusive contract with the
Farmers-General, which had had the disastrous effect of cutting
down the American planter's price by nearly fifty per cent and
had "thrown the commerce of that article in agonies"; and in
December, 1786, Mr. Jefferson confides to Monroe a suspicion
that "my proceedings to redress the abusive administration of
tobacco by the Farmers-General have indisposed towards me a
powerful person in Philadelphia who was profiting from that
abuse." He had not suggested an annulment of the contract,
however, chiefly because if the contract were broken, the price
of tobacco in the French market would break with it. He merely
sought that "after the expiration of this contract, no similar one
should be made, and that meanwhile the Farmers-General should
be obliged to purchase annually about fifteen thousand hogs-
heads of American tobacco, imported directly from the United
States in French or American vessels, at the same price or on the
same conditions which have been stipulated by the contract with
Mr. Morris." This arrangement was effected—at least on paper—
and it was probably the thing that first brought Mr. Jefferson
in for the unfavorable attention of the alert and growing brood

of American speculative interests outside his native state. With his customary dislike of explaining any course of conduct that he deemed proper to follow, he told Monroe that while he had not actually gone to the lengths that Morris might suspect from a certain paragraph which Calonne had written on the subject of the tobacco contract, he had done what he conceived to be the right thing all around, "and I will not so far wound my privilege of doing that, without regard to any man's interest, as to enter into any explanations of this paragraph with him. Yet I esteem him highly, and suppose that hitherto he had esteemed me."

The King of Prussia, who hated England, alone was prompt and businesslike toward the American commercial envoys. "Old Frederic of Prussia met us cordially and without hesitation, and, appointing the Baron de Thulemeyer, his Minister at the Hague, to negotiate with us, we communicated to him our *projet* which, with little alteration by the King, was soon concluded." Denmark and Tuscany also nibbled at the bait. But "other Powers appearing indifferent, we did not think it proper to press them. They seemed in fact to know little about us but as rebels who had been successful in throwing off the yoke of the mother country." In the general field of diplomacy, Mr. Jefferson found little to do. The Barbary States were at the time making such a success with piracy on the Mediterranean that they had brought it up to something like the dimensions of a national industry; and Mr. Jefferson had not been long at his post before a Moroccan cruiser captured and confiscated an American ship and held her crew for ransom. The maritime powers of Europe were finding it cheaper to pay tribute than to fight and were getting along comfortably on that basis; but under the Articles of Confederation the United States had little money for tribute or for fighting or for anything. Disliking the idea of tribute, Mr. Jefferson organized a provisional combination of the smaller maritime powers with the United States to police the North African coast with a dozen men-of-war, having first made sure that the French government would not interfere or permit England to interfere with this joint enterprise. Congress, however, could not see its way to supply the American quota of one frigate, so nothing was done.

His only other diplomatic concern of importance was in international finance; and his principal achievement in that line was to head off his impetuous colleague, John Adams, who had been elected Vice-President, from going off home, incontinently leaving the dead and malodorous albatross of American credit hung to his neck. Adams, while at the Hague, before his transfer to London, had a general authority to deal with the Dutch bankers as best he could, in pursuance of a hand-to-mouth national policy of borrowing oneself out of debt. "Interest on the public debt, and the maintenance of the diplomatic establishment in Europe, had been habitually provided in this way." The ice was getting thin under this policy, however, and Adams, with his vigorous single-track mind full of the Vice-Presidency, was hastening his preparations homeward, telling the bankers that they should see Mr. Jefferson in case anything came up. "I was daily dunned by a company who had formerly made a small loan to the United States, the principal of which was now become due; and our bankers in Amsterdam had notified me that the interest on our general debt would be expected in June; that if we failed to pay it, it would be deemed an act of bankruptcy, and would effectually destroy the credit of the United States and all future prospect of obtaining money there." This was serious. "I had no powers, no instructions, no means and no familiarity with the subject," he wrote, pathetically. "It had always been exclusively under his [Adams's] management." Fortunately, Adams's preoccupied brain had somehow made room for the idea that before sailing he ought to take time for a farewell visit of courtesy at the Dutch court, to which he had been formerly accredited; and by a fortunate coincidence, Mrs. Adams communicated the tidings of his departure in a *pour prendre congé* which Mr. Jefferson "received on the very day on which he [Adams] would arrive at the Hague." Mr. Jefferson accordingly set out at once by the shortest way, through Brussels, Antwerp, and Rotterdam. There was no time to lose; "a consultation with him, and some provision for the future, was indispensable while we could yet avail ourselves of his powers; for when they would be gone, we should be without resource." He paused long enough at the Hague to pull John Adams's head down from the clouds and stow him aboard his carriage for Amsterdam, where by some marvel of persuasion they managed to peg the nondescript young republic's finances for another period.

Aside from these matters and from writing official reports on the state of European politics, his duties were of a minor and routine character. The impecunious American turned up pretty regularly in his day's work. "Gave Alex^r Learmouth, a poor American, 36 f," "Gave Hicks, an American, 12 f"—such entries occur in his account books about as often as one would expect. Then there were the private creditors of the United States, largely French officers who had served in the American war and who had not been paid—the United States not having been in shape at the time to pay even its own soldiers in anything better than paper. These creditors were a great pest, the worst of it being that their claims were valid, that almost without exception they needed the money, and that the poor American representative was utterly unable to give them anything more substantial than sympathy. Then there were the American sailors whom the Farmers-General caught in a prohibited port with a cargo of tobacco and promptly jailed. They said they had been driven into port by a storm; the Farmers-General said they were smugglers; perhaps both were right. Mr. Jefferson did what he could to soften the rigors of a French prison and worked long and hard for their release. Then there were the travelers—and then there were the young, the ingenuous, the sentimental travelers! He did his best by them in unfailing equanimity, like that other "dainty and high-bred Stoic," as Walter Pater calls Marcus Aurelius, "who still thought manners a true part of morals, according to the old sense of the term, and who regrets now and then that he can not control his thoughts equally well with his countenance." Gouverneur Morris, whom Robert Morris had sent over to Paris to keep an eye on the tobacco contract with the Farmers-General, left this significant observation in his diary:

May 30th—Call on Mr. Jefferson and sit a good while. General conversation on character and politics. I think he does not form very just estimates of character, but rather assigns too many to the humble rank of fools, whereas in life the gradations are infinite and each individual has his peculiarities of fort and feeble.

Then there was Ledyard. John Ledyard, of Connecticut, had been with Captain Cook on the Pacific, had given an excellent account of himself, and had published details of the voyage, putting Cook's treatment of the natives in an unfavorable light; thereby, Mr. Jefferson said, "lessening our regrets at his fate." When Mr. Jefferson reached Paris, Ledyard was there, trying to form a company to engage in the fur trade on the Pacific coast. This was not wholly a rattle-brained idea, for the French were then inclined to look with interest in that direction, and the expedition of la Pérouse, in 1785, was thought to have among its objects the examination of the northern American coast region with a view to establishing trading posts. Like Patrick Henry, Ledyard seems to have exercised a curious fascination upon Mr. Jefferson, by virtue of his great natural powers; and besides, Mr. Jefferson had been for years interested in geographical exploration, especially of the trans-Mississippi regions of America. Seeing Ledyard then "out of business and of a roaming, restless character, I suggested the enterprise of exploring the western part of our continent by passing through St. Petersburg to Kamchatka, and procuring a passage thence in some of the Russian vessels to Nootka Sound, whence he might make his way across the continent." Mr. Jefferson undertook to interest Catherine II in this extraordinary project, to the extent at least of permitting Ledyard to pass through her domains unmolested. He seems to have counted too much on the complaisance of Catherine's representatives in Paris, for there is record of his having given Ledyard "600 f. on account Empress of Russia." Catherine, however, put the enterprise down at once as sheer insanity and refused to have anything to do with it or to allow Ledyard within her frontiers. To her way of thinking, apparently, Russia had lunatics enough of her own, without importing any. Nevertheless Ledyard started and "pursued his course to within two hundred miles of Kamchatka, where he was overtaken by an arrest from the Empress, brought back to Poland and there dismissed." Poor Ledyard was a man of humor as well as pertinacity. In 1787, Mr. Jefferson writes, "I had a letter from Ledyard lately, dated at St. Petersburg. He had but two shirts, and yet more shirts than shillings. Still, he was determined to obtain the palm of the first circumambulator of the earth. He says that having no money, they kick him from place to place, and thus he expects to be kicked around the globe."

Mr. Jefferson got one more glimpse of this strange being who, as he wrote dryly to Charles Thomson, had "too much imagination." Ledyard somehow found his way from Poland to London, where he "engaged under the auspices of a private society formed there for pushing discoveries into Africa." On his way to embark at Marseilles, he stopped at Paris, where he promised Mr. Jefferson that if he returned from his explorations of the Nile and the Niger, he would go to Kentucky and penetrate to the western side of the continent. But he never returned. There is possibly just the faintest suggestion of emotion discernible in Mr. Jefferson's few words to Carmichael in 1789, "My last accounts of Ledyard were from Grand Cairo. He was just then plunging into the unknown regions of Africa, probably never to emerge again."

II

But the true business of life in Europe, as in America, lay outside the routine of politics and diplomacy. One of the first matters that came under Mr. Jefferson's notice in Paris was the theory of Buffon that hot countries produce large animals and moist countries small ones; and the variant of the same theory, fathered by the Abbé Raynal, that the transplanting of Europeans to America tends to degeneration of physique. He collided sharply with Buffon on both these assumptions, denying that the atmosphere of America was more humid than that of Europe, and maintaining that neither heat nor humidity had anything to do with determining the size of animals. He got data on the minor point from Franklin, proving that there was more moisture in the air of Paris and London than in the air of Philadelphia. This did not amount to much, to be sure, but it was all that could be shown on the basis of observation and experiment until more facts were collected. "In the meantime," he says, "doubt is wisdom."

Even admitting the "superior humidity of America," however, he contended that Buffon's theory still ran aground on the mammoth, for instance; and, among living animals, on the cat tribe, on birds, on certain types of deer, and on the elk and moose—on nearly everything, in fact. Buffon had his doubts; he was polite about them, but imperturbable. A mammoth was probably the same thing as an elephant. As for the others, one must see them in order to make up one's mind. The moose seemed interesting, as Mr. Jefferson described it, but it was no doubt the same thing as a reindeer. Mr. Jefferson was an American, and these well-meaning children of the forest were imperfectly informed and likely to exaggerate. There must be some mistake about it; the moose could hardly be a distinct species. As for the elk, Buffon would like to see its horns; "this would decide whether it be an elk or a deer."

Buffon was the greatest of men in his line and worth convert-

ing; not for the sake of a mere theory, still less of deciding the
petty personal question of who was right and who was wrong, but
for the sake of attracting the eye of science everywhere to the
unsuspected resources of the new country. "He did not know our
panther. I gave him the stripped skin of one I bought in Phila
delphia, and it presents him a new species. . . . I have convinced
him that our deer is not a chevreuil." This was something, but
the whole matter might as well be settled first as last. Mr. Jefferson accordingly asked John Sullivan, President of New Hampshire, to send over the horns, bones, and skin of a moose, particularly, and those of such other animals on the list as could be
conveniently got hold of. In his eagerness, he forgot to suggest a
limit of expense in the matter, and the bill of sixty guineas was
a heavy blow. The mystified Sullivan had taken him at his word
and made a good workmanlike job of it. "He had made the
acquisition the object of a regular campaign, and that too of
a winter one. The troops he employed sallied forth, as he writes
me, in the month of March—much snow—a herd attacked—one
killed—in the wilderness—a road to be cut twenty miles—to be
drawn by hand from the frontiers to his house—bones to be
cleaned, etc., etc., etc." Mr. Jefferson paid the costs of this expedition without flinching, when he found out how they had
been incurred, and shortly had the satisfaction of presenting
Buffon with "the bones and skin of a moose, the horns of another
individual of the same species, the horns of the caribou, the elk,
the deer, the spiked-horned buck, and the roebuck of America."
Buffon was graceful, as became a man of science, and wound up
the controversy by saying, "I should have consulted you before
publishing my natural history, and then I should have been sure
of the facts."

An unauthorized French edition of Mr. Jefferson's *Notes on
Virginia*, the book which gave rise to this little brush with Buffon,
was just now putting its author in something of a quandary. The
volume had been originally compiled offhand for the information
of the French representative in the United States. In two respects
it remains a literary curiosity of the first magnitude; in the range
of observation, information, and memory that it exhibits and in
the extraordinary interest that it carries for the general reader,
without showing any mark whatever of literary effort. It is a book
of statistics, without pretence of being anything else, and it is
probably the most interesting statistical work ever produced—

interesting, that is, to a reader who has no antecedent interest in the statistics it presents. Mr. Jefferson did not publish the book in America, chiefly from diffidence; besides, it contained observations on slavery and on the state constitution that he feared might "produce an irritation" which would stand in the way of reform. When he went to France, he had a few copies privately printed for the benefit of acquaintances whom he could trust; and one of these copies getting into the hands of a French publisher, it was surreptitiously translated and put on the press. Mr. Jefferson was quite as willing to have the book appear in Europe as he was unwilling to have it appear in America; it was not bad advertising for the United States. But the translation was a botch. Mr. Jefferson succeeded in delaying publication while he struggled with some of its worst errors, when the Abbé Morellet came forward, to his great relief, with an offer to retranslate the work *de novo*. By way of providing a frontispiece to the book, Mr. Jefferson mustered his talents as a surveyor and mathematician, and produced a map, on the scale of one inch to twenty miles, which he caused to be engraved in London. "It comprehends from Albemarle Sound to Lake Erie, and from Philadelphia to the mouth of the Great Kanawha, containing Virginia and Pennsylvania, a great part of Maryland, and a part of North Carolina." He enlisted Dr. Bancroft, in London, to arrange for the engraving and printing; and he added a postscript stipulating that his name should not appear on the map, partly out of regard to the original authors whom he had consulted in its compilation, but chiefly and characteristically, "because I do not wish to place myself at the bar of the public."

His letters in the early summer of 1785 describe at great length the ill-fated experiment in aerial navigation made by Pilâtre de Rozière, who lost his life in attempting to cross the English Channel in a balloon; and also a curious anticipation of the screw propeller, which worked in the air instead of in the water. "I went to see it. . . . The screw, I think, would be more effectual if placed below the surface of the water." He sends the president of Yale College the star catalogues of de la Caille and Flamsteed and discusses briefly the identity of the planet Jupiter with the 964th star of Mayer. He comments on Pigott's discovery of periodical variations of light in the star Algol. "What are we to conclude from this? That there are suns which have their orbits of revolution too? But this would suppose a wonderful harmony in their planets, and present a new scene, where the attracting powers should be without and not within the orbit. The motion of our sun would be a miniature of this."

He notes the superior availability of "the metal called platina, to be found only in South America," for the specula of telescopes, since "it is insusceptible of rust, as gold and silver are, none of the acids affecting it excepting the *aqua regia.*" Noticing that the royal cabinet of natural history was without specimens of the American grouse and pheasant, he asks Hopkinson to stuff and send over a pair of each and to send also two or three hundred pecan nuts, of which he always thought uncommonly well, for some reason or other, and believed that the French would take great interest in cultivating—a belief which turned out to be illusory. In behalf of literature, he would be all for the expulsion of the Turks from Greece, "if they meant to leave the country in possession of the Greek inhabitants. We might then expect once more to see the language of Homer and Demosthenes a living language. . . . But this is not intended. They only propose to put the Greeks under other masters; to substitute one set of barbarians for another."

Whenever he heard of a new mechanical process or device, he promptly went to see it, and if it had value, he put his mind on it until he got it to work as he wished. Thus he patiently tinkered with the model of an English stationary copying press, until he succeeded in making one that was portable; and then in great delight he sent them to one after another of his friends in America. When the Argand lamp came out, he was immediately on hand to test it and ship it over. Hearing of a mechanic who had standardized the parts of muskets, "I went to the workman. He presented me the parts of fifty locks taken to pieces and arranged in compartments. I put several together myself, taking pieces at hazard as they came to hand, and they fitted in the most perfect manner." A few days afterward, he went "to see a plough which was to be worked by a windlass, without horses or oxen. It was a poor affair. With a very troublesome apparatus, applicable only to a dead level, four men could do the work of two horses." He comments on the new acid process of copperplate engraving as an art which will be "amusing to individuals," evidently with no great notion of its importance. He considers attentively the new steam pumps of Paris, finding them nothing more in point of principle than "the fire-engine you have seen described in the books of hydraulics"; and the steam grist mill at London, which by his calculation "makes a peck and a half of coal perform exactly as much as a horse in one day can perform." This is much worth while, because "America has abundance of fuel." On its first trial flight from its nest in the inventor's brain, he caught Drost's method of minting coins, which works "so as to strike both faces and the edge at one stroke, and makes a coin as beautiful as a medal." Here was a real find. As yet, Drost had made only a few coins by way of sample, "to show the perfection of his manner. I am endeavouring to procure one to send to Congress as a model for their coinage." He examined Renaudin's metronome and writes Hopkinson that a little Yankee ingenuity can make one plenty good enough for anybody out of a plumb bob and a piece of string. The colloquy with Buffon on the relative humidity of the American climate led him to inquire in London for a hygrometer made on the principles laid down by Franklin; and he presently began keeping daily hygrometric observations in addition to the thermometric and barometric records which he always kept. He complains to M. de Crèvecoeur that the newspapers are "robbing us of another of our inventions to give it to the English, . . . that is, the making the circumference of a wheel of one single piece. The farmers in New Jersey were the first who practiced it, and they practiced it commonly." He then tells how the London patentee got the idea originally from Franklin, who labored with him for some weeks in showing him how to make his first pair of wheels. "The writer in the paper supposes the English workman got his idea from Homer. But it is more likely the Jersey farmer got his idea from thence, because ours are the only farmers who can read Homer." Besides, he adds, the Jersey practice is precisely that stated by Homer, while the English practice is quite different:

Homer's words are (comparing a young hero killed by Ajax to a poplar felled by a workman) literally thus, "He fell on the ground like a poplar which has grown smooth in the west part of a great meadow, with its branches shooting from its summit. But the chariot-maker with the sharp axe has felled it, that he may bend a wheel for a beautiful chariot. It lies drying on the banks of the river." Observe the circumstances which coincide with the Jersey practice. 1. It is a tree growing in a moist place, full of juices and easily bent. 2. It is cut while green. 3. It is bent into the circumference of a wheel. 4. It is left to dry in that form. You who write French well and readily should write a line for the Journal, to reclaim the honour of our farmers.

After vindicating the New Jersey wheelwright's competence in classical literature, he takes note of a new departure in wagon making, whereby the axletree turns with the wheel, "thought to be proved best by experiment, though theory has nothing to urge in its favour." He is hospitably disposed toward a forthcoming life preserver or "hydrostatic waistcoat," which a person puts on either over or under his clothes in one minute and can inflate "by blowing with the mouth, in twelve seconds." He sends George Wythe the best editions of Polybius and Vitruvius, acknowledging "my debt to you for whatever I am myself." He makes drawings of a cabriolet and a phaeton for the Baron de Geismer, "made with such scrupulous exactness in every part that your workman may safely rely on them." With them also "I enclose you a pretty little popular tune which will amuse you for a day or so." The watches one could buy in Paris were something really beyond belief. Madison ought to have one: "I can get for you here one made as perfect as human art can make it, for about twenty-four louis." This should be a great inducement to the careful little man; but who could stand out against the insinuating intimation that "for twelve louis more you can have in the same cover, but on the back and absolutely unconnected with the movements of the watch, a pedometer, which shall render you an exact account of the distances you walk"? Mr. Jefferson was charmed with the pedometer, although from the whole pageful of intricate directions that he subsequently sends to Madison, when the Father of the Constitution finally capitulated, it must have been a frightful nuisance. Madison was not the only one who felt the tempter's power. "Are you become a great walker?" Mr. Jefferson suddenly drops in as a guileless *obiter dictum* in a letter to Bannister, "You know I preach up that kind of exercise. Shall I send you a *conte-pas*? It will cost you a dozen louis, but be a great stimulus to walking, as it will record your steps."

Later on, when the east wind of the Revolution was beginning to blow upon spiritual activity in France, Mr. Jefferson speaks despondently of "the crumbs of science on which we are subsisting here." He doubts the theory of promoting vegetable growth by electricity or by light until it is better confirmed by observation. "It is always better to have no ideas than false ones; to believe nothing, than to believe what is wrong." He notes a new process of engraving on glass and the experiments of chemists engaged in "the dispute about the conversion and reconversion of water and air." Concerning the latter, again, he thinks it "laudable to encourage investigation, but to hold back conclusion." Buffon frankly disparaged "the present ardour of chemical inquiry," much to Mr. Jefferson's surprise. "He affected to consider chemistry but as cookery and to place the toils of the laboratory on a footing with those of the kitchen. I think it, on the contrary, among the most useful of sciences, and big with future discoveries for the utility and safety of the human race." Nevertheless he thought it "probably an age too soon to propose the establishment of a system," and that the attempt of Lavoisier in this direction was premature. "One single experiment may destroy the whole filiation of his terms, and his string of sulphates, sulphites and sulphures may have served no other end than to have retarded the progress of the science by a jargon, from the confusion of which, time will be requisite to extricate us." His uneasy sense of the inhibiting power of words and of the tendency by which words come to do duty for ideas caused him invariably to nibble with long teeth at such attempts. "Upon the whole, I think the new nomenclature will be rejected, after doing more harm than good." Experimental chemistry, however, was producing results; a first-rate improvement in the bleaching process was already established in France, and "I believe they are beginning to try it in England." There was news also of a most important improvement in the composition of gunpowder, the details of which were not yet made public. Something was stirring, too, in the way of manufacturing artificial pearls, enough to be worth one third of a long letter to Francis Hopkinson, who was making some experiments of the kind himself.

The trouble is that until the whole field of chance is canvassed, one can never tell when some awkward fact will get in the way of the finest generalization and wreck it. In fact, it is best to keep generalization down to the minimum. "It is always better to have no ideas than false ones; to believe nothing than to believe what is wrong." Here in Paris, for instance, is a little abbé, a humble son of the church, who has "shaken, if not destroyed, the theory of de Dominis, Descartes and Newton, for explaining the phenomenon of the rainbow." If his observations were correct —and though they were borne out in part by Mr. Jefferson's own observations, one must be duly cautious—"it appears to me that these facts demolish the Newtonian hypothesis, but they do not support that erected in its stead by the abbé. . . . The result is that we are wiser than we were, by having an error the less in our catalogue; but the blank occasioned by it must remain for some happier hypothesist to fill up."

Indeed, it seems that "a patient pursuit of facts and cautious combination and comparison of them is the drudgery to which man is subjected by his Maker, if he wishes to attain sure knowledge." Such drudgery can hardly be overdone; it is all worth while. Sullivan's expedition in the wintry wilds of Massachusetts and New Hampshire was worth while, and so were the sixty guineas. Here in Paris again, for instance, there comes word from America of a brilliant conjecture that the Creek Indians are descendants of the Carthaginians who had in some way become separated from the main fleet of Hanno and drifted to a new shore. Very well; one may "see nothing impossible in his conjecture," but the way to find out is to find out. "I am glad he means to appeal to similarity of language, which I consider as the strongest kind of proof it is possible to adduce. I have somewhere read that the language of the ancient Carthaginians is still spoken by their descendants inhabiting the mountainous interior parts of Barbary, to which they were obliged to retire by the conquering Arabs. If so, a vocabulary of their tongue can still be got, and if your friend will get one of the Creek languages, a comparison will decide. He probably may have made progress in this business; but if he wishes any inquiries to be made on this side the Atlantic, I offer him my services cheerfully."

Yet a chaste platonic love of theory, unsoiled by "the rage of drawing general conclusions from partial and equivocal observations," and indulged with those by whom one may not be misunderstood, is not inadmissible. Mr. Jefferson had mentioned to the Marquis de Chastellux that "the sea breezes which prevail in the lower parts of Virginia during the summer months, and in the warm parts of day, had made a sensible progress into the interior country; that formerly, within the memory of persons living, they extended but little above Williamsburg; that afterwards they became sensible as high as Richmond; and that at present they penetrate sometimes as far as the first mountains, which are above a hundred miles further from the sea coast than Williamsburg is." The Marquis published this fact in a book; it came under the notice of the Academy of Science; and M. le Roy, member of the Academy, wrote Mr. Jefferson a "polite and learned letter," asking his views on the cause of this phenomenon.

Mr. Jefferson, writing with his left hand, his right wrist having been lately fractured by a fall, composed a letter of nine pages octavo, setting forth in full detail the theory of climatic changes induced by deforestation:

The first settlements of Virginia were made along the sea coast, bearing from the south towards the north, a little eastwardly. These settlements formed a zone in which, though every point was not cleared of its forest, yet a good proportion was cleared and cultivated. The cultivated earth, as the sun advances above the horizon in the morning, acquires from it an intense heat which is retained and increased through the warm parts of the day. The air resting on it becomes warm in proportion, and rises. On one side is a country still covered with forest, on the other is the ocean. The colder air from both of these then rushes towards the heated zone to supply the place left vacant there by the ascent of the warm air. The breeze from the West is light and feeble, because it traverses a country covered with mountains and forests, which retard its current. That from the east is strong, as passing over the ocean, wherein there is no obstacle to its motion. It is probable therefore that this easterly breeze forces itself far into, or perhaps beyond, the zone which produces it. This zone is, by the increase of population, continually widening into the interior country. The line of equilibrium between the easterly and westerly breezes is therefore progressive.

But according to the lie of the land, these prevailing breezes ought to be southeasterly; whereas in fact they blow pretty directly from the east and sometimes from the northeast. How is this? "We know too little of the operations of nature in the physical world to assign causes with any degree of confidence." Yet making the best guess one can, one would say it is probably due to lateral pressure of the strong east wind of the tropics, plus the influence of the sun, which is more freely exercised outside the equatorial belt "in proportion as the surface of the globe is there more obliquely presented to its rays." Moreover, the northern air which flows down toward the equatorial parts "to supply the vacuum made there by the ascent of their heated air, has only the small rotatory motion of the polar latitudes from which it comes. Nor does it suddenly acquire the swifter rotation of the parts into which it enters. This gives it the effect of a motion opposed to that of the earth, that is to say, of an easterly one."

As a matter of free conjecture, "willing always, however, to guess at what we do not know," one might perhaps assume that all these causes taken together would account for the direction of the sea breezes on the Virginian coast.

When running on in the vein of pure conjecture, too, one's interest is always heightened if one can give one's scientific imagination a practical turn. Speaking of the strong tropical east winds, he goes on to observe to M. le Roy that "they are known to occasion a strong current in the ocean in the same direction." This current breaks on the wedge of land of which St. Roque is the point, the southern column of it probably turning off down the coast of Brazil. "I say probably, because I have never heard of the fact, and conjecture it from reason only." The northern column is probably the agency that scooped out the Gulf of Mexico, cutting the continent nearly in two. It reissues from the northern part of the Gulf, washes the whole coast of the United States with a warm current, and then turns off eastwardly to the Banks of Newfoundland. It goes by the name of the Gulf Stream.

Since the Gulf Stream, then, has already so nearly bitten its way through the continent, why not hurry up its work for civilization? The Spaniards were desirous of trading with the Philippine Islands by way of the Cape of Good Hope. The Dutch were opposing them under authority of the Treaty of Munster, thus forcing them to consider a trade route through the Straits of Magellan or around Cape Horn. Very well; then let the Spaniards cut a canal through the Isthmus of Panama! This would be "a work much less difficult than some even of the inferior canals of France," and almost any kind of cut would answer, because the current of the Gulf Stream would do the rest. "The tropical current, entering it with all its force, would soon widen it sufficiently for its own passage, and thus complete in a short time that work which otherwise will still employ it for ages." Great consequences would ensue. First, ships would have with them a steady wind and tide straight from Europe to Asia. Second, the Gulf of Mexico, "now the most dangerous navigation in the world, on account of its currents and movable sands, would become stagnant and safe." Then, too, the Gulf Stream on the coast of the United States would cease, and the "derangements of course and reckoning" which its motion brings upon mariners would cease also. Moreover, the fogs on the Banks of Newfoundland, which Franklin's ingenious conjecture has ascribed to "the vapours of the

Gulf Stream, rendered turbid by cold air," would no longer plague the seafarer. Finally, when the Banks were no longer continually supplied with sand, weeds and warm water, "it might become problematical what effect changes of pasture and temperature would have on the fisheries." As far as America was concerned, this last point was something for the New Englanders to worry about. Let John Adams scratch his head over it. In view of any larger good, the great agricultural republic at large need not consider these possibilities too carefully.

Speculation on the Panama Canal project and its consequences had often put a restless brain to sleep in the solitude of the Virginia hills, after an evening spent over some new geographical report or treatise. Other heads had been entertaining similar ideas. About a year and a half after broaching this theory to M. le Roy, Mr. Jefferson informs Carmichael of the assurance he had received from the Chevalier de Burgoyne, that a survey had been made of the Isthmus of Panama, "that a canal appeared very practicable, and that the idea was suppressed for political reasons altogether." De Burgoyne had seen the official report and given it a careful examination. Carmichael, as diplomatic and commercial representative of the United States at Madrid, might some time possibly be in a way to get track of it or even perhaps get a glimpse of it; so Mr. Jefferson casually drops a flea in his ear by saying that "this report is to me a vast desideratum, for reasons political and philosophical." At this time, the United States was bounded on the west and south by an unbroken line of Spanish territory and on the north by British territory. All the maritime American trade of the Mississippi Valley had to pass through the Spanish port of New Orleans. Some day, probably, these frontiers would be rectified, by one means or another, to the advantage of the United States. For the moment, however—indeed, for a good while to come—Spain would be a much more desirable neighbor than either of the two great predatory European powers which were just then running up into the early preliminaries of a mighty duel. The thing was to keep Spain's foot where it stood; at all costs to keep the border territory from falling into the hands of France which, for all its innumerable private excellences, was "a den of robbers"; and, on the other hand, to prevent any extension of territory on the part of the English, "a nation of buccaneers, urged by sordid avarice, and embarked in the flagitious enterprise of seizing to itself the maritime resources and rights of all other nations." Spain must be regarded hopefully; Spain must be kept on the blind side of American foreign policy. Therefore, with respect to the Isthmus of Panama, Mr. Jefferson tells Carmichael that he "can not help suspecting the Spanish squadron to be gone to South America, and that some disturbances have been excited there by the British. The court of Madrid may suppose we would not see this with an unwilling eye. This may be true as to the uninformed part of our people; but those who look into futurity further than the present moment or age, and who combine well what is with what is to be, must see that our interests, well understood, and our wishes, are that Spain shall (not forever, but) very long retain her possessions in that quarter; and that her views and ours must, in a good degree and for a long time, concur."

III

Mr. Jefferson's fiddle playing came to a sudden end on the afternoon of the fourth of September, 1786. Returning from a long walk in company with an acquaintance, he fell when about four miles from home and broke his right wrist. He did not permit the accident to interrupt the conversation, nor did he mention it at the moment to his companion, but grasping the broken wrist, he held it tight behind his back until he reached his house, where finally informing his acquaintance of what had happened, he made his excuses and sent for a surgeon. In the intervening hour, the wrist had swollen; the fracture was improperly set, and the wrist remained always weak, painful, and almost useless. This was the last of the violin—there was no help for that—but while one had one's left hand, one could still write fairly well with a little practice, and the sooner one got into practice, the better. Accordingly, on the same afternoon, he made the regular entries in his account book quite legibly; and in time he became ambidextrous with the pen, the weakness of the right hand somewhat offsetting the awkwardness of the left. The consciousness of being forever debarred from the execution of music did not apparently disincline him to music made by others, for according to his account book, he went alone to a concert on the eighth of September, four days after his misadventure, and on the ninth he went alone to the opera.

Presently he got in another surgeon for consultation with the first, and there are indications of others concerned with his case in an advisory capacity. After four months had gone by, this array of talent, seeming not to know what else to propose, recommended Mr. Jefferson to bathe his disabled wrist in mineral water. They suggested several resorts, and out of the lot Mr. Jefferson, who had little confidence in the proposal, with characteristic forethought chose Aix; because if the treatment were ineffectual, he would not have spent his time in vain. While in the neighborhood, he would be able to examine the canal of Languedoc, "acquiring knowledge of that species of navigation, which may be useful hereafter." The interest in canal projects in the United States was then gathering strength to become in a few years a sheer rage. In particular, there was the great Potomac Canal project, headed by George Washington, which, as a purely speculative enterprise, had so much to do with the establishment of the national capital in a most ineligible place. Mr. Jefferson had no financial interest in this or, indeed, in any speculative undertaking, never even acquiring a foot of land for speculative purposes in the whole course of his life. His personal distaste for money made in these ways, however, did not blind him to the "great view" presented by a project which "was to unite the commerce of the whole western country, almost, with the eastern." Similar projects were being talked up in New York—Mr. Jefferson still had a year to live after the completion of the Erie Canal—in Pennsylvania, in South Carolina, here, there and everywhere. Decidedly one should know something about canals, and where could one learn better than in France? Besides, one could "make the tour of the ports concerned in commerce with us, to examine on the spot the defects of the late regulations re specting our commerce, to learn the further improvements that can be made in it." Two or three months would be none too long for all this, "unless anything happens to recall me here sooner."

But an object of far more interest than canals, seaports, and the incidence of commercial regulations was the economic and social condition of the producing class. "You must ferret the people out of their hovels, as I have done," he wrote Lafayette, urging him to make a similar voyage of discovery, "look into their kettles, eat their bread, loll on their beds under pretence of resting yourself, but in fact to find if they are soft. You will feel a sublime pleasure in the course of this investigation, and a sublimer one hereafter, when you shall be able to apply your knowledge to the softening of their beds or the throwing a morsel of meat into their kettle of vegetables." Here one was once more on the ground of reality. The show of civilization, as one saw it in Paris, was all very fine, but it was secondary and dependent. Here, on the contrary, the appeal to the aesthetic sense is authoritative; one yields to it with all one's heart. "From the first olive fields of Pierrelatte to the orangeries of Hieres, has been continued rapture to me," he tells Lafayette, "I am never satiated with rambling through the fields and farms, examining the culture and cultivators with a degree of curiosity which makes some take me to be a fool, and others to be much wiser than I am."

He traveled alone, from the instinctive preference which kept him alone in most of his undertakings, and alone in spirit when he had company about him. "I think one travels more usefully when alone, because he reflects more." He had no respect for the tourist's or journalist's notion of travel, regarding it as a mere licentious itch for covering ground. "To pass once along a public road through a country, and in one direction only," he remarks to Professor Ebeling, "to put up at its tavern and get into conversation with the idle, drunken individuals who pass their time lounging in these taverns, is not the way to know a country, its inhabitants or manners." The daily record of his travels is an elaboration of the farm and garden journals that he kept in Virginia; it is written laboriously, now with the right hand and again with the left, at the end of each day's gleaning of information reported in a foreign tongue, chiefly in "a patois very difficult to understand." For example, he observes that as one approaches the Rhone, in the direction of Arles, "the soil becomes a dark grey loam with some sand, and very good. The culture is corn, clover, St. Foin, olives, vines, mulberries, willow and some almonds. There is no forest. The hills are enclosed in dry stone wall. Many sheep."

At Nismes the earth is full of limestone. The horses are shorn. They are (March 22) pruning the olive. A very good tree produces sixty pounds of olives, which yield fifty pounds of oil; the best quality sells at twelve sous the pound retail, and ten sous wholesale. . . . The horse chestnut and mulberry are leafing; apple trees and peas blossoming. The first butterfly I have seen. . . . The arches of the Pont St. Esprit are of eighty-eight feet. Wild figs, very flourishing, grow out of the joints of the Pont du Gard. The fountain of Nismes is so deep that a stone was thirteen seconds descending from the surface to the bottom.

At the outset of his journey, near Sens, he was puzzled to see that instead of living in scattered farmhouses, after the Virginia fashion, the people tended to cluster together in villages. "Are they thus collected by that dogma of their religion which makes them believe that to keep the Creator in good humour with his own works, they must mumble a mass every day?" He seems not to have inquired into the matter, but to have referred it arbitrarily to his general principle that the farther one keeps from one's neighbors, the better. "Certain it is that they are less happy and less virtuous in villages than they would be insulated with their families on the grounds they cultivate." He hears great things of the climate in certain quarters. At one place there had been a notable cold spell fifteen years before, when "from being fine weather, in one hour there was ice hard enough to bear a horse. It killed people on the road." Yet he is told, and apparently believes, that after all this, "the old roots of the olive trees put out again." Elsewhere he was informed that "about five years ago there was such a hail as to kill cats." After a winter in Paris, it seems, Mr. Jefferson's ears were open to almost any tall story of the weather. Rather oddly for one of his great strength and stature, he was always painfully sensitive to cold. He wrote to William Dunbar in 1801, no doubt with vivid memories of the climate of Paris, especially in the notable winter of 1788, which nearly finished him, that "when I recollect, on the one hand, all the sufferings I have had from cold, and on the other, all my other pains, the former predominate greatly"; and it is often a matter of wonderment to him "that any human being should remain in a cold country who could find room in a warm one." Still, although he could believe a great deal about the peculiarities of the French climate, the published reports of one hailstorm, even when supported by aristocratic authority, were almost too much for him. "I considered the newspaper account of hailstones of ten pounds weight, as exaggerations. But in a conversation with the Duke de la Rochefoucault the other day, he assured me that though he could not say he had seen such himself, yet he considered the fact as perfectly established."

The permanent interest of this journal is probably in its testimony to the amount of actual labor that a human being is capable of packing into a period of three months. One reads with great respect, for example, the record of two days' work in a wine-growing region:

March 7 & 8. From la Barque to Chagny. On the left are plains which extend to the Saone, on the right the ridge of mountains called the Cote. The plains are of a reddish-brown rich loam, mixed with much small stone. The Cote has for its basis a solid rock, on which is about a foot of soil and small stone, in equal quantities, the soil red and of middling quality. The plains are in corn; the Cote in vines. The former have no inclosures, the latter is in small ones of dry stone wall. There is a good deal of forest. Some small herds of small cattle and sheep. Fine mules, which come from Provence and cost twenty louis. They break them at two years old, and they last to thirty.

The corn lands here rent for about fifteen livres the arpent. They are now planting, pruning and sticking their vines. When a new vineyard is made, they plant the vines in gutters about four feet apart. As the vines advance, they lay them down. They put out new shoots and fill all the intermediate space, till all trace of order is lost. They have ultimately about one foot square to each vine. They begin to yield good profit at five or six years old, and last one hundred or one hundred and fifty years. A vigneron at Voulenay carried me into his vineyard, which was of ten arpents. He told me that some years it produced him sixty pieces of wine, and some not more than three pieces. The latter is the most advantageous produce, because the wine is better in quality and higher in price in proportion as less is made, and the expenses at the same time diminish in the same proportion. Whereas, when much is made, the expenses are increased, while the price and quality become less. In very plentiful years they often give one half the wine for casks to contain the other half. The cask for two hundred and fifty bottles costs six livres in scarce years and ten in plentiful. The Feuillette is of one hundred and twenty-five bottles, the Piece of two hundred and fifty, and the Queue or Botte of five hundred. An arpent rents at from twenty to sixty livres. A farmer of ten arpents has about three labourers engaged by the year. He pays four louis to a man, and half as much to a woman, and feeds them. He kills one hog and salts it, which is all the meat used in the family during the year. Their ordinary food is bread and vegetables. At Pommard and Voulenay I observed them eating good wheat bread; at Meursault, rye. I asked the reason of this difference. They told me that the white wines fail in quality much oftener than the red, and remain on hand. The farmer therefore cannot afford to feed his labourers so well. At Meursault only white wines are made, because there is too much stone for the red. On such slight circumstances depends the condition of man! The wines which have given such celebrity to Burgundy grow only on the Cote, an extent of about five leagues long and half a league wide. They begin at Chambertin, and go through Vougeau, Romanie, Veaune, Nuys, Beaune, Pommard, Voulenay, Meursault, and end at Monrachet. Those of the two last are white, the others red. Chambertin, Vougeau and Veaune are strongest, and will bear transportation and keeping. They sell therefore on the spot for twelve hundred livres the queue, which is forty-eight sous the bottle. Voulenay is the best of the other reds, equal in flavour to Chambertin, etc., but being lighter, will not keep, and therefore sells for not more than three hundred livres the queue, which is twelve sous the bottle. It ripens sooner than they do, and consequently is better for those who wish to broach at a year old. In like manner of the white wines, and for the same reason, Monrachet sells for twelve hundred livres the queue (forty-eight sous the bottle). It is remarkable that the best of each kind, that is, of the red and white, is made at the extremities of the line, to wit, at Chambertin and Monrachet. It is pretended that the adjoining vineyards produce the same qualities, but that belonging to obscure individuals, they have not obtained a name, and therefore sell as other wines. The aspect of the Cote is a little south of east. The western side is also covered with vines, and is apparently of the same soil, yet the wines are of the coarsest kinds. Such too are those which are produced in the plains; but there the soil is richer and less strong. Vougeau is the property of the monks of Citeaux, and produces about two hundred pieces. Monrachet contains about fifty arpents, and produces, one year with another, about one hundred and twenty pieces. It belongs to two proprietors only, Monsieur de Clarmont, who leases to some wine merchants, and the Marquis de Sarsnet of Dijon, whose part is farmed to a Monsieur de la Tour, whose family for many generations have had the farm. The best wines are carried to Paris by land. The transportation costs thirty-six livres the piece. The more indifferent go by water. Bottles cost four and a half sous each.

The amount of actual hard work represented by this review of a local industry is probably no more than most well-trained minds could get through in two days, but to keep up that pace for ninety consecutive days, like leaping hurdles, is another matter. It is nothing to leap two hurdles or three—any one can do it— but few can leap ninety hurdles at a stretch.

His journal takes account of many novelties and curiosities. At Pontac he is told of a seedless grape "which I did not formerly suppose to exist; but I saw at Marseilles dried raisins from Smyrna without seeds." He finds strawberries and peas on the table at Castres, "so that the country on the canal of Languedoc seems to have later seasons than that east and west of it. What can be the cause?" After giving this the benefit of some speculations, with which he is apparently dissatisfied, he remarks that there are ortolans at Agen, but none at Bordeaux. He devotes two

pages to a study of the phenomenon of alluvial formation in the
rivers running into the Mediterranean. "Has this peculiarity of
the Mediterranean any connexion with the scantiness of its tides,
which even at the equinoxes are of two or three feet only?" He
speculates on the origin of marine shells discovered on high
ground, away from the ocean, deciding finally that it was not
possible to accept any of the current hypotheses, although his
own guess that "some throe of nature has forced up parts which
had been the bed of the ocean," turned out to be a fairly good
one. He describes in detail the processes of butter making and
cheese making at Rozzano, of rice husking at Vercelli, two methods of vine planting which were new to him and one of planting
corn. Noli was remarkable for a great growth of aloes which never
flower; moreover, "a curious cruet for oil and vinegar in one piece,
I saw here. A bishop resides here, whose revenue is two thousand
livres, equal to sixty-six guineas. I heard a nightingale here." The
income of bishops seemed to interest him; he found a bishop
residing at Albenga who got as much as forty thousand livres.
He looked for plums at Brignolles, but found none, "which makes
me conjecture that the celebrated plum of that name is not
derived from this place." At Marseilles, "I measured a mule, not
the largest, five feet and two inches high." In examining the locks
of the canal of Languedoc, he calculated that five minutes were
lost at every basin on account of the archaic mechanism in use
for opening the gates; which in the aggregate came to one eighth
of the time spent in navigating the canal. He suggested a quad-
rantal gate, turning in a pivot and lifted by a lever, which "would
reduce the passage from eight to seven days, and the freight
equally." An interesting anticipation occurs in his suggestion of
a water-level highway from Spezia to Nice, whereby "travellers
would enter Italy without crossing the Alps, and all the little
insulated villages of the Genoese would communicate together,
and in time form one continued village along that road."

In the course of his excursion Mr. Jefferson remarks many
matters that are reminiscent of distant days on the Virginia
countryside. In Beaujolais, after mentioning "a very superior
morsel of sculpture done by Slodtz in 1740," a Diana and Endym-
ion, in possession of a certain local amateur, he adds, "The wild
gooseberry is in leaf; the white pear and sweet briar in bud." On
the ninth of April, near Nice, he writes, "The first frogs I have
heard are of this day," and nine days later, near Turin, "The

first nightingale I have heard this year is today." At Lyons he takes note that the nine arches of the Pont d'Ainay measure forty feet from center to center, and that "the almond is in bloom." On looking at the Italian Riviera he writes with a slight accent of wistfulness that "if any person wished to retire from his acquaintance, to live absolutely unknown, and yet in the midst of physical enjoyments, it should be in some of the little villages of this coast, where air, water and earth concur to offer what each has most precious."

IV

While in England, cooling his heels at the pleasure of the Marquis of Caermarthen, Mr. Jefferson employed his time in a methodical study of sixteen typical English gardens. He has some good things to say of the English technique of landscape gardening, but is highly critical of the architecture that goes with it. The Corinthian arch at Stowe "has a very useless appearance, inasmuch as it has no pretension to any destination." The architecture of the new house at Paynshill is "incorrect," but the Doric temple on the premises is beautiful. "Architecture has contributed nothing" to the sightliness of the Leasowes in Shropshire. Aside from this record, which carries a curious air of perfunctoriness and enervation, there is little to show for his occupations of two months in England. He remarks in a letter to Madame de Corny that "the splendour of the shops is all that is worth looking at in London." His account book carries an entry of the customary shilling for seeing Shakespeare's tombstone and another shilling for seeing the house where Shakespeare was born; but nothing more of consequence.

In the spring of 1788, when he set forth in haste to the Hague to overhaul John Adams and hold his nose to the grindstone of American national finance at Amsterdam, he took the occasion for a tour of nearly two months in the agricultural districts of the Rhine and the border provinces of Alsace-Lorraine. Here his journal comes back to the spirited and energetic tone of his French journal, and it is in great part a similar record of observations upon agricultural matters. This tour, however, carried him through several Dutch and German cities, where he noticed a whole world of minor novelties, some of which he illustrated by drawings sketched into the text of his descriptive notes. Thus the first thing in Amsterdam that caught his eye was the "joists of houses placed not with their sides horizontally and perpendicu-

larly, but diamondwise, thus: first, for greater strength;

second, to arch between with brick, thus:    ."

He also observed a new method of fixing a flagstaff to the mast of a ship; dining tables with folding leaves; "windows opening so that they admit air but not rain"—the upper sash swinging on a horizontal axis like a transom window, and the lower sash sliding up and down in the usual way. He made a minute description of the arrangement of a large private aviary kept by a rich merchant in the city, and he got detailed plans of a sawmill driven by wind power. He saw a lantern over a street door so arranged as to throw light both outdoors and indoors equally. "It is a hexagon, and occupies the place of the middle pane of glass in the circular top of the street door."

The only European art gallery ever singled out for special mention by Mr. Jefferson was the one at Düsseldorf, which he calls "sublime, particularly the room of Vanderwerff." Why this collection of pictures should have so impressed him as to gain notice over those to which he undoubtedly had access in Paris and the Dutch cities—especially in a journal devoted almost exclusively to practical affairs—is not clear. At Coblenz he saw a device that was immensely to his heart; it was a central-heating system in the Elector's palace, where "are large rooms very well warmed by warm air conveyed from an oven below, through tubes which open into the rooms." In the village of Bergen, between Frankfort and Hanau, the "things worth noting here are: 1. A folding ladder. 2. Manner of packing china cups and saucers, the former in a circle within the latter. 3. The marks of different manufactures of china. . . . 4. The top rail of a wagon supported by the washers on the ends of the axle-trees." At Mannheim, he took note of "an economical curtain bedstead," with an arrangement of bent iron rods to support the curtains. He saw with extreme disfavor the bird of household legend at Frankfort. "The stork, or crane, is very commonly tame here. It is a miserable, dirty, ill-looking bird." In Lorraine, as in Germany, he saw women doing all kinds of manual work, and their persistent love of ornament bore him eloquent testimony to the better way that things were managed in Virginia, where women did their duty in that station of life unto which it had pleased God to call them. He remarks this with a detachment so profound as to give his observations a patronizing air—one may charitably hope that they never fell under the eye of contemporary feminism, as represented by Mary Wollstonecraft, for example. "While one considers them as useful and rational companions, one can not forget that they are also objects of our pleasures; nor can they ever forget it. While employed in dirt and drudgery, some tag of a ribbon, some ring or bit of bracelet, earbob or necklace, or something of that kind, will show that the desire of pleasing is never suspended in them." This "barbarous perversion of the natural destination of the two sexes" was due to the swollen military establishment which kept so many men out of industry. It was a sorry sight, which one could never get out of one's memory. "Women are formed by nature for attentions, not for hard labour. A woman never forgets one of the numerous train of little offices which belong to her. A man forgets often."

v

In the course of five years, Mr. Jefferson may be said to have examined every useful tree and plant in Western Europe and studied its cultivation. He sends William Drayton "by Colonel Franks in the month of February last a parcel of acorns of the cork oak," for the Agricultural Society of South Carolina, and some seeds of the sulla grass, which, he explains, "is called by the names of Sulla and Spanish St. Foin, and is the *Hedysarum coronarium* of Linnaeus." To another correspondent he sends "some of the seeds of the *Dionoea Muscipula*, or Venus fly-trap, called also with you, I believe, the Sensitive Plant." To another he writes, "I am making a collection of vines for wine and for the table." He sends over to Monticello "a packet of the seeds of trees which I would wish Anthony to sow in a large nursery, noting well their names." He had great hopes for culture of the olive. "The olive tree is assuredly the richest gift of heaven," he wrote to his old preceptor, George Wythe, "I can scarcely except bread." He sent over two shipments of about five hundred olive plants to South Carolina, urging Drayton not to let unfamiliarity stand in their way. "The oil of the olive is an article the consumption of which will always keep pace with the production. Raise it, and it begets its own demand. Little is carried to America because Europe has it not to spare. We therefore have not learned the use of it. But cover the Southern States with it, and every man will become a consumer of oil within whose reach it can be brought in point of price." The South Carolinians did not share his faith, however; for in 1813 he wrote to James Ronaldson that "it is now twenty-five years since I sent my southern fellow-citizens two shipments . . . of the olive tree of Aix, the finest olives in the world. If any of them still exist, it is merely as a curiosity in their gardens; not a single orchard of them has been planted." He even tried to raise olives himself in Monticello, in company with a forlorn hope of Italian cherries, apricots, and four varieties of almonds! Nothing ever came of his efforts in the matter of olive culture; and nothing seems to have come of a consignment of caper plants which he sent over to South Carolina at about the same time that he sent the five hundred olive plants.

The fearful sacrifice of human life entailed upon Georgia and the Carolinas in the production of wet rice, "a plant which sows life and death with almost equal hand," caused Mr. Jefferson to take great interest in the culture of dry rice. In the last year of his foreign service he managed somehow to get hold of a cask of upland rice from Africa, which he promptly "dispersed into many hands, having sent the mass of it to South Carolina," where nothing came of the experiment; but being carried into the upper hilly parts of Georgia, "it succeeded there perfectly, has spread over the country and is now commonly cultivated." He also contrived to get his hands on a few pounds of Egyptian rice and sent it over. He got interested in Chinese rice, through reading a book by a French official who had traveled there, and he expresses "considerable hopes of receiving some dry rice from Cochin-China, the young prince of that country, lately gone hence, having undertaken that it shall come to me." The polite young Oriental's undertaking was probably perfunctory, for nothing was heard of the rice. Twenty years later Mr. Jefferson sent out a tracer in the person of a Dr. de Carro, who was going that way, but with no results. Inquiry among Parisian dealers brought the Piedmont rice to his attention. He could not be quite sure whether the difference between this and the Carolina rice was a difference in the grain or in the method of cleaning, and he made a note of the matter as something to be looked into when he went down into the south of France. "I had expected to satisfy myself at

Marseilles," but there seemed to be no one there who knew any more than the Parisians about the way of cleaning rice in Lombardy, or the style of machinery used. "I therefore determined to sift the matter to the bottom" by making "an excursion of three weeks into the rice country beyond the Alps, going through it from Cercelli to Pavia, about sixty miles." Here he found that the process and the machinery were nothing new, and hence "there was but one conclusion, then, to be drawn, to wit, that the rice was of a different species." He found moreover that the government of Turin was so well aware of this difference that "they prohibit the exportation of rough rice on pain of death." Nevertheless he reports to his superior in the Department of Foreign Affairs, who was then the exemplary John Jay, that "I have taken measures, however, which I think will not fail for obtaining a quantity of it, and I bought on the spot a small parcel."

He does not tell the profound and austere Secretary what these measures were; but they come out in the diary of his travels. "Poggio, a muleteer, who passes every week between Vercelli and Genoa, will smuggle a sack of rough rice for me to Genoa; it being death to export it in this form." To keep a sheet anchor to windward of this enterprise, since for some reason he had "no great dependence on its success," he stowed away the contents of the small parcel on his own person, "as much as my coat and surtout pockets would hold," and made his way unostentatiously across the frontier into free Genoa, his raiment bulging all over with contraband rice. Poggio turned out to be worthy of confidence; he also ran the blockade successfully; muleteer and diplomat met in triumph at Genoa and promptly shipped off the fruits of inquity to South Carolina and Georgia.

VI

It was all to the good; it would all come handy when one got back to the New World. First, there was Monticello, which one could make a great experiment station in everything that was new, practical, and beautiful. All the new ideas, the new agricultural processes, the new devices—the folding ladder, the hexagonal lantern, the "economical curtain bedstead," and all the rest— could be tried out there, perhaps improved, and disseminated among one's fellow workers. It had been a good five years; and now it was time to go home, reclaim one's property from "the ravages of overseers," and get to work in earnest. One might so easily have too much of a good thing. "Travelling makes men wiser, but less happy," Mr. Jefferson wrote a nephew. "When men of sober age travel, they gather knowledge which they may apply usefully for their country; but they are subject ever after to recollections mixed with regret; their affections are weakened by being extended over more objects; and they learn more habits which can not be gratified when they return home." The public service needed him no longer. He would retain his ambassador-ship, go back to Paris for a few months, more or less as a visitor, "to see the end of the Revolution, which I then thought would be certainly and happily closed in less than a year"; and that would end his office holding. The Constitution had been drafted; it did not suit him, but he had written long letters of advice to Madison and others concerning its amendment—advice which was being satisfactorily followed. He had heard of a political party division on an issue called Federalism. He did not know much about this, and when it was explained to him by letter, he took instinctively a Pauline view of it. "I am not a Federalist," he wrote Hopkinson shortly before leaving France, "because I never submitted the whole system of my opinions to the creed of any party of men whatever, in religion, in philosophy, in poli-tics, or in anything else where I was capable of thinking for my-self. Such an addiction is the last degradation of a free and moral agent. If I could not go to heaven but with a party, I would not go there at all. Therefore I am not of the party of Federalists. But I am much farther from that of the anti-Federalists." Being neither for the Jew nor for the Greek, he was for the new creature. When he returned to America, would he find himself alone in this view? He had an uneasy sense of the need to get acquainted with his countrymen; times change, and a people changes with them. There were rumors, indeed, that a great spiritual change had already come over America. "I hope to receive soon permis-sion to visit America this summer," he wrote Colonel Humphreys, "and to possess myself anew, by conversation with my country-men, of their spirit and ideas. I know only the Americans of the year 1784. They tell me this is to be much a stranger to those of 1789."

CHAPTER V

Washington, Hamilton, Adams

I

MR. JEFFERSON landed at Norfolk late in the autumn of 1789, bringing with him his fine French clothes and all the furnishings that he had bought for his two houses in Paris, carefully packed and ready for further use at Monticello; all the *toile de Jouy*, nearly a thousand francs' worth of it, the lawn curtains, the red damask window curtains, the blue damask bed curtains, the pictures and ornaments. His mind was full of happy anticipations— Christmas at Monticello and Martha's marriage early in the new year. The only cloud on his sky came out of a letter that he found waiting for him at Norfolk from President Washington, requisitioning his services as Secretary of State in the new government. He had already heard that something of the kind was in the wind; Madison had sounded him out some weeks before. He was not sure of his duty in the matter. Washington, for whom he had great respect, was in a difficult position, needing all the help he could get; this was the first consideration. Mr. Jefferson felt that he could manage foreign affairs well enough, probably, but if there were any domestic responsibilities attaching to the office, the case was different; he had been long out of contact with domestic matters and knew next to nothing about them. The proposal was disappointing, take it as one would, for the center of his interest in public affairs had, for the time being, shifted to France. Still, one must do the right thing. He could see that there was really no one else for the place. Of those who had had much practical experience in foreign affairs, Adams was now Vice-

President, John Jay was at the head of the newly formed Supreme Court, and Franklin was too old and ill to be at work. It would be delightful to go back to Paris for another year and see the end of the French Revolution, and Washington had given him a free option in the matter; yet, as things were, one might not be hard-headed about it.

Mr. Jefferson made a slow progress from Norfolk to Monticello, visiting along the way and gathering odds and ends of information about the state of the country. Madison came to see him. The precise little scholar set him straight about the duties of the new office. The Secretary of State was to look after foreign affairs, and all he needed to know about domestic concerns could easily be picked up as he went along. So much to the good. But politics at large were in a dubious way, and Madison was uncertain about them; the new government would not have easy going, by any means. The Constitution looked fairly good on paper, but it was not a popular document; people were suspicious of it, and suspicious of the enabling legislation that was being erected upon it. There was some ground for this. The Constitution had been laid down under unacceptable auspices; its history had been that of a *coup d'état*. It had been drafted, in the first place, by men representing special economic interests. Four fifths of them were public creditors, one third were land speculators, and one fifth represented interests in shipping, manufacturing, and merchandising. Most of them were lawyers. Not one of them represented the interest of production—*Vilescit origine tali*. In the second place, the old Articles of Confederation, to which the states had subscribed in good faith as a working agreement, made all due provision for their own amendment; and now these men had ignored these provisions, simply putting the Articles of Confederation in the wastebasket and bringing forth an entirely new document of their own devising.

Again, when the Constitution was promulgated, similar economic interests in the several states had laid hold of it and pushed it through to ratification in the state conventions as a minority measure, often—indeed in the majority of cases—by methods that had obvious intent to defeat the popular will. Moreover, and most disturbing fact of all, the administration of government under the Constitution remained wholly in the hands of the men who had devised the document or who had been leaders in the movement for ratification in the several states. The new

President, Washington, had presided over the Constitutional Convention. All the members of the Supreme Court, the judges of the Federal district courts, and the members of the Cabinet, were men who had been to the fore either in the Philadelphia Convention or in the state ratifying conventions. Eight signers of the Constitution were in the Senate and as many more in the House. It began now to be manifest, as Madison said later, who was to govern the country; that is to say, in behalf of what economic interests the development of American constitutional government was to be directed.

Mr. Jefferson was slow to apprehend all this. He had hitherto regarded the Constitution as a purely political document, and, having that view, he had spoken both for it and against it. He had criticized it severely because it contained no Bill of Rights and did not provide against indefinite tenure of office. With these omissions rectified by amendment, however, he seemed disposed to be satisfied with it. Its economic character and implications apparently escaped him; and now that for the first time he began, very slowly and imperfectly, to get a sense of it as an economic document of the first order, he began also to perceive that the distinction between Federalist and anti-Federalist, which he had disparaged in his letter to Hopkinson, was likely to mean something after all.

He set out on the first of March, 1790, for New York, the temporary capital, where he found himself a cat in a strange garret. Washington and his entourage greeted him cordially, and the "circle of principal citizens" welcomed him as a distinguished and agreeable man. He had grown handsomer as he approached middle age, and his elaborate French wardrobe set him off well. His charm of manner was a reminiscence of Fauquier; he was invariably affable, courteous, interesting. The people of New York could have quite taken him to their hearts if they had not felt, as everyone felt in his presence, that he was always graciously but firmly holding them off. Yet if they had any suspicions of his political sentiments and tendencies, they put them in abeyance; his attitude toward the French Revolution had shown that he was amenable to reason. As soon, no doubt, as this well-to-do, well-mannered, highly cultivated, and able man of the world saw which way the current of new national ideas was setting, he would easily fall in with it.

At any rate, everything should be made easy for him. "The

courtesies of dinner-parties given me as a stranger newly arrived among them, placed me at once in their familiar society." But every hour thus spent increased his bewilderment. Everyone talked politics, and everyone assiduously talked up a strong government for the United States, with all its costly trappings and trimmings of pomp and ceremony. This was a great letdown from France, which he had just left "in the first year of her revolution, in the fervour of national rights and zeal for reformation. My conscientious devotion to these rights could not be heightened, but it had been aroused and excited by daily exercise." No one in New York was even thinking of natural rights, let alone speaking of them. The "principal citizens" held the French Revolution in devout horror. "I can not describe the wonder and mortification with which the table-conversations filled me." Where indeed was the old high spirit, the old motives, the old familiar discourse about natural rights, independence, self-government? Where was the idealism that these had stimulated—or the pretense of idealism that these had evoked? One heard nothing here but the need for a strong government, able to resist the depredations which the democratic spirit was likely to make upon "the men of property" and quick to correct its excesses. Many even spoke in a hankering fashion about monarchy. All this, manifestly, was nothing to be met with the popgun of Constitutional amendments providing for a Bill of Rights and rotation in office; manifestly, the influential citizenry of New York would but lift their eyebrows at a fine theoretical conception of the United States as a nation abroad and a confederacy at home. Mr. Jefferson's ideas were outmoded; nothing was of less consequence to the people about him; he might have thought himself back in Paris in the days of Calonne, at a soirée of the Farmers-General. Other ideas were to the front; and when Washington's Cabinet came together, Mr. Jefferson confronted the coryphaeus of those ideas in the person of a very young and diminutive man with a big nose, a giddy, boyish, and aggressive manner, whom Washington had appointed Secretary of the Treasury.

II

Alexander Hamilton came to the colonies at the age of sixteen, from his home in the West Indies, dissatisfied with the prospect of spending his days in "the grovelling condition of a clerk or the like, . . . and would willingly risk my life, though not my character, to exalt my station . . . I mean to prepare the way for futurity." This was in 1772. He found the country ripe for him. There was something stirring all the time, something that an enterprising young man might get into with every chance to make himself felt. At eighteen he came forward in a public meeting with a harangue on the Boston Port Bill, and he presently wrote a couple of anonymous pamphlets on public questions, one of which was attributed by an undiscriminating public to John Jay, who, as Mr. Jefferson said, wielded "the finest pen in America" and therefore resented the imputation of authorship with a lively chagrin. He showed his bravery conspicuously on two occasions in resisting the action of mobs; once to rescue the Tory president of King's College, now Columbia, and once to rescue another Tory named Thurman. He saw that war was almost certainly coming on, bearing a great chance of preferment to the few in the colonies who had learned the trade of arms; so he studied the science of war, and the outbreak of hostilities found him established as an artillery officer. He had an unerring instinct for hitching his fortunes to the right cart tail. Perceiving that Washington would be the man of the moment, he moved upon him straightway, gained his confidence, and remained by him, becoming his military secretary and aide-de-camp.

But the war would not last forever, and Hamilton had no notion of leading the life of a soldier in time of peace. Arms were a springboard for him, not a profession. He served until the end of the campaign of 1781, when he retired with some of the attributes of a national figure and with the same persistent instinct for alliance with power. He always gave a good and honorable *quid pro quo* for his demands; he had great ability and untiring energy, and he threw both most prodigally into whatever cause he took up. Money never interested him. Although he inaugurated the financial system which enriched so many, he remained all his life quite poor, and was often a good deal straitened. Even in his career as a practicing lawyer, conducting important cases for wealthy clients, he charged absurdly small fees. His marriage in 1780 with one of the vivacious Schuyler girls of Albany made him a fixture in "the circle of principal citizens" of New York; it was a ceremony of valid adoption. He was elected to Congress in 1782; he served as a delegate to the Constitutional Convention in 1787; and now he was in the Cabinet, as the recognized head of the centralizing movement.

The four great general powers conferred by the Constitution upon the Federal government were the power of taxation, the power to levy war, the power to control commerce, and the power to exploit the vast expanse of land in the West. The task now before Congress was to pass legislation appropriate to putting these powers into exercise. There was no time to be lost about this. Time had been the great ally of the *coup d'état*. The financial, speculative, and mercantile interests of the country were at one another's elbow in the large towns, mostly on the seaboard; they could communicate quickly, mobilize quickly, and apply pressure promptly at any point of advantage. The producing interests, which were mostly agrarian, were, on the other hand, scattered; communication among them was slow, and organization, difficult. It was owing to this advantage that in five out of the thirteen states, ratification of the Constitution had been carried through before any effective opposition could develop. Now, in this next task, which was, in Madison's phrase, to *administration* the government into such modes as would ensure economic supremacy to the nonproducing interests, there was urgent need of the same powerful ally; and here was the opportunity for the great and peculiar talents that Alexander Hamilton possessed.

Perhaps throughout and certainly during the greater part of his life, Hamilton's sense of public duty was as keen as his personal ambition. He had the educated conscience of the *arriviste* with reference to the social order from which he himself had sprung. A foreigner, unprivileged, of obscure origin and illegitimate birth, "the bastard brat of a Scots pedlar," as John Adams testily called him, he had climbed to the top by sheer force of ability and will. In his rise he had taken on the self-made man's disregard of the highly favorable circumstances in which his ability and will had been exercised; and thus he came into the self-made man's contemptuous distrust of the ruck of humanity that he had left behind him. The people were "a great beast," irrational, passionate, violent, dangerous, needing a strong hand to keep them in order. Pleading for a permanent President and Senate, corresponding as closely as might be to the British model of a King and a House of Lords, he had said in the Constitutional Convention that all communities divide themselves into the few and the many, the first being "the rich and well-born, the other the

mass of the people. . . . The people are turbulent and changing;
they seldom judge or determine right. Give therefore to the first
class a distinct permanent share of government. . . . Nothing but
a permanent body can check the imprudence of democracy. Their
turbulent and uncontrollable disposition requires checks." He had
no faith in republican government, because, as Gouverneur Morris
acutely said, "he confounded it with democratical government,
and he detested the latter, because he believed it must end in
despotism, and be in the meantime destructive to public morality."

But republican government was here, and he could not change
it. Of all among "the rich and well-born" who talked more or
less seriously of setting up a monarchy, there was none doubtless
unaware that the republican system could hardly be displaced,
unless by another *coup d'état* made possible by some profound
disturbance, like a war. Hamilton, at any rate, was well aware of
it. The thing, then, was to secure the substance of absolutism
under republican forms; to *administration* republican government
into such absolutist modes as the most favorable interpretation of
the Constitution would permit. Here was the line of coincidence
of Hamilton's aims with the aims of those who had devised and
promulgated the Constitution as an economic document. These
aims were not identical, but coincident. Hamilton was an excellent financier, but nothing of an economist. In so far as he had
any view of the economics of government, he simply took for
granted that they would, as a matter of course and more or less
automatically, arrange themselves to favor "the rich and well-
born," since these were naturally the political patrons and pro-
tectors of those who did the world's work. In a properly constituted government, such consideration as should be bestowed upon
the producer would be mostly by way of *noblesse oblige*. The extent of his indifference to the means of securing political and
economic supremacy to "the rich and well-born" cannot be determined; yet he always frankly showed that he regarded over-
scrupulousness as impractical and dangerous. Strong in his belief
that men could be moved only by force or interest, he fearlessly
accepted the corollary that corruption is an indispensable instrument of government, and that therefore the public and private
behavior of a statesman may not always be answerable to the
same code.

Hamilton's general plan for safeguarding the republic from

"the imprudence of democracy" was at bottom extremely simple. Its root idea was that of consolidating the interests of certain broad classes of "the rich and well-born" with the interests of the government. He began with the government's creditors. Many of these, probably a majority, were speculators who had bought the government's war bonds at a low price from original investors who were too poor to keep their holdings. Hamilton's first move was for funding all the obligations of the government at face value, thereby putting the interests of the speculator on a par with those of the original holder and fusing both classes into a solid bulwark of support for the government. This was inflation on a large scale, for the values represented by the government's securities were in great part—probably sixty per cent—notoriously fictitious and were so regarded even by their holders. A feeble minority in Congress, led by Madison, tried to amend Hamilton's measure in a small way by proposing a fair discrimination against the speculator, but without success.

Before any effective popular opposition could be organized, Hamilton's bill was driven through a Congress which reckoned nearly half its membership among the security holders. Its spokesmen in the House, according to Maclay, who listened to the debate, offered little argument, and contented themselves with a statesmanlike recourse to specious moralities. "Ames delivered a long string of studied sentences. . . . He had public faith, public credit, honour, and above all justice, as often over as an Indian would the Great Spirit, and if possible, with less meaning and to as little purpose. Hamilton at the head of the speculators, with all the courtiers, are on one side. This I call the party who are actuated by interest." Hamilton's own defense of indiscriminate funding was characteristic; he declared that the impoverished original holders should have had more confidence in their government than to sell out their holdings and that the subsidizing of speculators would broadcast this salutary lesson.

Hamilton's bill contained a supplementary measure which reached out after the state creditors, united them with the mass of Federal creditors, and applied a second fusing heat. The several states which had at their own expense supplied troops for the Revolutionary army had borrowed money from their citizens for that purpose; and now Hamilton proposed that the Federal government should assume these debts, again at face value—another huge inflation, resulting in "twenty millions of stock divided among the favoured States, and thrown in as pabulum to the stock-jobbing herd," as Mr. Jefferson put it. Two groups of capitalist interest remained, awaiting Hamilton's attentions; one of them actual, and the other inchoate. These were the interest of trade and commerce and the interest of unattached capital looking for safe investment. There was no such breathless hurry about these, however, as there had been about digging into the impregnable intrenchments of funding and assumption. The first group had already received a small *douceur* in the shape of a moderate tariff, mostly for revenue, though it explicitly recognized the principle of protection; it was enough to keep them cheerful until more could be done for them. Considering the second group, Hamilton devised a plan for a Federal bank with a capital of ten million dollars, one fifth cf which should be subscribed by the government and the remainder distributed to the investing public in shares of four hundred dollars each. This tied up the fortunes of individual investors with the fortunes of the government and gave them a proprietary interest in maintaining the government's stability; also, and much more important, it tended powerfully to indoctrinate the public with the idea that the close association of banking and government is a natural one.

There was one great speculative interest remaining, the greatest of all, for which Hamilton saw no need of taking special thought. The position of the natural-resource monopolist was as impregnable under the Constitution as his opportunities were limitless in the natural endowment of the country. Hence the association of capital and monopoly would come about automatically; nothing could prevent it or dissolve it: and a fixed interest in the land of a country is a fixed interest in the stability of that country's government—so in respect of these two prime desiderata, Hamilton could rest on his oars. In sum, then, the primary development of republicanism in America, for the most part under direction of Alexander Hamilton, effectively safeguarded the monopolist, the capitalist, and the speculator. Its institutions embraced the interests of these three groups and opened the way for their harmonious progress in association. The only interest which it left open to free exploitation was that of the producer. Except in so far as the producer might incidentally and partially bear the character of monopolist, capitalist, speculator, his interest was unconsidered.

III

The debate over funding and assumption was at its height
when Mr. Jefferson took his place in the Cabinet. There was
relatively little trouble about funding, but assumption was drag-
ging its keel; it failed in the House, but was restored by the
Senate and sent back to the House for reconsideration. "Going to
the President's one day," Mr. Jefferson wrote in a private letter
two years later, "I met Hamilton as I approached the door. His
look was sombre, haggard and dejected beyond description; even
his dress uncouth and neglected. He asked to speak with me."
He walked Mr. Jefferson back and forth before the President's
house for half an hour, urging him to use his influence with the
Virginian members in behalf of assumption. He put it as a matter
of preserving the Union, and quite sincerely; there was a great deal
in what he said. New England, which comprised the principal
creditor states, was in a position to hold the threat of secession
over the rest of the country, as in fact it did at intervals for many
years. Mr. Jefferson, aware, as he wrote Dr. Gilmer, that "the
question had created greater animosities than I ever yet saw take
place on any occasion," was properly impressed by Hamilton's
representations. If assumption failed outright, he could see that
the failure might amount to "something very like a dissolution
of the government." He had no sentimentalist's repugnance to
the idea of secession. At the end of his first term in the Presidency,
he wrote frankly to Dr. Priestley that "whether we remain in one
confederacy, or break into Atlantic and Mississippi confederacies,
I believe not very important to the happiness of either part." If
now he "could scarcely contemplate a more incalculable evil than
the breaking of the Union into two or more parts," or if he con-
demned with indignation "the machinations of parricides who
have endeavoured to bring into danger the Union of these States,"
it was because of his ever-present fear that the country would be
picked up piecemeal by "the plundering combinations of the old
world." Assumption in some form, then, should be admitted;
but, as he told President Washington, he hoped it would be
"put into a just form, by assuming to the creditors of each State
in proportion to the census of each State, so that the State will
be exonerated towards its creditors just as much as it will have to
contribute towards the assumption." More than this he could

he useless employment of money is so much more lucra-
He had already written Edmund Pendleton in 1791, con-
Hamilton's general scheme, that "as yet, the delirium of
tion is too strong to admit sober reflection. It remains to
whether in a country whose capital is too small to carry
own commerce, to establish manufactures, erect buildings,
ch sums should have been withdrawn from these useful
s to be employed in gambling." In relation to the total
of the country, these sums were indeed so huge that one
ite understand a proximate and partial view of their em-
nt, to the exclusion of economic theory. While an earth-
is going on, one does not generalize about the persistence
e. Mercer estimated the entire public debt, after its egre-
nflation by Hamilton, at "one-fourth of the whole value of
operty" of the United States. This is probably an exaggera-
ut even cutting it down by one half, one can imagine the
ing predominance of a single vested interest equal to one
of a country's total wealth. No wonder Mr. Jefferson com-
bitterly that "the more debt Hamilton could rake up,
ore plunder for his mercenaries."

rest of all, Mr. Jefferson saw the political effect of Hamil-
fforts in rearing up "that speculating phalanx, in and out
ngress, which has since been able to give laws to change
olitical complexion of the Government of the United
." He wrote to President Washington in 1792, that "Alex-
Hamilton's system flowed from principles adverse to liberty,
as calculated to undermine and demolish the Republic by
ig an influence of his Department over members of the
ture. I saw this influence actually produced, and its first
to be the establishment of the great outlines of his project
votes of the very persons who, having swallowed his bait,
aying themselves out to profit by his plans." He gives a most
picture of the state of things ensuing upon the first trial of
ton's strength in Congress, with reference to the funding
sumption bill. When it became known what form the bill
take, "this being known within doors sooner than without,
pecially than to those in distant parts of the Union, the base
ble began. Couriers and relay-horses by land, and swift-sail-
lot-boats by sea, were flying in all directions. Active partners
gents were associated and employed in every State, town and
y neighbourhood, and this paper was bought up at five

not say. The formulation of the thing was in Hamilton's department, not his, and while he had an instinctive dislike of Hamilton's terms, he knew himself to be "really a stranger to the whole
subject." Moreover, he felt himself quite incompetent in financial
matters at large; he had naïvely written the Treasury Board from
Paris in 1785, that they were "very foreign to my talents."

With regard to the practical matter of effecting assumption,
however, he saw that it must be one of political trade-and-deal;
it could not be anything else. The *quid pro quo* was the location
of the national capital. The members from the middle states
wanted the capital at Philadelphia or Baltimore, and were indifferent about assumption, save as a trading point with "the Eastern
members, who have had it so much at heart." After hearing
Madison and Hamilton discuss the matter at his own dinner table,
the day after Hamilton had accosted him on the street, Mr.
Jefferson decided that "the least bad of all the turns the thing can
take" was to let Hamilton have his way on condition that the
capital should be established at Georgetown on the Potomac.
If there must be a bargain, it might as well be one from which
the producer as well as the speculator—especially the Virginian
and Middle-western producer—would stand to get something. He
had written Washington the year before that he considered the
union of the Ohio and Potomac rivers by the proposed Potomac
Canal, as "among the strongest links of communication between
the eastern and western sides of our confederacy. It will moreover
add to the commerce of Virginia, in particular, all the upper parts
of the Ohio and its waters." In view of this, he now thought that
placing the capital at the foot of the canal would tend to "vivify
our agriculture and commerce."

Thus Mr. Jefferson made what he afterward called, with some
exaggeration, the greatest political error of his life. Really, what
he did or did not do in the premises was of little practical consequence to the ultimate issue, namely: what economic interests
should control the government of the United States. He simply
did not see the end of Hamilton's plan; nor, it must be said, did
Hamilton himself clearly see it, except with the eye of instinct.
When one examines this collision of statesmanship, one is most
struck, perhaps, by the rapidity with which one's instincts invariably outrun one's own interpretation of them. Both men
represented an economic class interest in government; in any
proper use of the term, Mr. Jefferson seems to have been but

little more a theoretical democrat than Hamilton. To view him as a theoretical or doctrinaire democrat is to disregard the most inadmissible inconsistencies, both in his public acts and in his expressions of governmental theory—inconsistencies which resolve themselves immediately when one views him as the representative of an economic class interest. He was for control of government by the producing class; that is to say, by the immense majority which in every society actually applies labor and capital to natural resources for the production of wealth. His instincts reacted like the reflex action of an eyelid against anything that menaced that interest. Hamilton's instinct reacted as promptly against anything that threatened to disturb the preponderance of the exploiting class—the minority, that is, which in every society appropriates without compensation the labor products of the majority. The intellectual account which both gave themselves of the operation of this instinct, however, was as inadequate and sprawling as such accounts invariably are. Mr. Jefferson's infatuation with Hamilton's monarchism and Anglomania, for instance, his habitual view of him as "chained by native partialities to everything English," and his public character "bewitched and perverted by the British example"—all this, however sincere, is no more competent than Hamilton's own loose talk about "a womanish attachment to France and a womanish resentment against Great Britain."

Others were more quick than Mr. Jefferson to assess the economic implications of Hamilton's fiscal system. The science of economics was then in its cradle. By an odd coincidence, Mr. Jefferson had stood by the bedside of its birth in Paris; he knew its parents and godparents, both personally and by their writings, and yet seems never quite to have known what manner of child had been brought forth. As late as ten years before his death, he remarked that economics assumed the form of a science "first in the hands of the political sect in France, called the Economists. . . . Quesnay first, Gournay, Le Frosne, Turgot and Dupont de Nemours . . . led the way in these developments." But the tone of his discussion is purely academic, never showing a sense of the vital relation which the work of these men bore to the fiscal system which he instinctively opposed. He had occasional brilliant flashes of insight into fundamental economies and its relation to government, but they were too brief and unsteady to be illuminating; they but deepened the darkness that followed them.

Others, however, almost immediately system a kind of homespun economic anal bottom. In dealing with funding and a Maryland, Jackson of Georgia, and Taylo penetrated to the fundamental truth th speculator must ultimately be paid out of Hamilton's proposal therefore was actually lien on future labor. They also took the s policy in opposing the bank bill. The ban continuous monopoly of public funds, rais vestors in a semiprivate corporation—or, ra public but really private, since so large a pr and House were themselves investors who egregiously by funding and assumption, and become shareholders in the new bank. All t to be brought about at the uncompensated A levy of taxes for this purpose was, accord right conversion of labor-made values int vested in hands which had done nothing t annuity to a great amount is suddenly conj Taylor. ". . . It is paid out of labour, and falls on the poor. . . . But the aristocracy, cious, have contrived to inflict upon labour a ing for their emolument." Mercer also had principle a little earlier. "All public revenue he declared, "is a contribution, mediate o labour of the industrious farmer or mechanic

It does not appear that Mr. Jefferson's m through to this fundamental ground of ec Hamilton's fiscal system, or that it ever effec which did. He sometimes speaks somewhat Taylor and Mercer, but his precision of term than studied; as when, for instance, he wrot 1819, protesting against the sacrifice of "our erty and their labour, passive victims to the bankers and mountebankers." He had a clea system, considered by its aspect of pure fina has just notified its proprietors," he wrote in call for a dividend of ten per cent on their ca months. This makes a profit of twenty-six p Agriculture, commerce and everything useful shillings, and often as low as two shillings in the pound, before the holder knew that Congress had already provided for its redemption at par. Immense sums were thus filched from the poor and ignorant. . . . Men thus enriched by the dexterity of a leader would follow of course the chief who was leading them to fortune, and become the zealous instrument of all his enterprises."

In great measure, no doubt, his concern with the immediate political bearings of Hamilton's system diverted his attention from its theoretical economics. In this he was far from exceptional. On the one side, Oliver Wolcott, one of Hamilton's most interested supporters, wrote explicitly that he attached no importance to the funding measure save as "an engine of government," and that "without assumption, the political purposes which I have enumerated can not be attained." On the other side, Jackson brought out the historical parallel, taken from Blackstone, of the political reasons for creating the British national debt; "because it was deemed expedient to create a new interest, called the moneyed interest, in favour of the Prince of Orange, in opposition to the landed interest which was supposed to be generally in favour of the King." Mr. Jefferson wrote Washington to the same effect, that "this exactly marks the difference between Colonel Hamilton's views and mine, that I would wish the debt paid tomorrow; he wishes it never to be paid, but always to be a thing wherewith to corrupt and manage the Legislature." Of the bank project also, he wrote in retrospect, nearly twenty years after the event, "The effect of the Funding system and of the Assumption would be temporary. It would be lost with the loss of the individual members whom it had enriched, and some engine of influence more permanent must be contrived while these myrmidons were yet in place to carry it through all opposition. This engine was the Bank of the United States."

Perhaps naturally, then, Mr. Jefferson's official memorandum on the constitutionality of the bank bill does not lead into the large question of public policy exhibited by the economics of the measure. When the bill came up for the President's signature, Washington asked the four members of his Cabinet each to prepare him a written opinion for his guidance. Hamilton wrote an affirmative opinion, of great ability; General Knox, Secretary of War, a good soldier, quite out of his depth in any matter of this kind, agreed with him. Mr. Jefferson and Edmund Randolph, the Attorney General, wrote negative opinions. Mr. Jefferson took strictly legalistic ground, not passing from this to the ground of public policy, though it was well open to him. He enumerated the legal principles contravened by the bill, demolished the doctrine of the Federal government's "implied powers," and laid down as fundamental to the Constitution the formula of the Tenth Amendment, that "all powers not delegated to the United States by the Constitution nor prohibited by it to the States, are reserved to the States or to the people." Beyond this he did not go; it was a lawyerlike pronouncement, but in the premises hardly, perhaps, to be called statesmanlike.

It was not, at all events, the production of a man desirous of making himself the focus of a great popular movement of insurgency. It had a curious effect upon his reputation as a public man—curious, that is, until one remembers the tendency of terms originally fresh, vivid, and special in their significance to divest themselves of their original meaning and either degenerate into mere petrifactions or else to take on a new and different content. Mr. Jefferson's legalistic attitude toward Hamilton's fiscal system placed him before the country as a doctrinaire advocate of state rights and of strict Constitutional construction; whereas he was really neither. His advocacy of both was occasional. Class interest led him almost always to the side of the smaller political unit against encroachment by the larger, because the greater the power of local self-government, as a rule, the better for the producer and the worse for the exploiter. Thus he was quite regularly for state rights against the Union, for county rights against the state, for township rights or village rights against the county, and for private rights against all. But in this he was far from doctrinaire; when the producer's interest lay in the other direction, he promptly changed sides. He showed himself as little doctrinaire, also, toward construction of the Constitution. He was always well aware that law, even fundamental law expressed in a Constitution, is merely something that succeeds in getting itself measurably well obeyed, and that a Constitution must therefore be, in the last analysis, a device by which anything can be made to mean anything. "Some men look at Constitutions with sanctimonious reverence," he wrote in his old age, "and deem them like the ark of the covenant, too sacred to be touched." He had seen too much lawmaking and lawmongering to entertain any such illusions; his view was always practical. "I am certainly not an advocate for frequent and untried changes in laws and Constitutions.

I think moderate imperfections had better be borne with; because when once known, we accommodate ourselves to them, and"—he adds, suggestively—"find practical means of correcting their ill effects." As Secretary of State, in 1792, he says in an official opinion that where a phrase in the Constitution is susceptible of two meanings, "we ought certainly to adopt that which will bring upon us the fewest inconveniences." Yet when the interest of the producer leaned that way, he could, and invariably did, stand out as stiffly as anyone for the letter of the law and for the "safe and honest meaning contemplated by the people of the United States at a time of its adoption."

Mr. Jefferson had always a sound and clear view of the function of capital as a factor in production, always drawing a sharp distinction between capitalism and monopoly. He would not have understood a condemnation of Hamilton's system because it was capitalistic any more than he would have sympathized with idle conjurations of a "menace of capitalism" in general. "To the existence of banks of discount for cash, as on the Continent of Europe, there can be no objection, . . . I think they should even be encouraged by allowing them a larger than legal rate on short discounts, and tapering thence in proportion as the term of discount is lengthened." He did not object, even, to a national establishment of merchant banking, but rather advocated it. "The States should be urged," he wrote in 1813, "to concede to the General Government, with a saving of chartered rights, the exclusive power of establishing banks of discount for paper." It was the monopoly feature, the element of law-created economic privilege, to which he objected. He perceived, in short, the difference in economic status held by the industrial or merchant banker, furnishing capital for productive enterprise, and the banker who underwrites and hawks a lien which a government imposes, through an exercise of the taxing power, upon the products of future labor.

The last of Hamilton's fiscal measures was a protective tariff; and here again Mr. Jefferson showed a sound instinct outstripping a rather hamstrung economic interpretation. He was a natural free trader. During the Revolution he had urged upon Franklin, then at the French court, the advisability of supporting public credit by securing "free trade by alliance with some naval power able to protect it," and in his official report on foreign commerce, in 1793, he recurs to the same step-by-step policy. "Would even a single nation begin with the United States this system of free commerce, it would be advisable to begin it with that nation; since it is one by one only that it can be extended to all." He saw international commerce in the large general terms of "an exchange of surpluses for wants between neighbour nations"; if this exchange could be made free, it would be a great natural stimulus to production all round—"the greatest mass possible would then be produced of those things which contribute to human life and human happiness; the numbers of mankind would be increased, and their condition bettered."

On the other hand, he accepted the doctrine of retaliatory tariffs, apparently without perceiving that as an economic weapon any form of tariff, boycott, or embargo kicks farther than it carries, and that the best reason for a tariff is invariably a better reason against one. He never anticipated, for example, the appalling economic consequences brought indirectly upon the producer by the great embargo which he imposed upon the country in 1807. Although he correctly calls tariff taxes "duties on consumption," he assumes that they are paid at first hand instead of being passed along. He also assumes that taxation should be based on ability to pay rather than on a rental basis determined by the value of economic privilege received from government. "Taxes," he says, "should be proportioned to what may be annually spared by the individual." The theory of taxation set forth by the Economists seems not to have stirred his usually sensitive curiosity. He regarded it as an academic matter of little interest. "Whatever may be the merit of their principles of taxation, it is not wonderful they have not prevailed; not on the questioned score of correctness, but because not acceptable to the people, whose will must be the supreme law." Hence it is not surprising to find him accepting a revenue tariff as a device for making the rich pay all the taxes. As the tariff taxes "fall principally on the rich," he writes the Comte de Moustier in 1790, "it is a general desire to make them contribute the whole money we want, if possible." This failure to trace the actual incidence of taxation may be said to have made his own fiscal measures almost as bad for the producer, in the long run, as Hamilton's.

In their economic judgment on the protective system, Mr. Jefferson's contemporaries again outran him. His Virginian neighbor, Taylor, seems to have caught sight of the fundamental principle that in international trade as well as in domestic trade goods can be paid for only in goods or services, and that money, or any form of credit which apparently pays for them, does not really pay for them, but is merely a device for facilitating their exchange. "Currency is the medium for exchanging necessaries"— it must have goods behind it, and whatever medium has the guarantee of goods behind it is valid currency. Trade, then, should follow the natural lines set by purchase in the cheapest market and sale in the dearest; and any mechanism of interference, like a tariff, is disabling. He also saw that a tariff, by artificially raising prices to the domestic consumer, is a "distribution of property by law"—by political means, in other words, rather than by economic means. Moreover, by successive shiftings, the final incidence of this tax falls inevitably on production, for any governmental "bounties to capital are taxes upon industry." Tightening his terms a little, the values absorbed by the "chartered monopoly" created by a tariff law must come from somewhere, and there is nowhere for them to come from, finally, but out of production. By the last analysis somebody, in Mr. Jefferson's phrase, must "labour the earth" to produce them.

Mr. Jefferson stood out against Hamilton in every Cabinet meeting, but he always lost. He was a poor disputant; contention of any kind was distasteful to him, as having at best a touch of vulgarity about it. Unable even formally to concur with Hamilton, as the President hoped he might, he at last told Washington that "my concurrence was of much less importance than he seemed to imagine; that I kept myself aloof from all cabal and correspondence on the subject of the Government, and saw and spoke with as few as I could. That as to a coalition with Mr. Hamilton, if by that was meant that either was to sacrifice his general system to the other, it was impossible. We had both, no doubt, formed our conclusions after the most mature consideration; and principles conscientiously adopted could not be given up on either side." At Washington's request he continued to hold office in an *ad interim* fashion for a time, but a series of stirring events in the following year, 1793, determined him; he resigned on the last day of that year and shortly afterward went home. Washington's administration was headed straight for the rocks; and Mr. Jefferson, quite indisposed to martyrdom for a cause he did not believe in, went overboard and struck out for Monticello and safety.

England went into a counterrevolutionary war with the new-born French Republic in 1793. In the spring of that year, a stormy petrel made its way from France to the United States, in the person of Edmund Charles Genêt, the first French republican minister accredited to this country. The terrible latter phase of the French Revolution was a windfall to the American economic interests represented by Hamilton, since it enabled them to manufacture a serviceable public sentiment. By holding up the Revolution as a movement for democracy and illustrative of democracy in action, they could say a great deal for Hamilton's general view of the people as "a great beast," needing a strong centralized government to keep its excesses in check; and at the same time they could effectively divert attention from the economics of the French revolutionary movement and from the economic character of the strong centralized government that they were advocating for the United States. "The Anglomen and monocrats had so artfully confounded the cause of France with that of freedom that both went down in the same scale." To represent the French Revolution in terms of political theory, rather than in terms of economics, was highly advantageous for their immediate purposes; just as in the American Revolution it was advantageous for the New England traders to express their revolutionary doctrine in the political terms of the Declaration, rather than in terms of molasses, rum, codfish, and the carrying trade, or for the Virginians in terms of free land, tobacco, and debts due British creditors. The idea liberated by a successful revolution is always greater than the idea actually animating it. The American and French revolutions released upon the world the idea of the right of individual self-expression in politics; but neither was actually animated by that idea.

In the promotion of this myth, however, sincerity and interest played, as they always do, alternate and indistinguishable parts. With Washington and Hamilton, sincerity was certainly uppermost; they were shocked and horrified by the Red Terror of Democracy. The sincerity of the Vice-President, John Adams, was transparent. "You never felt the terrorism of Shays's Rebellion in Massachusetts, . . ." he wrote Mr. Jefferson plaintively, years later. "You certainly never felt the terrorism excited by Genêt in 1793, when ten thousand people in the streets of Philadelphia, day by day, threatened to drag Washington out of his house and effect a revolution in the Government, or compel it to declare war in favour of the French Revolution and against England. . . . I have no doubt you were fast asleep in philosophical tranquillity when . . . Market Street was as full of men as could stand by one another, and even before my door; when some of my domestics, in frenzy, determined to sacrifice their lives in my defence." It was all very well for Mr. Jefferson, safe and sound in Monticello, to view the French Revolution with complacency and stand by his declaration that "rather than it should have failed, I would have seen half the earth desolated; were there but an Adam and Eve left in every country, and left free, it would be better than it is now." Bearing the burden and heat of the day in Philadelphia, holding off a rabble of discontented scallawags incited by a rascally French incendiary, was another matter. There was something in this, perhaps; still, Mr. Jefferson had given a pretty good account of himself in the revolutionary cause—and given it without complaint. Cornwallis had been a reality to him, and so were the hoodlums of Paris who had twice robbed his house.

The French had the measure of matters in America. They knew that no issue of academic political theory had set the country by the ears. State rights, anti-Federalism, antimonarch-ism, and all that kind of thing were but the American equivalent of their own *liberté, egalité, fraternité*. What really had divided the country, in their view, was a mode of constitutional develop-ment inaugurated by a bold seizure of power and designed to subordinate the economic interests of the producing class to those of the monopolist and exploiting class. The French agents in America were able men, hard-baked realists, no better and no worse than the average run of men who hold such positions. Their reports to the French Foreign Office showed that they knew their game. Fauchet, in so many words, ascribes to Hamilton's policy the solid intrenchment of a class which "shows a threatening prospect of becoming the aristocratic order," nontitular, indeed, but in solid substance of economic control, precisely like that which the French proletarians had just ousted; and Fauchet puts his finger firmly upon the consequent formal opposition between the producing interest, *l'intérêt foncier ou agricole*, and the mo-nopolist exploiting interest, *l'intérêt fiscal*.

Here was something to be taken advantage of, and the French

agents knew how to do it. Ternant, the predecessor of Genêt, had already embarrassed the government by politely suggesting that it pay its debts to France. The government mulled the matter over a while, and as politely replied that it could not pay at the moment—France must wait until things looked up a little. Genêt pressed upon Washington the obligation of the treaty of 1778, which bound the United States to fight on the side of France, on demand, in any European war. When he received the cold shoulder, he went over the head of the government with an appeal to the people, making himself the center of a popular demonstration too lively to be disregarded. If the government and its supporters could get up a great current of idealism in behalf of law and order, he could get up a countercurrent of the same serviceable motive power in behalf of the warmed-over spirit of '76. Even the glossary of '76 was but so recently out of currency that Genêt had no trouble in putting it into circulation again, almost as good as new. He could talk in quite the old familiar phrases about liberty, natural rights, democracy, and the like and get first-rate effects with them; and all this he promptly did. He was helped, too, by several matters of economic discontent that affected even upholders of the established order; such as the British war policy of seizing neutral ships engaged in the newly opened and highly profitable French West Indian trade, which made important commercial interests restless under what they regarded as the slackness of the administration in protecting them.

Washington was in a tight place; he declared that he would rather be in his grave than in his present situation. War with England was impracticable, for the best of reasons. John Jay, with great acuteness, had put the whole doctrine of war in a dozen words, when he said that "nations in general will go to war whenever there is a prospect of getting anything by it"; and if the United States took the part of France against England, the dominant interests must face the prospect of loss. England, conscious of the strength of her position with these interests, was offering America every provocative indignity; yet the inexorable fact remained that trade with England was five times greater than with France, that war with England meant a stoppage of credit, depreciation of securities, a check on land speculation—one American speculator, Robert Morris, had sold as much as a million acres of American land in England in 1791—and it would thus tend powerfully to embarrass and disintegrate the solid body of supporters which Hamilton had built up for the government. There was good reason for Hamilton to be "panic-struck," as Mr. Jefferson contemptuously wrote Monroe, "if we refuse our breech to every kick which Great Britain may choose to give it."

Moreover, if the government kept faith with the treaty of 1778, it would have to reckon with the turbulent masses of excited citizenry at home—"all the old spirit of 1776," wrote Mr. Jefferson, "rekindling the newspapers from Boston to Charleston." The whole debtor class was involved; a quarrel with England would void the stipulations for payment written into the treaty of 1783, and to a man they were determined, as Wolcott put it, "to weaken the public force so as to render the recovery of these debts impossible." From this it would be a short step to summary dealing with domestic exploiting interests. Hatred of Hamilton's "corrupt squadron of paper-dealers" in Congress and resentment at the oppressive ascendency of their affiliated interests outside, the "stock-jobbers and king-jobbers," were being busily organized; so-called "democratic societies" were springing up everywhere and propounding what seemed to the government a thinly veiled Jacobinism. If America took the side of France, Hamilton wrote, "it was to be feared that the war would be conducted in a spirit which would render it more than ordinarily calamitous. There are too many proofs that a considerable party among us is deeply infected with those horrid principles of Jacobinism which, proceeding from one excess to another, have made France a theatre of blood. . . . It was too probable that the direction of the war, if commenced, would have fallen into the hands of men of this description. The consequences of this, even in imagination, are such as to make any virtuous man shudder."

Washington's perplexity was as deep as his difficulties. A sincere republican, he was really friendly to the French struggle toward republicanism. An honest man, he felt the profound inconsistency of his position if, as head of the new Western republic, he should discountenance or discourage that struggle. Sensitive to oppression in its gross and obvious forms, he believed in revolution—had he not been a revolutionist himself?—as long as its conduct remained in the right hands and brought the right kind of people out on top. He could see the point of a revolution against the British King and his ministers, for instance, but not of one against American revenue officers in Pennsylvania or against the merchant-creditor ring in Massachusetts. He under-

stood rebellion against taxation arbitrarily imposed by an interested foreign power, but not against taxation as arbitrarily imposed by an interested native minority. His mind was "slow in
operation," Mr. Jefferson said, "being little aided by invention or
imagination," and his education had been rudimentary, "merely
reading, writing and common arithmetic, to which he added sur-
veying at a later day." He read little. He was one of the richest
men in the country, and though a Virginian and a planter, neither
his instincts nor his pursuits were primarily those of a producer.
His chief interests were in landholding and money lending; and
his predilections followed his interests no less closely and no more,
probably, than is the case with the average of upright men.
Paine's bitter condemnation of him for having turned the country over to the tender mercies of monopolists and speculators
merely wounded his sensibilities without ever reaching his understanding. Why, to whom else should the country be turned over?
—to the ignorant rabble of workingmen and farmers? He had
done the best he could. Had he not himself bitterly deplored
speculation when it got out of the hands of the judicious and
began to run wild among Tom, Dick, and Harry? He was, in
short, a thoroughgoing liberal of the best type, eager to see "with
what dose of liberty man could be trusted for his own good," but
"with all a liberal's nervous horror of an overdose and all a"
liberal's naïve assumption of competent natural authority to pre-
scribe and regulate the dose.

Washington set himself against the French. The treaty of 1778
did not trouble his conscience; he had gone far enough in state-
craft to become aware that a treaty is merely the memorandum
of an accommodation of interests, usually made under duress, and
that it imposes no moral obligation when the balance of those
interests shifts. He therefore announced that the treaty had been
made with the French monarchy, now defunct, and that he could
not recognize the right of a succeeding government to claim
American assistance under its provisions.

One of Mr. Jefferson's last acts as Secretary of State was to
arrange for the recall of Genêt. He was disgusted with the bad
manners, so necessary to successful popular agitation, which Genêt
displayed in the character of *agent provocateur* to embroil Washington with Congress and the whole administration with the
people. Never, he thought "was so calamitous an appointment
made as that of the present minister of France here. . . . His
conduct is indefensible by the most furious Jacobin." Yet he dealt

with him patiently, "doing everything in my power to moderate the impetuosity of his movements," and thought he should be put up with as long as possible, believing that his heated indecencies would overreach themselves and that the net effect of his presence might be to make some weight in favor of "a fair neutrality," which was what Mr. Jefferson most desired.

He too had no scruples or superstitions about the treaty of 1778, always having strong notions of the value of American neutrality as a bargaining point whereby the incessant wars of Europe might be regularly used as leverage for the promotion of American producing interests. In a letter from Paris in 1788, he had urged this upon Washington as a continuous national policy; and a sense of it had most to do, probably, with his inveterate aversion to entangling alliances abroad. Though he disliked war, he was never a doctrinaire pacifist; he kept his sentiments and preferences quite separate from his practical view of national circumstances. He saw peace, in the present instance, as simply the most profitable asset of the American producer, and war as the most profitless sacrifice of the producer's welfare. "I hope France, England and Spain will all see it their interest to let us make bread for them in peace, and to give us a good price for it." America could well afford to put up with a good deal of chivvying for the sake of this hope, and though he feared that at first "a fair neutrality will prove a disagreeable pill" to the French, he knew that only a fair neutrality could realize his hope, and he was confident that self-interest would in the end cause France to worry down the pill without overmuch retching.

What he most feared was that Washington's proclamation of neutrality would not really mean a fair neutrality. He had an inkling of the conscious solidarity of Anglo-American monopolistic and capitalistic interest. He wrote Madison in May, 1793, that "the line is now drawn so clearly as to show on one side, 1. The fashionable circles of Philadelphia, New York, Boston and Charleston (natural aristocrats). 2. Merchants trading on British capital. 3. Paper men (all the old Tories are found in some one of the three descriptions). On the other side are, 1. Merchants trading on their own capital. 2. Irish merchants. 3. Tradesmen, mechanics, farmers, and every other possible description of our citizens." Would the government, in its international relations, take the same side that it had always taken in its domestic relations? Would it go over to the side of the producer by "a manly neutrality, claiming the liberal rights ascribed to that condition by the very Powers at war," or would it, by "a sneaking neutrality," really pro-English, keep on the side of the international monopolist and exploiting interests? There was no doubt about the disposition of the President's advisers; a good deal depended upon the President's own disposition; but much more depended upon the producer's own vigilant readiness to assert himself. "If anything prevents its being a mere English neutrality," Mr. Jefferson wrote his anxious friend Madison, "it will be that the penchant of the President is not that way, and above all, the ardent spirit of our constituents."

Washington made his proclamation. He then sent to London the best Anglo-American in the country, Chief Justice Jay, a man of flawless character and great ability, whose devotion to Hamilton's principle of preponderance for "the rich and well-born" was austerely conscientious. He was downright candid in declaring that "those who own the country should govern the country." John Jay negotiated a treaty with the British Foreign Office, which William Cobbett, then acting as a propagandist in the United States, afterward described in a letter to Pitt as a victory for England, "infinitely more important than all [Lord Melville's] victories in the West Indies put together, which latter victories cost England thirty thousand men and fifty millions of money." Mr. Jefferson, in retirement at Monticello, spoke of it indignantly as "really nothing more than a treaty of alliance between England and the Anglomen of this country against the Legislature and people of the United States." News of the treaty shook the country. "I have never," Mr. Jefferson wrote Monroe, who was then minister in Paris—poor soul!—trying in sincere puzzlement to smooth down the irate French, "I have never known the public pulse beat so full and in such universal union on any subject since the Declaration of Independence." Jay was burned in effigy from one end of the country to the other, and Hamilton was stoned from the platform while speaking in defense of the treaty.

Even Washington, whose second term was about expiring, went under a cloud. When he refused the demand of the House of Representatives that he should lay before them a copy of Jay's instructions and the correspondence relating to the British treaty, the people lost faith in him. Mr. Jefferson, whose estimate of him was always singularly just, defended him stanchly. "He errs as other men do," he wrote to a wrathful neighbor in Virginia, "but he errs with integrity"; and somewhat more informally he wrote later to Madison, "I wish that his honesty and his political errors may not furnish a second occasion to exclaim, 'Curse on his virtues, they have undone his country!'" Resentment against Washington, however, did not last. Indeed, in the long run quite probably, as Mr. Jefferson said, his reputation came to be even "more deeply seated in the love and gratitude of the republicans," whose regard for his virtues was disinterested, "than in the pharasaical homage of the federal monarchists," whose main concern was with making use of him and with building a supporting tradition around him in behalf of their policies. Long after the death of the three men whose names are most closely associated with the establishment of America's economic system, John Adams wrote Mr. Jefferson a rambling disquisition on the "abuses of grief," in which he made a vivid incidental reference to this technique of tradition building.

The death of Washington diffused a general grief. The old Tories, the hyperfederalists, the speculators, set up a general howl. Orations, prayers, sermons, mock funerals, were all employed, not that they loved Washington, but to keep in countenance the funding and banking system; and to cast into the background and the shade all others who had been concerned in the service of their country in the Revolution.

The death of Hamilton, under all its circumstances, produced a general grief. His most determined enemies did not like to get rid of him in that way. They pitied, too, his widow and children. His party seized the moment of public feeling to come forward with funeral orations and printed panegyrics, reinforced with mock funerals and solemn grimaces, and all this who have buried Otis, Sam Adams, Hancock and Gerry in comparative obscurity. And why? Merely to disgrace the old Whigs, and keep the funds and banks in countenance.

The death of Mr. Ames excited a general regret. His long consumption, his amiable character and reputable talents, had attracted a general interest, and his death a general mourning. His party made the most of it by processions, orations and mock funeral. And why? To glorify the Tories, to abash the Whigs, and maintain the reputation of funds, banks and speculations.

Mr. Jefferson foresaw that Washington's retirement was coming on the nick of time to carry over a rich legacy of trouble to the succeeding administration. "The President is fortunate," he wrote Madison, "to get off just as the bubble is bursting, leaving others to hold the bag. Yet, as his departure will mark the moment when the difficulties begin to work, you will see that they will be ascribed to the new Administration, and that he will have his usual good fortune of reaping credit from the good acts of others, and leaving to them that of his errors." He was interested in this, inasmuch as he had just been elected to play a kind of supernumerary part in the new administration, as Vice-President under John Adams.

v

Mr. Jefferson made the most of his three years' retirement from the disheveling squalor of routine politics. For a long time he did not even read the newspapers. He wrote his former colleague, Edmund Randolph, who had succeeded him as Secretary of State, "I think it is Montaigne who has said that ignorance is the softest pillow on which a man can rest his head. I am sure it is true as to everything political, and shall endeavour to estrange myself to everything of that character. I indulge myself on one political topic only, that is, in declaring to my countrymen the shameless corruption of a portion of the representatives to the First and Second Congresses, and their implicit devotion to the Treasury. I think I do good in this, because it may produce exertions to reform the evil." He shortly gravitated into the position, quite alien to his natural bent, of leadership in a great popular movement; and he also came to be regarded, by no means properly, as the philosopher and thinker of that movement. All this came about because a double bill of availability had to be filled, and there was no one else to fill it. Among the profounder students of public affairs, like Taylor, none was enough of a national figure to be a vote getter; and among those who relished popular leadership and had a gift for it, none had Mr. Jefferson's peculiar record of aloofness from the general scuffle for easy money. Patrick Henry, for example, in the best sense of the word a great demagogue, had been busy in various speculative enterprises and had done well out of them—so well that the Federalists thought it safe to approach him as a possible candidate for the Presidency.

Thus Mr. Jefferson was projected into the campaign of 1796, and finally found himself in the one public office that exactly suited him. He was a born Vice-President. He wrote Madison that "it is the only office in the world about which I am unable to decide in my own mind whether I would rather have it than not have it," which was a great concession. He wrote Gerry that "the second office in the government is honorable and easy; the first is but a splendid misery," and to Volney that it seemed possible "you may see me in Philadelphia about the beginning of March, exactly in the character which if I were to reappear at Philadelphia, I would prefer to all others; for I change the sentiment of Clorinda to *l'alte temo, l'humile non sdegno*." Gossip went abroad that he would refuse the Vice-Presidency as *infra dig.*, and this rumor set off the only flash of interest that he manifested in the whole campaign. He wrote at once in great consternation to several friends that there was nothing in it; that he had always played second fiddle to John Adams, and had every desire to keep on doing so. "I am his junior in life, was his junior in Congress, his junior in the diplomatic line, his junior lately in the civil Government." He wrote Madison that the election was likely to be close; if it reached the danger point, "I pray you, and authorize you fully, to solicit on my behalf that Mr. Adams may be preferred." Toward the close of the same letter he let the cat out of the bag with the observation that public affairs, as he saw them, "never wore so gloomy an aspect since the year 1783. Let those come to the helm who think they can steer clear of the difficulties. I have no confidence in myself for the undertaking."

The best thing for the opposition movement for the next four years was to let it precipitate itself into solidarity, like accretions of limestone, around the fossil of the Vice-Presidency. The election turned out that way by a scary margin of three votes; and there was uncommon warmth in Mr. Jefferson's letter of thanks to his old friend Dr. Benjamin Rush, for "your congratulations on the public call on me to undertake the second office in the United States, but still more for the justice you do me in viewing as I do the escape from the first. I have no wish again to meddle in public affairs, being happier at home than I can be anywhere else. Still less do I wish to engage in an office where it would be impossible to satisfy either friends or foes, and least of all at a moment when the storm is about to burst, which has been conjuring up for four years past. If I am to act, however, a more tranquil and unoffending station could not have been found for me, nor one more analogous to the dispositions of my mind. It will give me philosophical evenings in the winter, and rural days in summer."

John Adams's position as a candidate was somewhat like Mr.
Jefferson's. Both sides were about equally hard up for just the
right kind of man. Able men, for the most part, naturally preferred to profit by politics rather than engage in them, especially
in a land whose resources made the opportunities for quick profit
so great; and hence the practice of politics began quite early to
go into the hands of mere professional agents. Washington had
great difficulty in filling up his second cabinet and in the end had
to be content with poor figures. Of the few first-rate men available for the Presidency in 1796, the best by far was Jay; but with
the odium of the British treaty reeking in the public's nostrils, he
would have been an utter failure as a vote getter. As Mr. Jefferson
sardonically wrote Monroe, he was "completely treaty-foundered."
Hamilton himself never had any popular following; he was never
able to attract the confidence of the public in any large way, and
he was aware of it. About the only thing left in stock that stood
any chance of suiting the market was Adams, and there were
prayerful misgivings about him.

The figure of Adams is perhaps the most congenial—one may
say perhaps the most lovable—of any made on the page of
history by an American of his period. Franklin said, and Mr.
Jefferson often quoted it with approval, that Adams was always
an honest man, often a great man, and sometimes absolutely in-
sane. His faults were all faults of temper; they laid him continually
open to deception and betrayed him on occasion into incredible
inconsistency and pettiness. He was vain, irascible, truculent, suspicious; and these faults were offset by a corresponding excess of
the virtues that usually accompany them and are often, in a sense,
colored by them—even his integrity was pugnacious. He never
cared to conceal anything that was in his mind, and perhaps the
most prepossessing thing about him was his utter inability to do
so if he had. Engaging as the sum of his qualities undoubtedly
was, it did not precisely recommend him to those who, in their
search for a candidate, were considering it by the dry light of
partisan exigency. They knew, moreover, that while he was in
a general way on their side, he differed sharply from them in certain important particulars, and it was a question how well he
could be managed into "going along." Hamilton, indeed, was so

uncertain about this that he tried a piece of political sharp practice to defeat him in the electoral college in favor of Thomas Pinckney, but with no result except to earn for himself the fine old man's imperishable hatred.

Not long before the campaign, Adams had published a large treatise on the theory of government, which marked him as a political *tertium quid*. He was for government by "the rich and well-born," on the ground of their superior competence, but only under definite checks and restraints. He frankly acknowledged that all politics rests on the basis of economics. He was therefore against democracy, because it meant that the poor and low-born would use politics to despoil the rich and well-born; and here, from a partisan point of view, he was sound. But he also saw that an unchecked aristocracy would use politics to despoil the poor and low-born, and that by virtue of their superiority in intelligence and cunning, they would carry this spoliation to the point of mastery over all a country's economic resources and a consequent reduction of the poor and low-born to a state of living on sheer sufferance. He was as much afraid of the rich, in short, as of the poor; and his book was an effort to devise a scheme of governmental mechanics which should impartially restrain the rapacity of both. Without such apparatus, he said, "The struggle will end only in a change of impostors. When the people, who have no other property, feel the power in their hands to determine all questions by a majority, they ever attack those who have property, till the injured men of property lose all patience and recur to finesse, trick and stratagem to outwit those who have too much strength, because they have too many hands to be resisted in any other way."

On the veiled issue of the campaign, therefore, which was its real issue, his position was questionable. One could never be sure whether, on some special point of division, he might not be found heretical. In foreign affairs, also, his attitude was anomalous. He was perhaps the only man in public life whose sentiments were not in some degree pro-English or pro-French; he did not care twopence for the fortunes of either France or England. Hence it was again a question whether on occasion he could be managed into a proper service of international interests in monopoly and finance; it would be quite like him to go blustering off into some commitment against the one country or the other, on the strength of a petty issue of schoolboy's patriotism, like impressing sailors or rifling cargoes, when really serious considerations made it imperative that he should do nothing of the kind. Managing Mr. Adams would be a very delicate business, and his political sponsors contemplated it with trepidation; yet he was the only shot in their locker, and the alternative, as they put it, was the red and ruthless Jacobinism of an enraged majority.

The French had a splendid chance at Mr. Adams, and threw it away; yet it was a chance that only an extraordinary political sagacity could improve. If they had so far masked their dislike of the Jay treaty as to abstain from further hectoring tactics against the American government, they would have had no trouble with Adams and would have profited by the popular dissatisfaction which was bound to keep on in their favor if only let alone to take its own course. Adams sent commissioners to France to reach a *modus vivendi;* they came back, saying that they had been badly received, that the French government had dealt with them only at second hand through three unofficial representatives (whom Adams designated in his report to Congress as Mr. X, Mr. Y, and Mr. Z), and that these men had demanded a cash bribe and an annual cash tribute as the price of French good will.

Unfortunately it was never clear how far these men actually represented the French government or whether anything like these fatuous˙ demands was actually authorized—whether, indeed, any such thing was ever in Talleyrand's mind. Mr. Jefferson exculpated the Directory on the strength of a parallel case. "When the Portuguese Ambassador yielded to like attempts of swindlers, the conduct of the Directory in imprisoning him for an attempt at corruption, as well as their general conduct, really magnanimous, places them above suspicion." He made no bones of his belief that whatever basis of fact the incident may have had, the commissioners, led by John Marshall, had made an utterly unscrupulous use of it in behalf of damming the current of pro-French sentiment in America. "You know what a wicked use has been made of the French negotiation," he wrote Edmund Pendleton, "and particularly the X.Y.Z. dish cooked up by Marshall, where the swindlers are made to appear as the French Government." The one certain thing is that the French Government had behaved in such a high-handed way as to give color to almost any kind of report that Marshall saw fit to make. Adams promptly communicated Marshall's report to Congress, and its publication as promptly turned the tide of popular feeling. "The odiousness of the corruption supposed in these papers excited a general and high indignation among the people," Mr. Jefferson wrote. "Unexperienced in such manoeuvres, they did not permit themselves even to suspect that the turpitude of private swindlers might mingle itself unobserved, and give its own hue to the communications of the French Government, of whose participation there was neither proof nor probability."

The American people, never difficult to stir up, and never troubling itself to inquire too closely into politico-economic motive, went into a violent war hysteria, fomented by every effort of the economic interests affected. This went on increasing in volume until suddenly one day, without a word to his Cabinet or to Congress, John Adams took all the wind out of it by appointing a minister to France. He somehow heard that the French government had disavowed the X.Y.Z. incident, that it quite wished to be friendly and would gladly receive a minister. Well, if that were so, that was all there was to it; with the *casus belli* removed, there was no point to keeping on with war preparations just because they had been started in good faith, and there was even less point to keeping on with them merely to gratify a spirit of interested and more or less meretricious belligerency—and so, with one motion, the sturdy old man split his whole political organization from end to end.

The organization, indeed, had already overreached itself with the people. The powers behind it had had such easy going since the X.Y.Z. incident that their strength seemed impregnable. Naturally disposed to make all the hay they could while the sun shone, they fostered a reckless Congressional prodigality with public money. Adams had gone along splendidly in this, for he had been as warm as anyone over the X.Y.Z. proposals up to the moment when he smelt a rat in them, and for the first and only time in his life he was the idol of his party. He recommended measures for establishing a navy, for raising an army, for defending harbors, for purchasing supplies. All this meant money, money meant taxes, and taxes meant a certain recrudescence of the old critical spirit against the economic interests which were so obviously capitalizing resentment against France and raking money out of it with both hands—Wolcott, Secretary of the Treasury, for example, opened a loan of five million dollars *at eight per cent!* The organization of civil recalcitrance, however, like the organization of war, must have a pretext as well as a cause; and the administration itself furnished a pretext that fitted as if made to order by the passage of the Alien and Sedition Acts.

These laws were intended as a clincher for the stability of the existing order by providing for the deportation of foreign propagandists who were on the wrong side, like Genêt, and for the jailing of disaffected native editors, spellbinders, and publicists. The Alien Act was never enforced: there seems to have been no occasion. The Sedition Act was enforced in a strictly partisan way. In themselves, however, these laws were probably not objectionable to the people. Americans were never sticklers for theory; they have been always more concerned with the inconveniences of despotism than with its iniquities. The fate of a few aliens or of a few homegrown seditionists might therefore not have troubled them much—and least of all, perhaps, would they have been disturbed by the inconsistency of such laws with the libertarian principles so lately set forth on dress parade in the First Amendment. But they looked at these laws with eyes already jaundiced by various afflictions, which Mr. Jefferson enumerated as "the vexations of the Stamp Act, the disgusting particularities of the direct tax, the additional army without an enemy, and recruiting-officers lounging at every court-house, a navy of fifty ships, five millions to be raised to build it, on the ruinous interest of eight per cent, the perseverance in war on our part when the French Government shows such an anxious desire to keep at peace with us, taxes of ten millions now paid by four millions of people, and yet a necessity in a year or two of raising five millions more for annual expenses."

Mr. Jefferson took a strong position in precipitating popular sentiment against the Alien and Sedition Acts. Some malcontents in Pennsylvania made a move toward insurrection, which Mr. Jefferson disapproved, believing that "anything like force would check the progress of the public opinion, and rally them around the Government." He was for getting the state legislatures to declare these laws null and void, himself writing a pattern resolution for the legislature of Kentucky. Mr. Jefferson apparently never believed that the important function of constitutional interpretation should be vested in any one branch of the government, probably perceiving that such an investiture would be equivalent to the establishment of an oligarchy. He seems to have regarded Constitutional interpretation as an occasional function in the general system of checks and balances, to be exercised by the legislature, judiciary or even by the executive, whenever one or another should display any tendency to usurpation or tyranny. "Our country has thought proper to distribute the powers of its government among three equal and independent authorities constituting each a check upon one or both of the others in all attempts to impair its Constitution." Thus when during the administrations of Washington and Adams, minority class control was carried on chiefly through the instrumentality of Congress and the executive, he was for nullification by the judiciary or the state legislatures. When during his own administration, minority class control was carried on through the judiciary, he was for nullification by Congress and the executive. A letter to Mrs. John Adams, written at the end of his first term in the Presidency, shows how far he thought fit to go, and did go, in the nullification by executive order of laws duly passed and pronounced valid by a preceding administration. "I discharged every person under punishment or prosecution under the Sedition law, because I considered, and now consider, that law to be a nullity, as absolute and as palpable as if Congress had ordered us to fall down and worship a golden image; and that it was as much my duty to arrest its execution in every stage as it would have been to rescue from the fiery furnace those who should have been cast into it for refusing to worship the image."

The *opera buffa* character suddenly put by Adams upon all the high-pressure patriotism vented in preparedness for the French war made the populace look at one another in the blank and rueful fashion of those who feel themselves "sold." The administration had set off all the thunder and lightning in the world, and not a drop of rain fell. They counted up the cost of this eccentric exhibition and decided that they had seen enough. Hamilton and all that he represented turned viciously upon Adams, who boiled with rage. Conscious of having done the right thing, he struck out blindly against friend and enemy. He stood for re-election in 1800, but got no support. "The rich and well-born" saw that their entrenchment in the legislative and executive branches of the government was no longer safe and that they must shift it to the judiciary. As Wolcott wrote to Ames, "The steady men in Congress will attempt to extend the judicial department, and I hope that their measures will be very decided. It is impossible in this country to render an army an engine of government; and there is no way to combat the State opposition but by an efficient and extended organization of judges, magistrates and other civil officers." Here Adams, in sheer pique and resentment, was easily influenced to do them an incalculable service. At the very fag end of his administration, the Judiciary Act was passed, creating twenty-three new Federal judicial districts. Adams sat up half the last night of his term, signing commissions to fill these judgeships with men whom, for the most part, he did not know, but who were of the right stamp. He also appointed John Marshall, author of the X.Y.Z. reports, Chief Justice of the Supreme Court, first offering the position to John Jay, who declined it. Then, having made all the political trouble possible for his successor— and with no idea that his acts had any deeper significance—he packed up in high dudgeon and set forth for his home in Massachusetts, disregarding the customary formality of attending his successor's inauguration.

CHAPTER VI

Eight Years of "Splendid Misery"

I

Previous to the election of the elder Adams to the Presidency, a most veracious stump orator from Providence addressed the Old Britoners and Hardscrabblers, on which occasion . . . he felt he could impart to such intelligent citizens as those before him a profound secret which, when learned, could not fail to convince every independent freeman present who had any regard for the honour and well-being of his country, how immensely in all respects John Adams, the profound and fearless patriot and full-blooded Yankee, exceeded in every respect his competitor, Tom Jefferson, for the Presidency, who, to make the best of him, was nothing but a mean-spirited, low-lived fellow, the son of a half-breed Indian squaw, sired by a Virginia mulatto father, as was well-known in the neighbourhood where he was raised wholly on hoe-cake (made of coarse-ground Southern corn), bacon and hominy, with an occasional change of fricaseed bullfrog, for which abominable reptiles he had acquired a taste during his residence among the French at Paris, to whom there could be no question he would sell his country at the first offer made to him cash down, should he be elected to fill the Presidential chair. . . .

At the conclusion of the speech, it was unanimously voted by the assembled freemen present that any Old Britoner or Hardscrabble freeman who should not vote for the glorious John Adams at the coming election, ought to be deemed guilty of treason and shunned by all his neighbours accordingly; whilst in case any *individual* or *individuals* should dare to vote for that half Injun, half nigger, half Frenchman, with a touch of the bullfrog, Tom Jefferson, he or they should be rode on a green split chestnut rail, sharp side up.

The Jonnycake Papers.

The campaign of 1800 had many diverting features. The moral and religious forces of the country had already largely enlisted themselves in the service of partisan politics, with an immense preponderance on the Federalist side, since, to paraphrase Jay's dictum, those who owned the churches governed the churches. "The rich and well-born" in New York and New England gave special attention to this mode of propaganda, getting such good results out of it that Hamilton presently proposed to organize it formally on a permanent basis by establishing a "Christian Constitutional Society." This was to be, in principle, a cheap popular edition of the Order of the Cincinnati, to offset the "Jacobin clubs" and the "democratic societies." Hamilton's prospectus for this interesting project set forth its objects as, first, "the support of the Christian religion," and, second, "the support of the Constitution of the United States." Rather oddly, not a word more is said about the first object, but a great deal about the second. The society was to attend to "the cultivation of popular favour by fair and justifiable expedients," such as, first and foremost, "the diffusion of information. For this purpose not only the newspapers but pamphlets must be largely employed. . . . It is essential to be able to disseminate *gratis* useful publications." Next, "the use of all lawful means in *concert* to promote the election of *fit* men." Finally—most interesting anticipation of all—"the promoting of institutions of a charitable and useful nature in [i.e., under] the management of Federalists. The populous cities ought particularly to be attended to; perhaps it would be well to institute in such places—1st, societies for the relief of emigrants; 2d, academies, each with one professor, for instructing the different classes of mechanics in the principles of mechanics and the elements of chemistry."

Hamilton sketched this plan in a letter to Bayard, who deprecated it as unnecessarily obvious. All these desirable objects would in a little time be attained naturally and informally—much better so than by a national organization to "revive a thousand jealousies and suspicions which now began to slumber." A little patience and two or three years "would render every honest man in the country their proselyte." Hamilton's immense genius for organization stood in the way of his recognition of the imponderabilia; he never really understood the mighty force which has been so well called "the cohesive power of public plunder," though it was all along his most effective ally—his entire practical statesmanship, indeed, might be not unfairly summed up as merely an agency for its release—and Bayard's instinct for trusting to it to compass all the objects of Hamilton's plan was the instinct of the better politician.

The informal confiscation of moral, religious, and patriotic sentiment, in fact, had yielded excellent returns during the Presidential canvass and was still producing a good steady revenue. Mr. Jefferson's early efforts for the establishment of religious freedom in Virginia and his long immersion in the supposititious atheism and impurity of French social life furnished the basis for an endless playing up of his ungodliness and immorality. One clergyman compared him to Rehoboam; another gave warning of his "solicitude for wresting the Bible from the hands of their [i.e., the congregation's] children." Another set forth that he had "obtained his property by fraud and robbery; that in one instance he had defrauded and robbed a widow and fatherless children of an estate to which he was executor, of ten thousand pounds sterling."

The clergy of Connecticut in particular, under the leadership of Dr. Timothy Dwight, organized a kind of jehad. Dr. Dwight had a threefold responsibility to bear. He was a clergyman, president of Yale College, and related by blood or marriage to nearly the whole of the little politico-economic oligarchy that had controlled Connecticut from its colonial beginnings. Some person of a genealogical turn tabulated this connection and published it during the campaign.

The Family Compact of Connecticut

1. Dr. Timothy Dwight, president of Yale, generally known as the Pope.

2. James Hillhouse, United States Senator. He and Dwight married sisters.

3. Theodore Dwight, candidate for Congress. A brother to the Pope.

4. Mr. Morris, the extraordinary chairman of Sedgwick in Congress. Married Pope Dwight's sister.

5. Mr. Hosmer, member of Congress. Related to Hillhouse by marriage.

6. Chauncy Goodrich, member of Congress. Married Oliver Wolcott's sister.

7. Oliver Wolcott, Secretary of Treasury.

8. Elizur Goodrich, brother of Chauncy.

9. Long John Allen, brother-in-law of Elizur Goodrich.

10. Mr. Austin, collector of customs at New Haven, is the step-father of Long John Allen.

11. Son of Gov. Trumbull married the daughter of

12. Jeremiah Wadsworth.

13. Roger Griswold, candidate for Congress, a cousin of Hillhouse.

Dr. Dwight dictates the policy and prayers of the Illuminati; Mr. Hillhouse holds the purse, as Treasurer.

With all this moral momentum behind him, Dr. Dwight prophesied faithfully the terrible consequences of permitting the ungodly Virginian and his desperadoes to seize the reins of political power. In a single "discourse preached on the Fourth of July," he managed to get them all in, even to the nationalization of women.[1] "For what end shall we be connected with men of whom this is the character and the conduct? . . . Is it that we may change our holy worship into a dance of Jacobin frenzy, and that we may behold a strumpet personating a goddess on the altars of Jehovah? Is it that we may see the Bible cast into a bonfire, the vessels of the sacramental supper borne by an ass in public procession, and our children, either wheedled or terrified, uniting in chanting mockeries against God, and hailing in the sounds of Ça ira the ruin of their religion and the loss of their souls? Is it that we may see our wives and daughters the victims of legal prostitution; soberly dishonoured; speciously polluted; the outcasts of delicacy and virtue, the loathing of God and man? . . . Shall our sons become the disciples of Voltaire and the dragoons of Marat; or our daughters the concubines of the Illuminati?"

Such efforts in behalf of righteousness could not fail to have a great effect; and in fact, when Mr. Jefferson became President, certain pious women in New England buried their Bibles in their gardens for fear that he would at once send out janizaries to confiscate them. The interesting thing about all this, however, is that John Adams had always let his mind play as freely on

[1] On the secular side, it is also to be noticed how promptly the familiar plea for the widows and orphans came into the campaign. "Tremble then in case of Mr. Jefferson's election, all ye holders of public funds," wrote one impassioned charitarian, "for your ruin is at hand. Old men who have retired to spend the evening of life upon the fruits of the industry have invested their moneys in the public debt, will be involved in one of their youth. Widows and orphans with their scanty pittances. Public banks, insurance companies, literary and charitable institutions, who, confiding in the admirable principles laid down by Hamilton and adopted by Congress, and in the solemn pledges of national honour and property, common, certain and not very distant ruin."

religious matters as Mr. Jefferson's; he had always said a far more piquant say than Mr. Jefferson's about the vices and hypocrisies of organized Christianity and about the pernicious influence of its authoritarianism. But his economics were orthodox, at least in the main, and this made him a fit subject for the exercise of Christian tolerance, as much so as the erring brethren who made up the "corrupt squadron" in Congress. A sharp-witted pamphleteer of the period put it that "while our legislative majorities continue to serve an apprenticeship in the Hamiltonian academy of morals, it is of very small consequence whether they are atheists, Anabaptists, profess any religion or none."

Meanwhile, the object of these attentions was tranquilly looking after his husbandry at Monticello and baking brick for an addition to his house. He took no notice of either slander or abuse. It was really impracticable to notice them, even if one cared to do so, for "while I should be answering one, twenty new ones would be invented." Besides, his experience of human nature was such as to make it seem little worth while to upset one's equanimity to so slight purpose. "Dost thou wish to be praised by a man who curses himself thrice every hour?" asked Marcus Aurelius, searchingly. What really distressed Mr. Jefferson was that these people did not look at political differences disinterestedly and objectively. "It has been a source of great pain to me," he wrote to Richard Johnson, "to have met with so many among our opponents who had not the liberality to distinguish between political and social opposition; who transferred at once to the person the hatred they bore to his political opinions." He felt as he did when he wrote to the British officer, Phillips, in 1779, in the matter of the prisoners of Burgoyne's army, that "the great cause which divides our countries is not to be decided by individual animosities," or when, in the Virginia Statute for Religious Freedom, he declared that "the opinions and belief of men depend not on their own will, but follow involuntarily the evidence proposed to their minds." Opinions are determined by the general sum of experience and knowledge, and there is a childish failure in dignity in permitting them to act as a divisive force between individuals. He had never permitted himself to bear this mark of immaturity, even in his disagreements with Hamilton; they always got on well in a social way, and Mr. Jefferson gave his great political opponent all possible evidence of personal esteem.

Curiously, it was this very failure on the part of Hamilton to draw a firm line between personal and political opposition, that had most to do with seating Mr. Jefferson in the Presidential chair. Hamilton had had a sharp collision with Aaron Burr in the spring election in New York State, in which Burr had outgeneraled him at every point, ensuring the electoral vote of New York for the anti-Federalist ticket. When the national election came on, the popular vote for Mr. Jefferson was so large as to admit no doubt of the will of the country; but the vote in the electoral college resulted in a tie between Mr. Jefferson and Aaron Burr, who was not even a candidate for the Presidency. This threw the election into the House of Representatives, where the Federalists were strong enough to hold the matter at a deadlock. Thus Hamilton was confronted by a sorry choice among evils. He had tried hard at the outset to dislodge Adams and elect Thomas Pinckney, whom the Federalists had chosen to go on the ticket as a running mate with Adams, but it could not be done. His resentment against Burr was no less than that against Adams. Both of them had mightily dynamited his prestige, and he could not bring himself to support either. When Adams was eliminated and the issue reduced to a miserable option between Aaron Burr and Mr. Jefferson, the more casehardened of the Federalist leaders were rather in favor of Burr. Things were looking pretty dark, and there was a bare chance that Burr would be fairly corruptible; perhaps the Federalists might come to some kind of satisfactory pre-election understanding with him.

This was intolerable to Hamilton, and he threw himself with frantic energy into compassing the defeat of Burr. After all, Hamilton was a good patriot; it was not out of character that he should expect Burr to treat the country as cavalierly as he had treated him, Alexander Hamilton—*l'Etat, c'est moi*. All Hamilton's differences with Mr. Jefferson had been above the plane of political sharp practice, and Mr. Jefferson had always been scrupulous; all the personalities injected into them had been injected by himself. Of the two calamities, therefore, Mr. Jefferson's election was preferable. "Upon every virtuous and prudent calculation," Hamilton wrote Wolcott, "Jefferson is to be preferred. He is by far not so dangerous a man; and he has pretentions to character."

Hamilton's authority had by this time so far weakened, however, that if Burr had done a hand's turn for himself, he would no doubt have got enough Federalist support to carry him through. But he had said he would not contest the election with

Mr. Jefferson, and he kept his word, behaving, according to Mr. Jefferson's testimony, in an "honourable and decisive" way. One may say without the least disparagement of Burr, that this was wise. The country was in an ugly and dangerous mood, exasperated by the obstructionist tactics displayed at the election, and quite up to the mark of violence, if need be, in behalf of seeing the popular mandate carried out. Burr would not treat, would not put in an appearance; he remained in seclusion at Albany. Mr. Jefferson was warily approached for an understanding. If he would not disturb the fiscal system, not lean too far to the French side, not shut off development of the navy and not sweep out all the Federalist officeholders, there would be no trouble about electing him. He declared unequivocally "that I would not receive the government on capitulation, that I would not go into it with my hands tied." On these terms he stood, and on these terms he was finally elected, after protracted obstructionism by the "circle of cabal, intrigue and hatred" had brought the country to the verge of general insurrection.

II

What was needed was peace. In his first month of office, Mr. Jefferson wrote his old friend John Page that he was "very much in hopes we shall be able to restore union to our country. Not indeed that the Federal leaders can be brought over. They are invincibles; but I really hope their followers may. The bulk of these last were real republicans, carried over from us by French excesses. . . . A moderate conduct throughout, which may not revolt our new friends and may give them tenets with us, must be observed." In the same month he made similar professions to Gerry and Gates of his hopes of "uniting a great mass of confidence." In fact, the opposition party was pretty well disintegrated, and its flotsam and jetsam were in an approachable mood. The thing now was to soften asperities and let them melt out of minds already tired of them, to cultivate confidence and good temper.

Hamilton's general system, he saw, was a fixture. "We can pay off his debts in fifteen years," he said, mournfully, "but we can never get rid of his financial system." If the government had only started differently—but a ship cannot turn around in its own length. "When the government was first established, it was possible to have kept it going on true principles, but the contracted, English, half-lettered ideas of Hamilton destroyed that hope in the bud." This was a characteristically sanguine view and hardly tenable, underestimating as it does so grotesquely the lure of "public plunder." Hamilton's achievement could not be seriously meddled with; one must trust to time and a wider-spread enlightenment for that. "It mortifies me to be strengthening principles which I deem radically vicious, but this vice is entailed on us by the first error. . . . What is practicable must often control what is pure theory." To be a Strafford and go in for a policy of "thorough" ended disastrously, even under a monarchy; and the end of the Federalists showed what would happen in a republic.

Nevertheless a great deal could be done for the producer. Deflation of the public debt was out of the question, but the debt could be paid, thus drying up one contaminating stream at its source. On the eve of taking office, Mr. Jefferson wrote Samuel Adams of the "portentous aspect" presented by a "debt of a hundred millions, growing by usurious interest, and an artificial paper phalanx overruling the agricultural mass of our country." To get rid of this, he was "applying all the possible savings of the public revenue." The Administration began its program of economy, which Mr. Jefferson placed "among the first and most important of republican virtues," with the appropriations for military purposes. The army was cut down to a skeleton, and naval construction was stopped—and thus perished the Federalists' covert plans for summary dealing with proletarian insurrection at home and contested markets abroad. The newly created courts were abolished, and the Secretary of the Treasury, Gallatin, was set at work to ratproof every avenue of access to public money. The law was laid down to him by an exacting and realistic master. Mr. Jefferson was ready to acknowledge always that the technique of finance was "foreign to his nature," but he knew well enough what general results he wanted and, in a general way, how to get them. He had told Madison four years before, that "the accounts of the United States ought to be, and may be, made as simple as those of a common farmer, and capable of being understood by common farmers." He now served notice on Gallatin of his desire to see "the finances of the Union as clear and intelligible as a merchant's books, so that every member of Congress and every man of any mind in the Union, should be able to comprehend them, to investigate abuses and consequently to control them."

He was severe upon the esoteric methods pursued by Gallatin's predecessors, especially by Hamilton—methods which came under particular suspicion by reason of the outbreak of unaccountable fires among the Treasury records on the eve of Gallatin's accession to office. "Alexander Hamilton," Mr. Jefferson wrote in a memorandum to Gallatin,

in order that he might have the entire government of his [political] machine, determined so to complicate it that neither the President nor Congress should be able to understand it or to control him. He succeeded in doing this, not only beyond their reach, but so that at length he could not unravel it himself. He gave to the debt in the first instance, in funding it, the most artificial and mysterious form he could devise. He then moulded up his appropriations of a number of scraps and remnants, many of which were nothing at all, and applied them to different objects in reversion and remainder, until the whole system was involved in impenetrable fog; and while he was giving himself the airs of providing for the payment of the debt, he left himself free to add to it continually, as he did in fact, instead of paying it.

Plain going was to be the rule. Along with the enormous reduction in governmental expenditure went a considerable lightening of taxes on production. The excise was abolished, to the great relief of a multitude of small remote farmers, especially in Pennsylvania, who could neither transport their corn nor find a market for it until they had converted it into whisky. Direct taxes of various kinds, projected in the war fever of 1798, all went. At the end of his first term, Mr. Jefferson was able to proclaim that "it may be the pleasure and pride of an American to ask what farmer, what mechanic, what labourer, ever sees a tax-gatherer of the United States." This was literally true; yet there were taxes remaining on certain articles of ordinary use, such as salt, sugar, tea, and coffee, which the consumer paid indirectly, beside a tariff on foreign goods, which had the inevitable stiffening effect upon general prices. Mr. Jefferson's imperfect acquaintance with economics comes out in a suggestion to Gallatin about the tax on sugar and salt, which worried him a little, but which he could hardly see a way to get rid of without too much loss of revenue. In the strange belief that a tariff tax stays where it is put, he wrote Gallatin that he wished "it were possible to increase the impost on any articles affecting the rich chiefly, to the amount of the sugar-tax, so that we might relinquish that at our next session."

Nor did he foresee the most unwholesome social consequence of the immense impetus that would be given to unlimited private land monopoly by his cherished plan to clear off the public debt by the sale of Western lands.

He was able to do another great service to the producing interests, as he thought, by the purchase of the territory known as Louisiana—comprising, roughly, everything between the Mississippi River and the Rocky Mountains—which had lately been ceded to France by Spain. There was also good politics in the purchase. The Mississippi was the avenue of transportation for all the products of the West, and with its outlet at New Orleans in possession of an energetic, marauding foreign power, there was bound to be trouble. The contingency that he foresaw while ambassador at Paris had come to pass. "Spain might have retained [New Orleans] quietly for years," he wrote Robert Livingston. "Her pacific dispositions, her feeble state, would induce her to increase our facilities there, so that her possession of the place would hardly be felt by us. . . . Not so can it ever be in the hands of France." What Mr. Jefferson chiefly dreaded in the event of a brush with France was the inevitable political *rapprochement* with the other great predatory power, England. "The day that France takes possession of New Orleans . . . seals the union of two nations who in conjunction can maintain exclusive possession of the ocean. From that moment we must marry ourselves to the British fleet and nation. We must turn all our attention to a maritime force . . . and . . . make the first cannon which shall be fired in Europe the signal . . . for holding the two continents of America in sequestration for the common purposes of the united British and American nations."

This was a detestable prospect, for English influence had already far too strong a foothold in America to suit him. Curiously, however, it was always the external and superficial aspects of this influence that mostly concerned him. He continually mistook these for its underlying reality, and hence his exertions against it were robbed of a good deal of force. Three years before, for example, he wrote Gates that he wished "any events could induce us to cease to copy [the British governmental] model, and to assume the dignity of being original. They had their paper system, stockjobbing, speculations, public debt, moneyed interest, etc., and all this was contrived for us. They raised their cry against Jacobinism and revolutionists, we against democratic societies and

anti-Federalists." It was never thoroughly clear to Mr. Jefferson
that this fiscal apparatus was contrived for America by no means
because it was British, but because there was money in it—because
it was the most effective engine of exploitation by the "rich and
well-born." The only essential difference between government by
the "rich and well-born" in a hereditary aristocracy, as in the
France of Mr. Jefferson's day, and in a republic is that the former
is a closed corporation, while the latter, by an indefinite extension
of the cohesive power of public plunder, admits a steady accession
of outsiders. In these respects Britain, being so largely an industrial and trading nation, most nearly resembled a republic, and
her institutional safeguards of exploitation were most appropriate
to republican conditions.

Mr. Jefferson sometimes caught glimpses of the root vice of
British influence in America, but his mind quickly reverted to its
superficial appearances in matters of mere mode, fashion, predilec-
tion. Thus after the war of 1812, he wrote Caesar Rodney that
"their merchants established among us, the bonds by which our
own are chained to their feet, and the banking combinations inter-
woven with the whole, have shown the extent of their control."
But he is chiefly worried by externalities that by comparison appear insignificant, by "the mimicry I found established of royal
forms and ceremonies" under Washington; by "monarchism
which has been so falsely miscalled Federalism"; by those who
have "covered their devotion to monarchism under the mantle of
Federalism." There is great unconscious humor in his fine-spun
analysis written to John Mellish as late as 1813. "Anglomany,
monarchy and separation [i.e., secession] then, are the principles
of the Essex Federalists, Anglomany and monarchy those of the
Hamiltonians"—when, as the most obscure pamphleteer of the
period knew, what really animated and held these people together
was a predatory economic interest.

The purchase of Louisiana, then, would keep the country politically independent of England. It would also close the possibility
of capture by British forces. In one of Mr. Jefferson's first official
opinions as Secretary of State, he had committed himself un-
reservedly upon this peril. "I am so impressed with the magnitude
of the dangers which will attend our government if Louisiana and
the Floridas be added to the British Empire, that in my opinion
we ought to make ourselves parties in the general war expected to
take place, should this be the only means of preventing the

calamity." Mr. Jefferson had long contemplated buying the territory, but did not imagine at the moment, apparently, that Bonaparte would let it go. He gave large discretionary powers to Monroe, but opened negotiations only for New Orleans and the adjacent Floridan regions. Bonaparte backed and filled awhile, and ended by abruptly offering to close out the entire French possession. This was good business on both sides. Bonaparte needed the money, and he had too many military engagements on his hands to take care of pregnable holdings so far away. On the American side, there were Constitutional difficulties in the way of incorporating foreign territory into the United States, but the administration went ahead on its own, and the bargain was closed.

In themselves, these difficulties did not worry Mr. Jefferson greatly. He had no doubt about the sentiment of the country. "It is the case of a guardian," he wrote Breckenridge, "investing the money of his ward in purchasing an important adjacent territory, and saying to him when of age, I did this for your own good; I pretend to no right to bind you; you may disavow me and I must get out of the scrape as I can." What worried him was that any play of fast and loose with the Constitution "presents a handle to the malcontents among us" and might offset the overtures he had been making to the rank and file of the opposition. But as it turned out, he had little to fear. The "invincibles," especially those of the Essex Junto, had an uncommonly keen business sense. They did not like the prospective attenuation of New England's hegemony through the admission of Western states; yet Louisiana was a dazzling vision for the land monopolist —if it was a boon to the agrarian producer, it was a godsend to the speculator. So, after some formal objection and a vote of record in the Senate, the question of constitutionality was quietly allowed to lapse. On the popular side, too, the purchase rather let the wind out of current gossip about Mr. Jefferson's pro-French predilections. Apprehensions of objection from the British government likewise turned out to be groundless. When the news of the sale reached the British Foreign Office, Lord Hawkesbury said graciously that he was very glad to hear it. There seems no reason why not. Loose British capital could, as it so abundantly did, find a safe investment there and wax fat indefinitely on the rise in land values produced by the continuous increase of population. American labor and capital would do all the work of development, and the British monopolist would appropriate the increment of value; and this, naturally, from the point of view of the British Foreign Office, would be a fair and laudable division of responsibility.

The industrial and commercial interests fared better under Mr. Jefferson than they expected. He did not harry them, and his views on the tariff and his unconcern with land monopoly helped them. At the end of a year, Hamilton congratulated him and praised the impartiality of his administration; and so did his old colleague in Washington's Cabinet, General Henry Knox, who had lately gone into bankruptcy for $400,000 and was in a chastened frame of mind. Mr. Jefferson had an extremely low opinion of Knox in his public capacity, leaving record that he thought him a fool and a blabber; but he replied politely, though rather dryly, that "union is already effected from New York southward almost completely. In the New England States it will be slower than elsewhere, from peculiar circumstances better known to yourself than to me. But we will go on attending with the utmost solicitude to their interests and doing them impartial justice, and I have no doubt they will in time do justice to us." In his dealings with the banks, he showed that two could play the game of building up capitalist support by the use of public money. "It is certainly for the public good," he wrote Gallatin in 1802, "to keep all the banks competitors for our favours by a judicious distribution of [public funds in deposit] and thus to engage the individuals who belong to them in support of the reformed order of things, or at least in an acquiescence under it." Some months later he wrote him again that "I am decidedly in favour of making all the banks Republican by sharing deposits among them in proportion to the dispositions they show. . . . It is material to the safety of Republicanism to detach the mercantile interest from its enemies and incorporate them into the body of its friends."

This little transaction with the banks, however, was about all he attempted to do by power of the loaves and fishes. By cutting down the number of Federal offices by about one half, he made an astonishing and spectacular voluntary reduction in his resources of patronage; nor, except in one instance, did he employ the remainder for partisan purposes. On the personal side, he saw as clearly as anyone the practicability of a strong political machine, and he was well aware that no ruler on earth had such enormous machine power as the Constitution permitted a President to develop and use. "A person who wishes to make [patronage] an engine of self-evaluation may do wonders with it," he wrote James Sullivan in 1808, and as he surveyed the "madness and extravagance" of the Federalists in 1798, he wrote John Taylor that "those who have once got the ascendency and possessed themselves of all the resources of the nation, their revenues and offices, have immense means for retaining their advantage." This was part of the Constitutional system devised in behalf of the "rich and well-born"; the Constitution was meant to work that way, and it did. But he was not disposed to take advantage of this. "The elective principle becomes nothing," he said, "if it may be smothered by the enormous patronage of the General Government." He made few removals, and those only "who had signalized themselves by their own intolerance in office"—about fifteen, in all—with some who were removed "for such delinquencies as removed the Republicans equally." All this wretched peddling business of office mongering was gall and wormwood to him. "The ordinary affairs of a nation offer little difficulty to a person of any experience," he wrote Sullivan plaintively, "but the gift of office is the dreadful burthen that oppresses him." Republican officeseekers were like any other; they came to Washington hungry, and, when disappointed, were ready to fry the President alive for breakfast. "Every office becoming vacant, every appointment made, *me donne un ingrat et cent ennemis.*" In 1799, before he had practical experience of the fact, he remarked to Tench Coxe the great truth that "whenever a man has cast a longing eye on offices, a rottenness begins in his conduct"; and now he found that "the task of appointment is a heavy one indeed. He on whom it falls may envy the lot of a Sisyphus or Ixion. Their agonies were of the body; this of the mind. Yet, like the office of hangman, it must be executed by some one. It has been assigned to me and made my duty. I make up my mind to it therefore, and abandon all regard to consequences."

The one exception to his impartial use of patronage was in the case of the implacable state of Connecticut. At the outset he served notice on his Attorney General, Levi Lincoln, a Massachusetts man, as explicitly as he did on Gallatin, that the hardshelled irreconcilables of the Federalist group should be fed on the bread of affliction until they brought forth works meet for repentance. Sedgwick, Cabot, Gore, Higginson, Pickering, and the Family Compact of Connecticut, were fair prey; the game law was out on them. "While we associate with us in affairs, to a certain degree, the Federal sect of Republicans, we must strip of all the means of influence the Essex Junto and their associate monocrats in every part of the Union." Connecticut stood out stiffly; no Republican need apply for a state office in Connecticut. Mr. Jefferson noted this with disapproval, and put his back up. "Our gradual reformations seem to produce good effects everywhere except in Connecticut. Their late session of Legislature has been more intolerant than all others. We must meet them with equal intolerance. When they will give a share in the State offices, they shall be replaced in a share of the general offices. Till then, we must follow their example."

Economy furnished Mr. Jefferson a good pretext for indulging his inveterate dislike of ceremonial formalities. "We have suppressed all those public forms and ceremonies which tended to familiarize the public eye to the harbingers of another form of government," he wrote Kosciusko in 1802. When the House cut down Washington's official title to a bare designation of office, Mr. Jefferson wrote Carmichael that he hoped "the terms of Excellency, Honour, Worship and Esquire, forever disappear from among us from that moment. I wish that of Mr. would follow them." All his life, when writing formally in the third person, he rarely applied this last title to himself, except when not using it would have been at the price of ostentation; but on the other hand, he was invariably punctilious about the formal title of address to others. As President, he made a clean sweep of levees, parades, reviews, and public functions of a decorative character. These things cost money. Rules of precedence were superseded by the simple arrangements established by general good taste in ordinary unofficial society. Mr. Jefferson's associates in office were men of dignity and good manners, so the plan worked well and produced a good effect at large. Thomas Moore, the poet, did not relish it; he was highly critical of the undistinguished treatment he received at the White House. The British Minister, too, an odd kind of fussbudget who bore the ill-assorted name of Merry, and who, as Mr. Jefferson remarked, had learned nothing of diplomacy but its suspicions, most unhumorously worked himself up into a great tantrum over a dinner at the White House, because Mr. Jefferson, who had asked Mrs. Madison to preside at his table, offered his arm to her instead of to Mrs. Merry. Poor Mr. Merry's confidence in republican institutions was still further undermined when, calling at the White House on business at an irregular hour, he was received by Mr. Jefferson in slippers and a dressing gown. Mr. Merry seems to have made these incidents the basis of a report to his government, and to one of them is probably due the persistent tradition, otherwise quite devoid of foundation, that Mr. Jefferson was habitually careless and slipshod in his dress. According to Mr. Jefferson, however, the gray mare was so much the best horse in Mr. Merry's stable that Mr. Merry had to trot to her gait, though otherwise "personally as desirable a character as could have been sent us," and Mr. Jefferson would be sorry to lose him "as long as there remains a possibility of reclaiming him to the exercise of his own dispositions." Every concession, every allowance should be made to the wretchedness of a henpecked man, and "if his wife perseveres, she must eat her soup at home, and we shall endeavour to draw him into society as if she did not exist."

At the beginning of his administration, Mr. Jefferson wrote a friend that "the path we have to pursue is so quiet that we have nothing scarcely to propose to our Legislature. A noiseless course, not meddling with the affairs of others, unattractive of notice, is a mark that society is going on in happiness." At the end of his first term, he recapitulated the achievements of his administration during four years of strict sticking to this noiseless course. "To do without a land tax, excise, stamp tax and the other internal taxes, to supply their place by economies so as still to support the government properly and to apply $7,300,000 a year steadily to the payment of the public debt; to discontinue a great portion of the expenses on armies and navies, yet protect our country and its commerce with what remains; to purchase a country as large and more fertile than the one we possessed before, yet ask neither a new tax nor another soldier to be added, but to provide that that country shall by its own income pay for itself before the purchase-money is due; to preserve peace with all nations, and particularly an equal friendship to the two great rival Powers, France and England, and to maintain the credit and character of the nation in as high a degree as it has ever enjoyed; are measures which I think must reconcile the great body of those who thought themselves our enemies."

Indeed, they commanded the praise even of the unreconciled, for never since the time of the Antonines, if then, was seen anything comparable to the disinterestedness of this administration. Erasmus made it a mark of true Christians that "they should be so blameless as to force infidels to speak well of them." In 1828, after years spent in vitriolic hatred of Mr. Jefferson, John Randolph of Roanoke said in a public speech, "Sir, I have never seen but one Administration which seriously and in good faith was disposed to give up its patronage, and was willing to go farther than Congress, or even the people themselves, so far as Congress represents their feelings, desired; and that was the first Administration of Thomas Jefferson. He, sir, was the only man I knew or ever heard of, who really, truly, and honestly, not only said *Nolo episcopari*, but actually refused the mitre."

III

In the full tide of a popularity as great as Mr. Jefferson's, at about the same age, and from a far more exalted eminence in life—a solitary stylite, indeed, upon the august and unapproachable pinnacle of Roman rulership—Marcus Aurelius looked back upon the fate of famous men, "Camillus, Caeso, Valesus, Leonatus, and a little after also Scipio and Cato, then Augustus, then also Hadrian and Antoninus," his own foster father and predecessor. Even their names seemed now in a manner antiquated. "And this I say of those who have shone in a wondrous way. For the rest, as soon as they have breathed out their breath, they are gone and no man speaks of them. And, to conclude the matter, what is even an eternal remembrance? A mere nothing." As his first term in the Presidency ended, Mr. Jefferson's mind took the same turn. Great men had lately gone—Samuel Adams, Alexander Hamilton, Edmund Pendleton, S. T. Mason—and some less eminent but as much beloved, Mann Page, Bellini, Parson Andrews. "To these I have the inexpressible grief of adding the name of my youngest daughter"; for Maria too had gone, as her mother had gone, a sacrifice to the social expectations put upon wifehood in her day. "This loss has increased my anxiety to retire, while it has dreadfully lessened the comfort of doing it." But he had no serious thought of retiring. Midway of his policies, he felt obliged "to appeal once more to my country for a justification. I have no fear but that I shall receive honourable testimony by their verdict."

He kept the line clear between official and personal popularity, in the face of extraordinary temptations to further the one by use of the other. Even to the last days of his Presidency he returned insignificant presents made him by admiring friends. Four months before his final retirement, he sent back to Samuel Hawkins an ivory cane, with a courteous letter of thanks, mentioning the rule that he had laid down for himself and pleading his wish "to retain that consciousness of a disinterested administration of the public trusts which is essential to perfect tranquillity of mind." When citizens of Boston proposed to make his birthday a holiday, he wrote them that he did not approve of "transferring the honours and veneration for the great birthday of our Republic to any individual, or of dividing them with individuals," and that therefore he declined letting the date of his birth be known; and it remained unknown until some time after his death. He declined to make any public appearances. Sullivan suggested a swing around the circle, to let the people, particularly in the North, have a look at their popular President and see what he was like. He replied austerely that he was "not reconciled to the idea of a chief magistrate parading himself through the several States as an object of public gaze and in quest of an applause which, to be valuable, should be purely voluntary. I had rather acquire silent good will by a faithful discharge of my duties than owe expressions of it to my putting myself in the way of receiving them." After leaving the White House, his inveterate indisposition to placing himself in any personal way "at the bar of the public" became invincible. He never again went outside his native state; indeed, it may almost be said that he never again set foot off his own property.

With an Epicurean so strongly bent on hiding his life, not much can be done. During the campaign of 1804, Mr. Jefferson remained as usual inactive in his own behalf and silent under worse partisan defamation, if any could be worse, than was visited on him in 1800. He also kept an unsleeping eye on the political neutrality of his officeholders. Writing to Gallatin a month before the election, he mentions his fear that "the officers of the Federal Government are meddling too much with the public elections. Will it be best to admonish them privately or by proclamation?" No activity was needed, however, on any one's part; Mr. Jefferson carried every state but two. The inexorable state of Connecticut went solidly against him with nine electoral votes and Delaware with three. Two of Maryland's eleven votes were against him, and the total vote was one hundred and sixty-two to fourteen.

Undeniably he had a popular mandate; yet hardly had he begun to look about him in his second term before he saw signs of disaffection. He had for a year been anticipating something of the kind. In 1803 he wrote Gallatin that he suspected trouble in Pennsylvania "between the moderates and highflyers," and he predicted that "the same will take place in Congress whenever a proper head for the latter shall start up." Sure enough, John Randolph, after a period of restlessness, broke with him, and drew some other Republican leaders together into a small faction which, from its position as a political *tertium quid*, became known as the quid faction. Mr. Jefferson's former Vice-President, Aaron Burr, was also a prolific trouble breeder. Burr was one of the few toward whom it was temperamentally difficult for Mr. Jefferson to be strictly just. His sharp practice in securing a charter for a company in New York, nominally to provide the city with water but really to start a bank, was exactly the kind of thing that would stick in Mr. Jefferson's mind. Again, Burr's attitude toward public office during the preceding administrations, his way of showing "that he was always at market" when a high military or diplomatic appointment was pending, made a most unpleasant impression on Mr. Jefferson. Yet this distrust never degenerated into anything like personal enmity. Mr. Jefferson respected Burr's ability and, if Burr had not unexpectedly landed in the Vice-Presidency, would have given him a high appointment out of regard "for the favour he had obtained with the Republican party by his extraordinary exertions and successes in the New York election in 1800." But with the impressions that he had of Burr, "there never had been any intimacy between us and but little association." Characteristically, he treated Burr with distinguished civility, wished to be just to him, and avoided him as much as he could.

He was slow to believe that Burr's expedition was directed against the integrity of the Union, but when convinced, he behaved toward Burr with unjustifiable severity. His preceptors, Wythe and Small, might have shaken their heads gravely at their "man of science" prejudging Burr's guilt while the matter was still at issue before the court. It now seems improbable that Burr was guilty as charged. Quite possibly his advertised purpose of setting up a colonizing project on an old land grant issued to a Baron Bastrop was his real purpose, or at most, he may have contemplated ultimately some such land-grabbing enterprise as was carried out in 1836 by Houston. It is at all events certain that Mr. Jefferson's confidence in General Wilkinson, his principal informant, was misplaced. Probably therefore, Burr's trial resulted accidentally in substantial justice, notwithstanding its character of sheer travesty. The spirit of Mercutio may indeed have given an unconscious import to the action of a mob in Baltimore, which at the close of this discreditable performance burned in effigy both Burr and the presiding judge, John Marshall.[1]

Foreign relations involved Mr. Jefferson in further factional difficulties. England and France were again at war, each trying to draw in the United States against the other; England, moreover, according to her invariable policy, trying at the same time to cripple the rising commercial power of a potential rival. Both nations vigorously exercised piracy against American trade, leaving Mr. Jefferson's margin of choice a narrow one. War with both powers was out of the question; war with either was highly inadvisable at the time, since it meant not only a great debt, but an impracticable interruption of the policy of domestic development. "If we go to war now," Mr. Jefferson wrote Monroe, "I fear we may renounce forever the hope of seeing an end of our

---

[1] The mob also burned in effigy Luther Martin, one of Burr's counsel, an able jury lawyer and a mighty devotee of strong drink; and also Blennerhassett, the amiable amateur of music and chemistry, whom fate so sadly victimized through his casual acquaintance with Burr. The handbill inviting the public to this event is worth reproducing for the sake of its literary quality. It has been reprinted several times for other purposes, but perhaps never before for the sake of delighting a reader with the superb force and raciness of its style:

AWFUL!!!

The public are hereby notified that four choice spirits are this afternoon to be marshalled for execution by the hangman on Gallows Hill, in consequence of sentence passed against them by the unanimous voice of every honest man in the community. The respective crimes for which they suffer are thus stated in the record:

1. Chief Justice M———, for a repetition of his X. Y. Z. tricks, which are said to have been much aggravated by his strange capers in open court under pleas of irrelevancy.

2. His Quid Majesty, charged with the trifling crime of wishing to divide the Union and farm Baron Bastrop's grant.

3. Blunderhassett, chemist and fiddler, convicted of conspiracy to destroy the tone of the public fiddle.

4th and last, but not least in crime, Lawyer Brandy-Bottle, for a false, scandalous and malicious prophecy that before six months Aaron Burr would divide the Union.

N.B. The execution of accomplices is postponed to a later day.

national debt. If we can keep at peace eight years longer, our income, liberated from debt, will be adequate to any war, without new taxes or loans, and our position and increasing strength put us *hors d'insulte* from any nation." Any increase in the national debt, or any slowing up of its discharge, meant just so much strengthening of exploiting power directed against the producer. After the battle of Trafalgar, he saw that war with England was coming, but he was for holding off for a fair prospect that "by war we should take something and lose less than at present." Perhaps, too, if the United States persisted in passive neutrality, self-interest might induce the belligerents to stop their depredations on American trade; they might see that by sweeping American trade off the ocean, they hurt themselves more than they hurt the United States. Meanwhile, one of two things might be done. The administration might give formal notice of the state of war in Europe and proclaim that every American ship that left its native waters did so at its own risk. Instead of this, Mr. Jefferson proposed a measure wholly subversive of the principle of liberty and fraught with far more serious economic consequences and with political consequences at least as serious. In fact, the most arbitrary, inquisitorial, and confiscatory measure formulated in American legislation up to the period of the Civil War was the Embargo Act.

The agrarians bore its hardships with fair patience, and the other producing interests displayed a good measure of fortitude, but the capitalist, industrial, and trading interests went into paroxysms of indignation. In the long run, the act worked out far better for these latter than for the producing interests, but their view of its incidence was as short as Mr. Jefferson's own. The difficulty of enforcement was immense. "The Embargo law is certainly the most embarrassing one we have ever had to execute." Mr. Jefferson wrote naïvely to Gallatin, "I did not expect a crop of so sudden and rank growth of fraud and open opposition by force could have grown up in the United States." Its political consequences were easily predicable. "Our Embargo has worked hard," Mr. Jefferson wrote to Short. "It has in fact Federalized three of the New England States." It did worse than that; it brought a threat of secession, under which Congress repealed the measure, the repeal to become effective on the day that its author retired from the Presidency. "I yielded, with others," Mr. Jefferson said, "to avoid a greater evil." But he never lost faith in the policy of the Embargo, and seems never to have had an inkling of its economic unsoundness. He was aware in 1808 that "should neither peace nor a revocation of the decrees and orders in Europe take place, the day can not be distant when the Embargo will cease to be preferable to open hostility." He was also aware that since the Embargo had been running fifteen months, the loss in exports came to more than the cost of war, "besides what might be got by reprisal." This consideration helped somewhat in reconciling him to the repeal. Nevertheless he persisted in believing that a continuance of the Embargo for two months longer would have effected its purpose and would have averted the War of 1812.

IV

Mr. Jefferson's imperfect sense of the economic causes that lie behind political development did not permit him to foresee the shift of his adversaries to their permanent stronghold in the judiciary. Yet this shift was natural and inevitable. All that could be done through the legislative and executive branches had been done. The thing now necessary was to develop a central instrument of political power which should be permanent, independent of the elective principle, and able to overrule it when, as happened in 1800, a popular majority should vote itself into control of these branches and administer them into inimical courses. The power of the Federal judiciary was available as an instrument of absolutism, and to it accordingly the monopolist and exploiting interests of the country immediately took recourse.

Even after the fact, Mr. Jefferson was slow to get the bearings of this shift, and their economic rationale, indeed, he never got. Even in the last year of his life, he wrote about the subject with a simplicity almost naïve: his view of the process was so clear, and yet his understanding of its purpose remained so limited. "At the establishment of our Constitutions the judiciary bodies were supposed to be the most helpless and harmless members of the Government. Experience, however, soon showed us in what way they were to become the most dangerous; that the insufficiency of the means provided for their removal gave them a freehold and irresponsibility in office; that their decisions, seeming to concern individual suitors only, pass silent and unheeded by the public at large; that these decisions, nevertheless, become law by precedent, sapping little by little the foundations of the Constitution and working its change by construction, before any one has perceived that the invisible and helpless worm has been busily employed in consuming its substance."

Nothing could be clearer than this view of the dangers of centralization in government and that of the judiciary as a centralizing agency. If this process went on, he saw plainly that the condition of Americans would be "as in Europe, where every man must be either pike or gudgeon, hammer or anvil. Our functionaries and theirs are wares from the same workshop, made of the same materials and by the same hands." In 1800 he wrote Granger of his belief that "a single consolidated government would become the most corrupt government on earth"; and twenty-one years later he remarked to Macon that "our Government is now taking so steady a course as to show by what road it will pass to destruction, to wit: by consolidation first, and then corruption, its necessary consequence. The engine of consolidation will be the Federal Judiciary; the other two branches the corrupting and corrupted instruments." He also wrote William Johnson in 1823 that there was no danger he apprehended so much as "the consolidation of our Government by the noiseless and therefore unalarming instrumentality of the Supreme Court. This is the form in which Federalism now arrays itself, and consolidation is the present principle of distinction between Republicans and the pseudo-Republicans, but real Federalists."

But *why?* What was the substantial motive of this surreptitious movement toward centralization? Mr. Jefferson was almost in full view of it when he observed to Granger in 1800, "What an augmentation of the field for jobbing, speculating, plundering, office-building and office-hunting would be produced by an assumption of all the State powers into the hands of the General Government!" Twenty-five years later, with almost his last breath, he speaks to Giles of those who "now look to a single and splendid Government of an aristocracy founded on banking institutions and moneyed corporations, under the guise and cloak of their favoured branches of manufactures, commerce and navigation, riding and ruling over the plundered ploughman and beggared yeomanry." Here he comes plump upon the essential fact of a government fashioned for the distribution of wealth by political means rather than by economic means—for the economic exploitation of one class by another. But he did not recognize this fact when he saw it, for in his next sentence he reverts to his old bugbear—"This will be to them a next best blessing to the monarchy of their first aim, and perhaps the surest stepping-stone to it!" Yet the only conceivable practical gain by monarchy is absolutism, and if absolutism can be effected quite as well by the native mechanism of a Federal judiciary, why trouble to import the foreign mechanism of monarchy?

Yet, though his mind never correctly interpreted it, his instinct somehow felt this essential fact as the one that justified his opposition to a strong centralized government. It is mere idleness to think of the author of the Embargo Act as a doctrinaire enemy of strength in government. It is quite as idle to think of one who wrote as Mr. Jefferson did repeatedly in 1787 about the coercion of the states under the Articles of Confederation as a doctrinaire enemy of centralization. If the Articles were not specific enough, he was for construing them quite as loosely as John Marshall himself might have done. "The coercive powers supposed to be wanting in the Federal head, I am of opinion they possess by the law of nature which authorizes one party to an agreement to compel the other to performance." His instinctive objection was not to strength, but to irresponsibility; not to centralization in itself, but as an engine of exploitation. He never failed in respect to his old doctrine that "the people who constitute a society or nation [are] the source of all authority in that nation"; that they properly exercise that authority on the elective principle, as far as it will go, and then on the principle of revolution; and that "the people are the only censors of their governors." In purchasing Louisiana and in the matter of the Embargo, he had acted as an elected agent, answerable for the exercise of discretion in extraordinary circumstances. If the people did not like what he had done, they were "free to transact their common concerns by any agents they think proper; to change these agents individually, or the organization of them in form and function, whenever they please." His exercise of power in laying down the Embargo Act and in the unexampled severities of its enforcement was the act of a strong central authority, but a responsible authority. With the eye of instinct he saw a great difference between this and a progressive insidious refashioning of government with intent to nullify the elective principle and abrogate official responsibility— and all for the final purpose of putting the legality of economic exploitation forever beyond the reach of both.

His second term was a steady fight against this process. He saw the judiciary, led by "a crafty chief judge who sophisticates the law to his mind by the turn of his own reasoning," made up of nonelective officers installed for life and answerable to none— for impeachment, as he found in the case of Justice Chase, was "not even a scarecrow"—he saw these functionaries "construing our Constitution from a co-ordination of a general and special government to a general and supreme one alone. This will lay all things at their feet." When the case of *Marbury vs. Madison* was cited in the Burr trial, he took the ground that the material point in the Supreme Court's decision—the point that Constitutional interpretation was a fixed function of the court—was a "gratuitous opinion" on a hypothetical matter not properly within the contemplation of the court and was therefore not law. "The judges in the outset disclaimed all cognizance of the case, although they then went on to say what would have been their opinion had they had cognizance of it. This, then, was confessedly an extra-judicial opinion, and as such, of no authority." He moreover gave notice that, if need be, he would meet the court's encroachments with his old weapon of nullification by the executive. "I should be glad therefore," he wrote the Federal prosecutor in charge of the proceedings against Burr, "if in noticing that case you could take occasion to express the determination of the Executive that the doctrines of the case were given extra-judicially and against law, and that their reverse will be the rule of action with the Executive."

But he always lost. The Chief Justice's "twistifications in the case of Marbury, in that of Burr and the Yazoo case, show how dexterously he can reconcile law to his personal biases." They showed more than that; they showed how completely the Chief Justice was in the economic tradition of the Fathers. His decisions in these cases, with his subsequent decisions in the cases of McCulloch, Dartmouth College, and Cohens, made the economic system of the United States, which was contemplated by the Constitution, formulated by Hamilton, put in operation by the administrations of Washington and Adams, forever impregnable.

v

"The present principle of distinction between Republicans *and the bseudo-Republicans, but real Federalists.*" One may pause upon these words. In his reflections on the schisms and defections that took place in his second term, discovering himself so much alone in his resistance to the surreptitious structural refashioning of the government, Mr. Jefferson, like Hamilton, failed to reckon with one most important effect of the cohesive power of public plunder. With America opening as the land of unprecedented monopolist opportunity, men would of course be impelled to get out of the producing class and into the exploiting class as quickly as possible. It was not hard to foresee a time when, for instance, the greatest producing industry of the country, agriculture, would be exploited to the point of bankruptcy as an industry, leaving the rise in land values as the only source of profit to the agriculturists. Nor, considering the tendency just mentioned, would it be hard to predict that the political will of the landowning agriculturalists themselves would be chiefly responsible for this breakdown. Mr. Jefferson never seemed aware that the prospect of getting an unearned dollar is as attractive to an agrarian as it is to a banker; to a man who owns timber or mineral deposits as it is to one who owns governmental securities or who profits by a tariff. For this reason he could not understand why Republicanism almost at once became a mere name. Nothing could be more natural, however, than for Republicans who saw any chance of participation in monopoly to retain the name and at the same time resist any tendency within the party to impair the system that held out this prospect. The certain course of political development, therefore, was toward bipartisanship; nothing could stop it. Party designation would become, like ecclesiastical designation, a merely nominal matter, determined by family tradition, local or sectional habit, or other causes as insignificant as these. The stated issues between parties would become progressively trivial, and would more and more openly tend to be kept up merely to cover from scrutiny the essential identity of the parties. The effect of this upon the practical conduct of politics would precisely correspond to that which Mr. Jefferson remarked in England. "The nest of office being too small for all of them to cuddle into at once, the contest is eternal which shall crowd the other out. For this purpose they are divided into two parties, the Ins and the Outs."

Mr. Jefferson did not distinguish this process of development, even though it went on before his eyes. He had a fanciful theory of his own concerning the natural division of men into parties.

"The sickly, weakly, timid man fears the people and is a Tory by nature. The healthy, strong and bold cherishes them and is a Whig by nature." His only suggestion of an economic influence in the determination of partisanship is in a letter to Joel Barlow in 1802 and is more or less rhetorical. He there classifies "the rich and the corrupt" with the weakly and nerveless as disposed to see "more safety and accessibility in a strong executive." So far from seeing an economic interest in the factional divisions among Republicans and in their tendency to amalgamate with the Federalists, he said in 1805 that, while the divisions are distressing, they are to be expected, because "the opinions of men are as various as their faces, and they will always find some rallying principle or point at which those nearest to it will unite, reducing themselves to two stations with a common name for each."

Yet, curiously, no man ever drew a clearer picture of economic motive in party affiliation than Mr. Jefferson did in a letter to Professor Ebeling in 1795. Two parties, he said, exist in the United States:

They embrace respectively the following descriptions of persons. The anti-Republicans consist of:

1. The old refugees and Tories.

2. British merchants residing among us, and composing the main body of our merchants.

3. American merchants trading on British capital, another great portion.

4. Speculators, and holders in the banks and public funds.

5. Officers of the Federal Government, with some exceptions.

6. Office-hunters, willing to give up principles for places—a numerous and noisy tribe.

7. Nervous persons, whose languid fibres have more analogy with a passive than active state of things.

The Republican part of our Union comprehends:

1. The entire body of landholders throughout the United States.

2. The body of labourers, not being landholders, whether in husbanding or the arts.

Nothing could be more obvious than the generalizations to be made from this, but more than intelligence was needed to make them. The cooperation of the *Zeitgeist* was needed, and this was not yet to be had.

VI

Mr. Jefferson's popularity was temporarily broken in his second term, but he had recovered it at the time of his retirement. He could have been re-elected, but declined to stand. There was "but one circumstance which could engage my acquiescence in another election, to wit: such a division about a successor as might bring in a monarchist"—once more his man of straw. Otherwise, Washington's example was a good one. "If the principle of rotation be a sound one, as I conscientiously believe it to be, with respect to this office, no pretext should ever be permitted to dispense with it, because there never will be a time when real difficulties will not exist, and furnish a plausible pretext for dispensation." There was another consideration. Like many men of uncommon constitutional strength, whenever any little matter ailed him, he took it as a warning of approaching senility. "You suppose I am 'in the prime of life for rule,'" he wrote an importunate correspondent, "I am sensible I am not; and before I am so far declined as to become insensible of it, I think it right to put it out of my own power." He had the satisfaction, too, of knowing that Madison was the kind of successor "to whom I shall deliver the public concerns with greater joy than I received them."

He went back to Monticello quietly and contentedly, with no pride in his achievements in office and with a detached point of view upon the prospects for their continuance. John Adams, in one of his moments of greatness, which were many, wrote him in 1813 that "your character in history may easily be foreseen. Your Administration will be quoted by philosophers as a model of profound wisdom; by politicians, as weak, superficial and shortsighted." Well, possibly; something of the sort might turn out to be true—who can tell? But why attempt to anticipate the definitive judgment of a long future? In the realm of the spirit as in the realm of affairs, Mr. Jefferson's outlook was always sincerely practical. "We have set a good example," he said, and more than that he was not disposed to say. As for the ensuing course of public affairs, he was aware that "in every government on earth is some trace of human weakness, some germ of corruption and degeneracy, which cunning will discover, and wickedness insensibly open, cultivate and improve." One might always hope—indeed, it is one's duty to do that—but expectations are inadmissible. "A government regulating itself by what is just and wise for the many, uninfluenced by the local and selfish views of the few who direct their affairs, has not been seen, perhaps, on earth. Or if it existed for a moment at the birth of ours, it would not be easy to fix the term of its continuance. Still, I believe it does exist here in a greater degree than anywhere else, and for its growth and continuance I offer sincere prayers."

CHAPTER VII

Recommencements

I

Reaching Monticello in the middle of March, "having found the roads excessively bad, although I have seen them worse," Mr. Jefferson immediately wrote a letter to his successor in the White House, giving him news of the great world of reality outside the realm of politics. "The spring is remarkably backward" is his first observation to the man who was facing the problems of possible war with Old England and possible secession in New England. "No oats sown, not much tobacco-seed, and little done in the gardens. Wheat has suffered considerably. No vegetation visible yet but the red maple, weeping willow and lilac. Flour is said to be at eight dollars in Richmond, and all produce is hurrying down." War or no war, secession or no secession, men must live, and the only way the means of life can be produced is by "labouring the earth" in vigilant cooperation with the sunshine, the air, and the rain.

Mr. Jefferson at once set about picking up the sadly raveled odds and ends of his farm work, laying out his flowerbeds and gardens, and indulging his extravagant passion for architecture, both at Monticello and on his new house at Poplar Forest, in the county of Bedford. Monticello was really never finished; probably it was never meant to be finished, but to be kept as a kind of standing challenge to the ingenuity of its owner. "So I hope it will remain during my life," he is reported to have told a visitor, "as architecture is my delight, and putting up and pulling down, one of my favourite amusements." About the first thing he had done to occupy the "rural days in summer" which the sinecure of the Vice-Presidency afforded him, was to tear down the whole top story of Monticello and rebuild it as a votive offering to architectural style. Two weeks after his inauguration into that "honourable and easy office," he speaks of this discomposing performance with an enthusiasm which those in charge of his housekeeping may not have shared. "I have begun the demolition of my house, and hope to get through its re-edification in the course of the summer."

His interest in landscape gardening and architecture began early, and its principle was as practical as that of all his interests, whether in the realm of the flesh or of the spirit. This principle appears in his travel notes, already quoted, for the European tour of Shippen and Rutledge in 1788. Architecture, he says there, is worth great attention because the doubling of America's population every twenty years means doubling the number of houses; "and it is desirable to introduce taste into an art which shows so much." Houses, grounds, and towns should be planned with an eye to the effect made upon the human spirit by being continually surrounded by a maximum of beauty. Mean and hideous surroundings—in other words, surroundings that reflect a low, commonplace, or eccentric taste—have a debasing and dehumanizing effect upon the spirit. Cultivation of the instinct of beauty, therefore, is a primary practical concern, not only of the moralist but of the statesman; and especially so under a form of government which makes no place for the tutelage of an aristocracy.

Hence Mr. Jefferson seems always to have had a greater aesthetic delight out of the cultivation of art than out of contemplating it. "Here I am," he playfully wrote the Comtesse de Tesse from Nîmes, in 1787, "gazing whole hours at the Maison Quarrée, like a lover at his mistress. The stocking-weavers and silk-spinners around it consider me a hypochondriac Englishman about to write with a pistol the last chapter of his history." Yet, most of his interest was that of a participant; what he really saw with his mind's eye was a copy of the building, to be set up in Richmond from his own model, as the new state capitol. A non-participating interest in art never touched him deeply. He left but a brief record of his admiration for certain pieces of sculpture, and of painting he says almost nothing. As he told Shippen and Rutledge, America could do little with these arts; they were as yet "too expensive for the state of wealth among us. . . . They are worth seeing but not studying." Yet, when he saw them, it was to good purpose. Writing to Macon, in 1816, concerning the costume for a statue of Washington, he recommended the Roman style, remarking with point that "our boots and regimentals have a very puny effect."

But Americans must have houses; many of them must live in towns; many even of those in towns would have grounds about their houses. Here were practical opportunities for the exercise and cultivation of taste. It was therefore with a different and deeper emotion that he carefully studied the radial plan of cities, the lay-out of notable grounds and gardens, and that "while in Paris I was violently smitten with the Hôtel de Salm, and used to go to the Tuileries almost daily to look at it" and to renew the delightful experience of constructive conjecture concerning the accommodation of this or that architectural quality to the circumstances of the new land. He found, however, that he was in these respects rather out of the current of popular sentiment in America. He was well aware that "the first object of young societies is bread and covering," and made allowances accordingly; but beyond that lay the great preoccupation with turning the immense resources of the country into money as quickly as possible—and these factors of necessity and greed together put a heavy discount on any devotion to the arts, no matter how practical its purpose. An interest in art marked one as alien, a dawdler and effeminate, and not quite to be trusted in the serious businesses of life. Mr. Jefferson felt the force of this discriminative sentiment and once at least, attempted to vindicate himself against it in the eyes of an old friend. His enthusiasm for the arts, he wrote Madison in 1785, was one "of which I am not ashamed, as its object is to improve the taste of my countrymen, to increase their reputation, to reconcile to them the respect of the world and procure them its praise." But his countrymen cared little for having their taste improved. *Carpe diem!*—the thing was to grow rich as possible as quickly as possible, while yet one might. If ever art were wanted, one could always buy it. Nor were they interested in any enhancement of the world's respect and praise; whatever of these was not purchasable was negligible.

Hence it came to pass that in 1785 Mr. Jefferson was found pleading his bitter mortification at the news from Virginia that "the first brick of the Capitol would be laid within a few days," without waiting for the designs which he, in conjunction with the great Clerissault, had taken such devoted pains to work out from the model of the Maison Carrée. What could the Virginians be thinking of? These designs, he wrote distressfully to Dr. Currie, "are not the brat of a whimsical conception never before brought to light, but copied from the most precious, the most perfect model of ancient architecture remaining on earth." His standard was that of Socrates. An ardent innovator, and indefatigable experimenter and improver, he yet believed that the practical starting point in art is always with that which represents the longest experience and the greatest collective wisdom—τὰ πολυχρονιώτατα καὶ σοφώτατα τῶν ανθρωπίνων. The Maison Carrée "has obtained the approbation of fifteen or sixteen centuries, and is therefore preferable to any design which might be newly contrived." Changes and adaptations were always admissible; but their value likewise was not to be appraised contemporaneously, but by the collective experience of posterity.

His plans ought to have at least a fighting chance in competition for the suffrage of the Virginia legislature. "Pray try if you can effect the stopping of this work," he wrote Madison. "The loss will be only of the laying the bricks already laid, or a part of them. . . . This loss is not to be weighed against . . . the comfort of laying out the public money in something honourable, the satisfaction of seeing an object and proof of national good taste, and the regret and mortification of erecting a monument of our barbarism." The legislature thought he was making a great fuss over a small matter, but, like the unjust judge, finally let him have his way. They had some formal pride in their distinguished fellow citizen, notwithstanding his residence in Paris had apparently alienated him a little too much toward the exotic fripperies of a light and notoriously immoral people. So at last they carried his plans "into execution, with some variations, not for the better, the most important of which, however, admit of future correction."

While yet in his twenties, Mr. Jefferson made some rather elaborate notes of his ideas for the planning of a large property. These ideas were never carried out; the record of them is valuable only as marking the initial step in a painstaking development of taste. Perhaps the notes relating to the layout of a "burying-place" are as much worth citing as any, and they have a little additional interest because they show some trace of the emotion caused by the death of a young sister, Jane, whom he seems to have loved,

in his inward and difficult fashion of loving, all his life. The bury-
ing place should be

among ancient and venerable oaks; intersperse some gloomy ever-
greens. The area circular, about sixty feet diameter, encircled with
an untrimmed hedge of cedar, or of stone wall with a holly hedge
on it. . . . In the centre of it erect a small Gothic temple of antique
appearance. Appropriate one-half to the use of my own family, the
other of strangers, servants, etc. Erect pedestals with urns, etc., and
proper inscriptions. The passages between the walls, four feet wide.
On the grave of a favourite and faithful servant might be a pyramid
erected of the rough rockstone; the pedestal made plain to receive an
inscription. Let the exit of the spiral . . . look on a small and distant part of the Blue Mountains. In the middle of the temple, an
altar, the sides of turf, the top of a plain stone. Very little light, perhaps none at all, save only the feeble ray of a half-extinguished lamp.

Then follows an epitaph upon his sister, which even the native
language of elegiac inscription cannot quite liberate from a pinch-
ing constraint:

> Ah! Joanna, puellarum optima,
> Ah! aevi virentis flore praerepta,
> Sit tibi terra levis;
> Longe, longeque valeto.

But in the America of 1771, if one wished to indulge a cultivated taste in architecture and its allied arts—or indeed, in any
art—one pretty well had to work out the practical side of it for
oneself. One had to be largely one's own architect, designer, drafts-
man, master builder, and decorator; and the resources available
for self-education were extremely scanty. When Mr. Jefferson was
a student at William and Mary, he made the most of the few
works on architecture to be found in Williamsburg and later he
imported others, more or less taking a shot in the dark at their
serviceability. By the time he left for Paris, in 1784, he had in his
library about a dozen books on the subject. By favor of instinct,
luck, good sense, management, or whatever combination of all
these graces, he succeeded in eluding the great peril which be-
sets the *Autodidakt* to the end of his life and, oftener than nine
times out of ten, lays him low, namely: the inability to appraise
and grade one's authorities, the tendency to accept whatever appears on the printed pages as authoritative, even though its in-

trinsic recommendations may be quite specious. Thus Mr. Jefferson managed to keep clear of an undiscriminating rabbinism on the one hand and an eccentric neology on the other.

His friends soon discovered his proficiency and saw to it that he had plenty of practice. He designed houses for the two Madisons and for Monroe, among others, and one for his daughter Martha. He drew plans for several public buildings in Virginia, some of them of a rather special character—a prison, an Episcopalian church at Charlottesville, two county court houses, and the quadrangle of a university. He sketched two plans for the White House, one of which was submitted anonymously in the competition. Existing remains of his work show that he was competent to do anything that a professional architect can do; he could draft preliminary studies, make working plans, full-size details, and specifications. His farm book contains a series of minute and interesting observations on materials, most of which still have value.

He originated the rectangular layout of city streets with alternate blocks of park space, recommending this design particularly in the case of the Southern cities which were scourged with yellow fever. "Take, for instance, the checkerboard for a plan," he wrote Volney. "Let the black squares only be building squares, and the white ones be left open in turf and trees. . . . The atmosphere of such a town would be like that of the country, insusceptible of the miasmata which produce yellow fever." In this, obviously, he did not reckon with the ineluctable factor of realty values. He was lukewarm about the radial plan on which Washington was laid out, proposing instead that the streets should be "at right angles as in Philadelphia, and that no street should be narrower than one hundred feet, with footways of fifteen feet." The main trouble with the radial plan was the difficulty of avoiding fantastic and unsightly buildings at the flatiron corners. The French Revolution, however, had bred a great fear of mobs, which gave general favor to the radial plan. The *ronds-points* or "circles" of Washington are reminiscent of that fear; they were put there in order that soldiers drawn up in them might have full command of the streets in case of any popular uprising. Mobs had been busy in a small way in Philadelphia in the stirring days of the Jacobin clubs and Citizen Genêt; there should be no barricades in Washington.

II

On his last journey from Washington to Monticello, Mr. Jefferson met with a great and irreparable loss. He had sent some of his heavy freight around by water, and by direst misfortune the one trunk containing his Indian vocabularies was broken open and ransacked by thieves. His interest in the Indian tongues began in boyhood. "The Indians were in the habit of coming often and in great numbers to the seat of government [at Williamsburg] where I was very much with them. I knew much the great Ontasseté, the warrior and orator of the Cherokees; he was always the guest of my father, on his journeys to and from Williamsburg. I was in his camp when he made his great farewell oration to his people, the evening before he took his departure for England . . . his sounding voice, distinct articulation, animated action, and the solemn silence of his people at their several fires, filled me with awe and veneration, although I did not understand a word he uttered." His acquaintance with the Indians having begun in this way, he "acquired impressions of attachment and commiseration for them which have never been obliterated." He admired their anarchist polity and their highly integrated sense of manners; it was his observation of these that put into his mind the great idea that in so far as mankind needs any kind of government at all, it should be governed by customs rather than by laws. He lamented the effect of the "interested and unprincipled policy of England" and subsequently even more that of Anglo-American mercantilism upon these fine developments; foreseeing, as he wrote von Humboldt, that "the confirmed brutalization, if not the extermination of this race in our America is therefore to form an additional chapter in the English history of the same coloured man in Asia, and of the brethren of their own colour in Ireland, and wherever else Anglo-mercantile cupidity can find a twopenny interest in deluging the earth with human blood." At the time of writing his *Notes on Virginia*, his speculations had led him to consider a probable kinship of the Indians with the Eastern Asiatics; certain resemblances between them "would induce me to conjecture that the former are the descendants of the latter or the latter of the former, excepting indeed the Esquimaux," who, he thought, may have come originally from the northern parts of Europe by way of Greenland.

Regarding language as "the best proof of the affinity of nations which can ever be referred to," he proposed to collect tribal vocabularies, "preserving their appellations of the most common objects in nature, of those which must be present to every nation, barbarous or civilized, with the inflections of their nouns and verbs, their principles of regimen and concord." But this, again, was one of the things that one must do for oneself if it were to be done. "Very early in life, therefore, I formed a vocabulary of such objects . . . and my course of life having given me opportunities of obtaining vocabularies of many Indian tribes, I have done so on my original plan." At the time of his retirement in 1809, he had amassed about forty of these; and after they were scattered by the thieves, no more than a few fragments were ever recovered.

In a philological enterprise of this kind, "our reward must be the addition made to the philosophy of language." As a rule, Mr. Jefferson took a pretty strictly practical view of language as little more than something whereby one gets oneself understood. "I do not pretend that language is science. It is only an instrument for the attainment of science." The chief object of learning a language is to get a command of its literature, and the earlier one gets at languages, the better, since getting at them is so largely a matter of memory. "In general, I am of opinion that till the age of about sixteen we are best employed on languages." Still, the rule was not invariable; he had done most of his own learning of living languages after sixteen. One might do a great deal with languages at any time of life, if one but kept at it. Industriousness, as he remarked to Martha in one of his strange preachments to her while she was at school in Paris, begets a sense of the abundance of time and thus, more than anything, holds off the approach of age. "No person will have occasion to complain of the want of time who never loses any. It is wonderful how much may be done if we are always doing." So, when he was past thirty, and the members of the new Continental Congress were looking one another over with curiosity, and gossiping a bit about one another, John Adams wrote that "Duane says that Jefferson is the greatest rubber-off of dust that he has met with; that he has learned French, Italian, Spanish, and wants to learn German." With German, however, he never got far, perhaps seeing little practical use to be made of it. There are in existence one or two scraps of interlinear translation that he made from the German, not well done or even well copied: not well enough to indicate any great amount of care or interest.

Falle	doch	auf	Doris	augenlieder
Fall	oh	on	Doris's	eyelids
Holder	schlaf	leicht	wallend	sanft	hernieder
Gentle	sleep	light		soft	down

Hence his great contemporary Goethe, in whose workaday philosophy he might have found so much to his own mind—not the author of *Faust* or of the *Wahlverwandtschaften*, certainly, but the real Goethe of the *Conversations*, the Goethe who said that *die Zeit ist unendlich lang*—remained unknown to him. What an affinity of spirit, one cannot help thinking, would this libertarian practitioner of taste and manners have found with one who formulated the profound truth that *Alles was unsern Geist befreit ohne uns die Herrschaft über uns selbst zu geben, ist verderblich!* Although Mr. Jefferson never spoke any language but English except on a great pinch, and with no care for anything beyond making himself understood, he seems to have been unable to manage German even to that extent. While traveling in Germany, he made note of having heard that near Duisberg there were "remains of the encampment of Versus, in which he and his legions fell by the arms of Arminius (in the time of Tiberius, I think it was) but there was not a person to be found in Duysberg who could understand either English, French, Italian or Latin. So I could make no inquiry." Probably he never had the opportunity to pick up the vernacular by the ingenious and timesaving method which he employed to some extent in learning colloquial French, and which he recommended to his son-in-law, advising him to board in a French family where there were children: "You will learn to speak better from women and children in three months than from men in a year."

He defended the study of Greek and Latin on grounds which have rather a curious turn of practicality; though if anyone cared to maintain that these literatures are but an apparatus of intellectual luxury, he raised the pertinent question why luxury in science may not be "at least as justifiable as in architecture, painting, gardening, or the other arts." He reinforces this large view, however, by observing that "the utilities we derive from the remains of the Greek and Latin languages" are, among others, "first, as models of pure taste in writing"; and he adds with penetration, that "without these models we should probably have continued the inflated style of our northern ancestors, or the hyperbolical and vague one of the East." To get all this benefit, however, one had to have a certain amount of *Grundlichkeit*, and a due interest in the structure of language. So, in his latter days, when he had returned to an undistracted occupation with Greek and Latin literature, Mr. Jefferson wrote at great length to Edward Everett, in opposition to the doctrine of Buttman, who "goes with the herd of grammarians in denying an ablative case to the Greek language." All Buttman's pretended datives are ablatives, for good and sufficient reasons, carefully set forth and expounded. One may have too much *Grundlichkeit*—so much that it makes hay of one's common sense. "By analyzing too minutely, we often reduce our subject to atoms, of which the mind loses its hold."

In 1813, having resumed correspondence with John Adams, Mr. Jefferson gave him one day a few lines of Theocritus, by way of apposite quotation in a letter. It drew from Adams the whimsical complaint, "Lord! Lord! What can I do with so much Greek? When I was your age, young man, that is, seven or eight years ago, I felt a kind of pang of affection for one of the flames of my youth, and again paid my addresses. . . . It was to little better purpose than writing letters on a pail of water." This, however, was but a playful pretense, for his range of classical culture and his depth of scholarship were almost equal to Mr. Jefferson's. Some time later, "to compensate in some measure for this crazy letter," [1] John Adams sent Mr. Jefferson an essay on

---

[1] It is impossible to resist quoting the portion of this "crazy letter" which deals with the celebrated Mlle de l'Espinasse. One hears in it the voice of the best in a culture which sought its end so largely "through a process of moral reasoning," speaking to the best in a culture which sought the same end through the practice of taste and manners. This may be the place to say also that whoever wishes disinterestedly to know what manner of men John Adams and Mr. Jefferson were cannot do better than begin with their correspondence of 1812-1826. This alone will carry a reader a long way if he has any literary experience and a fair power of constructive imagination. Unhappily, this correspondence is as yet only to be picked out piecemeal from the standard volumes of "collected works." The Bobbs-Merrill Company deserves praise for a thin volume of extracts put out under the editorship of Mr. Paul Wilstach. As far as it goes, it could probably not be improved, but it goes only far enough to remind a reader of Oliver Twist's rations in the workhouse and the paternalism of Mr. Bumble. Perhaps the recent increase

the correct pronunciation of Greek. Mr. Jefferson replied with a letter amounting to a small treatise, summarizing the results of an investigation of the subject which he had made in Paris with the help of some cultivated Greeks whom he stumbled upon and promptly laid under contribution. He shows his reasons for having given up the Italian method of pronouncing Greek in favor of a more modern method, though he accounts with much force and ingenuity for a few exceptions that he insists on in the case of certain diphthongs. Even here his interest has a practical end in view. Acknowledging that "the whole subject is conjectural," he is nevertheless glad "to see the question stirred" in America. Nothing which starts the human mind going to good purpose is to be disregarded; even this matter, which appears academic, may very well "excite among our young countrymen a spirit of enquiry and criticism, and lead them to more attention to this most beautiful of all languages."

It is possible that his German went derelict in behalf of Anglo-Saxon, which he took up primarily to qualify himself as a "man of science" in law, in his early days when he pored over the "old

of interest in the literature of that period will touch the flinty heart of some publisher and induce him to let the world once more see, in accessible and convenient form, the best that the period could do.

February 23, 1819.
"As you were so well acquainted with the philosophers of France, I presume the name and character of Mlle. de l'Espinasse is not unknown to you.

"I have almost put my eyes out by reading two volumes of her letters, which, as they were printed in 1809, I presume you have read long ago. I confess I have never read anything with more ennui, disgust and loathing; the eternal repetition of *mon Dieu* and *mon ami, je vous aime, je vous aime éperdûment, je vous aime à la folie, je suis au désespoir, j'espère la mort, je suis morte, je prends l'opium,* etc., etc.

"She was constantly in love with other women's husbands, constantly violating her fidelity to her own keepers, constantly tormented with remorse and regrets, constantly wishing for death, and constantly threatening to put herself to death, etc., etc., etc. Yet this great lady was the confidential friend of M. Turgot, the Duke de la Rochefoucauld, the Duchess d'Enville, M. Condorcet, the only lady who was admitted to the dinners which Mme. Geoffrin made for the literati of France and the world, the intimate friend of Mme. Boufflers, the open, acknowledged mistress of the great d'Alembert, and much admired by Marmontel.

"If these letters and the fifteen volumes of de Grimm are to give me an idea of the amelioration of society and government and manners for France, I should think the Age of Reason had produced nothing better than the Mahometans, the Mamelukes or the Hindoos, or the North American Indians have produced in different parts of the world."

dull scoundrel" Coke under George Wythe. The subject stayed
in his mind so well that latterly he wrote a good monograph on
it for the benefit of some young men at the University of Virginia who were studying under his guidance. His instruction in
Anglo-Saxon seems to have been rather popular, for in speaking
of his renewed interest in the subject as "a hobby which too often
runs away with me," he says that "our youth seem disposed to
mount it with me, and to begin their course where mine is end-
ing." He proposed an interesting simplification of Anglo-Saxon,
which might lessen "the terrors and difficulties presented by the
rude alphabet and unformed orthography" and make it a regular
part of a common English education. Why give Anglo-Saxon so
formidably learned a form, mounting it "on all the scaffolding of
the Greek and Latin," and loading it with the impedimenta of
imputed paradigms. What were the facts? Simply that our ancestors did so little with either reading or writing that they had no
fixed orthography. To represent a given sound, "every one jumbled
the letters together according to his unlettered notion of their
power, and all jumbled them differently." The thing to do, therefore, is to drop the superfluous consonants and give the remaining
letters their present English sound; "because, not knowing the
true one, the present enunciation is as likely to be right as any
other, and indeed more so, and facilitates the acquisition of the
language."

Macpherson's *Ossian* came his way when he was about thirty
years old and nearly swept him off his feet. "I am not ashamed
to own that I think this rude bard of the North the greatest poet
that has ever existed." Nothing would do but that he must learn
Gaelic. It so happened that a relative of the ingenious Macpherson had once been in Virginia and to him accordingly Mr.
Jefferson wrote posthaste a letter full of enthusiasm for the great
literary discovery. "Merely for the pleasure of reading his works
I am become desirous of learning the language in which he sung,
and of possessing the songs in their original form." Would Mr.
Charles Macpherson look into the matter and see what could be
done about forwarding a Gaelic grammar and dictionary, and
having a manuscript copy made of the Gaelic originals? Money
was no object. "The glow of one warm thought," he says finely,
was worth any outlay of money and trouble. One is reminded
again of the largeness and lucidity of Goethe, himself a devoted
student of natural science, who yet could perceive that "a teacher

who can arouse a feeling for one single good action, for one single good poem, accomplishes more than he who fills our memory with rows on rows of natural objects, classified with name and form." Charles Macpherson replied with an agreeable and somewhat canny letter. There was very little literature that could be sent over: some odds and ends of religious matter, possibly, but no grammar or dictionary. Gaelic was a spoken tongue, its uses passing from mouth to mouth; it would be quite difficult for a foreigner—and so forth. Mr. Jefferson broke off his quest after Gaelic. The Revolution interrupted it in the first instance, and no doubt also his ardor was dampened by the general suspicion that his favorite poems were a literary hoax. Yet his pleasure in *Ossian* always stood steadfast. "If not ancient," he wrote stoutly to Lafayette in 1823, "it is equal to the best morsels of antiquity." The practical function of poetry is, after all, as Hesiod said, to furnish "a release from sorrows and a truce from cares." If a poem did that, what matter whether it were written by this hand or by that?

In his views of literature generally, Mr. Jefferson's sense of beauty and his sense of practicality operated in good balance. The exception was in English poetry; there his sense of beauty did not quite hold its ground, and in consequence, his repertory of favorite English poems is on the whole prosaic and dissatisfying, and the few ventures which he made in original English verse are much more so. He copied lyrics occasionally all his life. In the case of those set to music, his choice was of course largely affected by the setting; but the others reflect no very sound or discriminating poetic taste. Yet in 1813 he wrote John Adams a long criticism on the unpoetic quality of Tate and Brady's metrical translation of the Psalms. Even the best English version, which he thinks to be that of "the Octagonian dissenters of Liverpool," is bad, "not a ray of poetical genius having been employed on them." In themselves, these strictures imply no great amount of discernment—almost anyone would make them—but in their context, probably, they have some significance. They are an *obiter dictum* on some praise which Adams had bestowed on the hymn of Cleanthes to Jupiter. Mr. Jefferson admitted the high poetic quality of this hymn, but thought the Psalmist should have "the palm over all the hymnists of every language and of every time," and that this superiority was manifest even when apprehended through the medium of a humdrum and jogtrotting translation.

Literary style interested him, but purism did not. "I readily sacrifice the niceties of syntax to euphony and strength," he told Edward Everett. Thus he was as far from the utilitarian or wheelbarrow theory of written style as he was from purism. He was enough of a musician to know that one should write for the ear as well as for the eye. "Fill up all the ellipses and syllepses of Tacitus, Sallust, Livy, etc., and the elegance and force of their sententious brevity are extinguished." He had a strong sense of the power of words and felt that much of this power lay in precision. "I am not scrupulous about words when they are once explained." Hence he was always "a friend to the encouragement of a judicious neology; a language can not be too rich." While new words should be allowed to make their way freely, there should be no interference with one's reverent regard for the stupendous resources of the English language and for the immeasurable privilege one has in possessing a native use of them. "It is much to be wished," he wrote in the last year of his life, "that the publication of the present county dialects of England should go on. It will restore to us our language in all its shades of variation. It will incorporate into the present one all the riches of our ancient dialects; and what a store this will be may be seen by running the eye over the county glossaries, and observing the words we have lost by abandonment and disuse, which in sound and sense are inferior to nothing we have retained."

He quite early anticipated the growth of an American variant of English and took issue with the Edinburgh Reviewers on their assumption that such a development would be a culpable adulteration. In his observations on this, he clearly intimates the discrimination to be made between the development and the degeneration of a living language. "Certainly so great growing a population spread over such an extent of country, with such a variety of climates, of productions, of arts, must enlarge their language to make it answer the purpose of expressing all ideas, the new as well as the old. . . . But whether will these adulterate or enrich the English language? . . . Did the Athenians consider the Doric, the Ionian, the Aeolic, and other dialects as disfiguring or as beautifying their language? Did they fastidiously disavow Herodotus, Pindar, Theocritus, Sappho, Alcaeus, as Grecian writers? On the contrary, they were sensible that the variety of dialects, still infinitely varied by poetical license, constituted the riches of their language and made the Grecian Homer the first of poets, as he must ever remain until a language equally ductile and copious shall be spoken."

III

"I think," wrote Mr. Jefferson to a young relative who was making choice of studies in college, "it is lost time to attend lectures on moral philosophy. He who made us would have been a pitiful bungler if He had made the rules of our moral conduct a matter of science. For one man of science, there are thousands who are not. What would have become of them?" The moral and religious nature of man presents many attractive problems to the metaphysician, but Mr. Jefferson had a pretty clear conviction, in the first place, that these problems are insoluble and, moreover, that their solution, even if one might attain it, would have so little bearing on the practical conduct of life that speculation about them had best be left to those who have nothing better to do. In these matters, it is interesting to see how completely, without being aware of it, he is in the tradition of such English churchmen as Whichcote, Jeremy Taylor, and Thomas Wilson. No doubt he was unacquainted with them, as he was unacquainted with Goethe; yet he was an independent and powerful continuator of their thought. The human sense of religion and morals "is submitted indeed in some degree to the guidance of reason; but it is a small stock which is required for this, even a less one than what we call common sense." First and last, one must be practical; this sense was meant to bear strictly on practice; and, as Bishop Wilson acutely said, while the practical truths of the Gospel are clear, no Christian need complain of a want of light. The worst of speculative system making was that it tended to interfere with practice; the tenets of these systems were inert. Mr. Jefferson was wholly with Whichcote in perceiving that "too many scholars have lived upon air and empty nothings; falling out about nothings, and being very wise about things that are not *and work not*." Furthermore, it was easy to assent to a speculative system, while a practical obedience to one's native sense of conduct was extremely hard—χαλεπὸν, Pittacus said, χαλεπὸν ἐσθλὸν ἔμμεναι—and therefore the tendency was to make the one do duty for the other. Mr. Jefferson had had a bitter experience of this in his collisions with the monstrous systematization of intolerance inculcated upon colonial Virginia by the Church of England.

"Why have Christians," he mused in 1776, "been distinguished above all people who have ever lived, for persecutions? Is it because it is the genius of their religion? No, its genius is the reverse. It is the refusing *toleration* to those of a different opinion"— toleration, which was of the essence of moral and religious practice. In this there is a distinct echo of Jeremy Taylor's insistence that "it is keeping the unity of the spirit in the bond of peace, and not identity of opinion, that the Holy Spirit requires of us."

Mr. Jefferson's repugnance to metaphysical system making and its resultant separatism was so strong that he kept fastidiously clear of all contact with the subject. "I not only write nothing on religion," he said in 1815, "but rarely permit myself to speak of it, and never but in a reasonable society." His experience of the Dwights, Smiths, and Masons of the period has satisfied him concerning the religious character bred by the official organization of Christianity, and therefore he was content to tell Dr. Ezra Stiles in 1819 that he was "of a sect by myself, as far as I know." Each person's particular convictions or principles "are a subject of accountability to our God alone"; it was quite enough for others to stay within the line laid down by Jesus and judge the tree by its fruits. It was a fair inference that if a life "has been honest and dutiful to society, the religion which has regulated it can not be a bad one"; and any attempt at a scrutiny closer than this was inadmissible. The worst thing for religion, indeed, was contention about it; therefore "it is a matter of principle with me to avoid disturbing the tranquillity of others by the expression of any opinion on the innocent questions on which we schismatize." Once more he is completely in Whichcote's penetrating view that "nothing is worse done than what is ill done for religion; that must not be done in defence of religion which is contrary to religion."

In the purview of teleology, especially, Mr. Jefferson was keenly aware of the vanity and viciousness of speculative constructions. He seldom spoke about his beliefs concerning the final destiny of man, and the little that he imparted to his more intimate correspondents is in a vein more nearly akin to the calm and profound thought of Marcus Aurelius than to post-Augustinian Christianity. The word *unimpassioned* is worth remarking in his suggestion to Mrs. John Adams in 1817, that "perhaps one of the elements of future felicity is to be a constant and unimpassioned view of what is passing here." A year later, he tells John Adams that presently "we shall only be lookers-on," and that *sub specie aeternitatis,* "we may be amused with seeing the fallacy of our own guesses, and even the nothingness of those labours which have filled and agitated our own time here." One might hazard such words to the Adamses, or to Edward Rutledge, or to good old conscientious John Dickinson, who would have liked the half-cooked omelette of demi-semi-independence back in 1776, but who could not bring himself to break any eggs by signing the Declaration. But the Reverend Isaac Story, dallying with a theory of the transmigration of souls, was another matter. "It is not for me to pronounce on the hypothesis you present. . . . When I was young, I was fond of the speculations which seemed to promise some insight into that hidden country, but observing at length that they left me in the same ignorance in which they had found me, I have for very many years ceased to read or think concerning them, and have reposed my head on that pillow of ignorance which a benevolent Creator has made so soft for us, knowing how much we should be forced to use it. I have thought it better, by nourishing the good passions and controlling the bad, to merit an inheritance in a state of being of which I can know so little, and to trust for the future to Him who has been so good in the past."

Mr. Jefferson surveyed the ancient and modern systems of moral and religious philosophy with an interesting impartiality. He considered the genuine doctrines of Epicurus as "containing everything rational in moral philosophy which Greece and Rome have left us." He drew up an excellent syllabus of these doctrines for his old diplomatic colleague, William Short, complaining of the sophistication of Epicurus at the hands of disciples and commentators, "in which we lament to see the candid character of Cicero engaging as an accomplice." Most of all, however, he felt at ease in the Christian system, again energetically discriminating against its sophistication and debasement. "There never was a more pure and sublime system of morality delivered to man than is to be found in the four Evangelists." His venerable Revolutionary compatriot, Charles Thomson, who was ornamenting a green old age by making a harmony of the Gospels, sent him a copy of his book. It then came out that Mr. Jefferson had to some extent anticipated him by putting together a *Verba Christi* in the interest of freeing this "pure and sublime system" from even the editorial comment and arrangement of the Evangelists themselves, letting it stand altogether clear of the influence of context. It was during his first term in the Presidency, he wrote Thomson, that he had employed several evenings in making "a wee-little book from the same materials, which I call the *Philosophy of Jesus*; it is a paradigma of his doctrines, made by cutting the texts out of the book and arranging them on the pages of a blank book in a certain order of time or subject. . . . If I had time, I would add to my little book the Greek, Latin and French texts, in columns side by side." He found time to do this almost at once, it appears, perhaps stimulated by Thomson's work; and he put together another book, making the four texts parallel, and styling it the *Morals of Jesus*.

IV

At the time of the Constitutional Convention, or even before, it was plain that by virtue of their superiority in mobility, in power of organization and in wealth, "the rich and well-born" would easily take command over the institutional voices of the new American society and cause them to say what they wished said; and that with this would go a rapidly developing technique of suppression and misrepresentation. It was a matter of great regret to Mr. Jefferson that no history of the Revolution, other than a mere chronology of external facts, could ever be written, "all its councils, designs and discussions having been conducted by Congress with closed doors, and with no members, as far as I know, having even made notes of them." Such records of post-Revolutionary political history as were made by Harper and Otis, for example, and by John Marshall in his biography of Washington, were only, he thought, about what might be expected: the first two, an endeavor to whitewash their party; and the last, a "party diatribe," conceived purely in an electioneering interest. Thus it was, he remarked, that "man is fed with fables through life, leaves it in the belief he knows something of what has been passing, when in truth he knows nothing but what has passed under his own eye." For what he so well called the "fan-colouring biographers" he had deep disrespect. "You have certainly practiced vigorously the precept of *de mortuis nil nisi bonum*," he wrote dryly to Patrick Henry's biographer, William Wirt. "This . . . constitutes perhaps the distinction between panegyric and history."

Yet he was aware that a long future belonged to such as these. He foresaw a protracted and diligent indoctrination of the public, an unquestioned sway of myth and legend over the popular imagination, in support of the politico-economic system of the United States. "We have been too careless of our future reputations, while our tories will omit nothing to place us in the wrong. Besides the five-volumed libel [Marshall's Life of Washington] which represents us as struggling for office, . . . the life of Hamilton is in the hands of a man who to the bitterness of the priest adds the rancour of the fiercest Federalism. . . . And doubtless other things are in preparation, unknown to us. On our part, we are depending on truth to make itself known, while history is taking a contrary set which may become too inveterate for correction." The cohesive power of public plunder, the appeal of America as the "land of opportunity" to get rich by the uncompensated appropriation of the labor products of others, by methods of speculation, monopoly, and forestalling—these would confirm contemporary history in its "contrary set." More than this, they would give direction to the whole institutional life of the country, to schools and colleges, the pulpit and the forum, to all forms of social organization, and especially to what Mr. Jefferson called the "cannibal newspapers." True, the years are never unjust, if one but reckon on enough of them—the self-preserving instinct of humanity attends to that—but while waiting for their justice, there is little else that one can do.

v

Yet, little as it might be, that little should be done. It was delightful to go on from day to day in the amiable social life of Monticello, cooperating with the august and unfailing periodicity of nature, keeping Homer and Sophocles, Tacitus and Pindar as one's intimates, playing at touch and go over the whole range of culture in one's correspondence with John Adams, Humboldt, Ticknor, Wistar, Cooper, Dupont de Nemours. It was well to enjoy the luxury of being a disinterested, irresponsible, and occasional observer of public affairs—

turbantibus aequora ventis,
E terra magnum alterius spectare laborem

—watching Madison struggle at the oar and sometimes giving him a bit of advice from the same footing of solid ground. These satisfactions were his by right; "having performed my *quadragena stipendia*, I am entitled to my discharge." One must be aware also that "nothing is more incumbent on the old than to know when they should get out of the way, and relinquish to younger successors the honours they can no longer earn and the duties they can no longer perform." When Mr. Jefferson was asked to become a candidate for the Presidency again in 1812, and when in the same year Madison asked him to go back to his old place as Secretary of State, he declined both invitations. "Good wishes," he wrote Thomas Law, "are all an old man has to offer to his country or friends." He owed his countrymen nothing, and he asked nothing of them. There is, one may be quite sure, no known instance of anyone having prosecuted a career in the service of the United States at so great personal sacrifice. He had the eminent consolation, as he wrote Count Deodati, in 1807, "of having added nothing to my private fortune during my public service, and of retiring with hands as clean as they are empty."

Yet, although in retirement, busy with the joys of a literary leisure so hardly earned, one might not be quite satisfied without giving one's waning activity some little turn for the public interest. Good wishes were not quite enough. Even for an old man, even to one's last hour, "*es ist nicht genug zu wissen*," his great German contemporary was insisting, "*man muss auch anwenden; es ist nicht genug zu wollen, man muss auch thun*." The wisdom of age, moreover, so improves the management and economy of activity and so clears and illuminates its direction that an old man with but little energy and with but little time before him should accomplish a work of more worth and permanence than could ever be done in youth. "*Wenn man alt ist*," said Goethe, again, "*muss man mehr thun als da man jung war*."

There were two public measures that Mr. Jefferson saw that he might still safely and effectively sponsor. One was for resisting centralization and promoting the principle of local self-government by the division of Virginia's counties into wards or townships. "These will be pure and elementary republics, the sum of all which, taken together, composes the State, and will make of the whole a true democracy as to the business of the wards, which is that of nearest and daily concern." If the transactions of the larger political units, which are necessarily carried on in a representative way, become "corrupt and perverted," the ward-system constitutes the people into a regularly organized power and furnishes the machinery whereby they may "crush regularly and peaceably the usurpations of their unfaithful agents." Probably not much could come of this, considering the way the country was going. "I have little hope that the torrent of consolidation can be withstood." Yet one might always try; it was just possible that in one State at least, the system might be put into effect, and that Virginia might set a good example, most of all to New England, which had the system, but was aborting its best fruit.

The second measure which Mr. Jefferson had at heart was "that of general education, to enable every man to judge for himself what will secure or endanger his freedom." This was a return to an old love. When he was employed in revising the Virginia Statutes, in 1779, he drew up a remarkable bill for a system of public schools. In the vulgar sense of the term—the sense by which anything merely indiscriminate may be called democratic—it was far from a democratic system. Mr. Jefferson's notion of the limitation of education at public expense was as explicit as his notion of a limited suffrage, which he set forth at the same time. Like his contemporary, the Iron Duke, he was well aware that it was possible for a man's education to be too much for his abilities. His bill provided that each ward in the county should have a school, open to all for instruction in reading, writing, and common arithmetic. Each year, "the boy of best genius in the school" —the girls, apparently, were out of reckoning—was to be picked out and sent to the grammar school, of which there were to be twenty, conveniently placed in the state. This élite of the primary schools should be continued at the grammar school one or two years and then dismissed, with the exception of "the best genius of the whole," who should be continued six years. "By this means," said Mr. Jefferson, "twenty of the best geniuses will be raked from the rubbish annually." At the end of six years, the best half of the twenty were to be sent to William and Mary, and the rest turned adrift. Children who paid their way might have use of the schools without restriction: this selective system showed only how far Mr. Jefferson thought the state's responsibility for free popular education should extend and the directions in which it should be discharged.

Throughout his life, Mr. Jefferson consistently maintained that "the most effectual means of preventing the perversion of power into tyranny are to illuminate as far as possible the minds of the people." He had no doubt that "if a nation expects to be ignorant and free, . . . it expects what never was and never will be." He seems never to have suspected, however, the ease with which mere literacy is perverted, and that it is therefore quite possible for a literate people to be much more ignorant than an illiterate people—that a people of well-perverted literacy, indeed, is invincibly unintelligent. His idea of literacy was mechanical, and he insisted on it mechanically; and he is thus, perhaps, as much as any one responsible for the general and calamitous overconfidence in literacy which prevailed in America unquestioned during the century that followed him. The astonishing exaggeration of his own confidence in literacy may be seen in a letter to the Chevalier de Ouis, in 1814, congratulating him upon the provision in the new constitution of Spain which disfranchised, after a certain time, all citizens who could not read and write. This, he said, "is the fruitful germ of the improvement of everything good, and the correction of everything imperfect in the present Constitution. This will give you an enlightened people, and an energetic public opinion which will control and enchain the aristocratic spirit of the government!"

VI

In his sixth annual message, Mr. Jefferson proposed the establishment of a national university, to which the élite of the whole land, according to his selective theory of public education, might resort. He suggested, though he did not precisely recommend, that this institution should get its supporting revenue from land grants, remarking that if Congress thought it should be maintained in this way, "they have it now in their power to endow it with those [lands] which will be among the earliest to produce the necessary income." He also made the interesting observation that land is the one and only imperishable security, in an economic sense, and that the income from land values is the only one whose continuity can be relied on in all emergencies. "This foundation would have the advantage of being independent on war, which may suspend other improvements by requiring for its own purposes the resources destined for them." This project, however, came to nothing. It was by no means popular; "people generally have more feeling for canals and roads than education." Since the public did not much insist on it, Congress did not move in the matter. The characteristic which John Bright remarked of the British Parliament in particular is common to legislative bodies in general; they sometimes do a good thing, but never do one merely because it is a good thing. Mr. Jefferson was aware of this. "A forty years experience of popular assemblies has taught me that you must give them time for every step you take." He therefore neither pressed the matter upon Congress nor made it an issue of popular agitation. "There is a snail-paced gait for the advance of new ideas on the general mind," he observed to Joel Barlow, "under which we must acquiesce. . . . If too hard pushed, they balk."

But one could always "set a good example"—indeed, perhaps, people are more effectively attracted by the force of example into the support of a great reform, than argued, browbeaten, or legislated into it. If the nation were not ready to establish a university, Virginia might be; so, on his retirement from the Presidency, Mr. Jefferson took up the project of a state university as "the last object for which I shall obtrude myself on the public observation." William and Mary would not answer the purpose under any kind of reorganization and renovation. As it stood, it was "just well enough endowed to draw out the miserable existence to which a miserable constitution has doomed it"—that is, its original constitution as a part of the establishment of the Church of England, which made it an object of immitigable jealousy on the part of other sects. It should be left as it was; the extension of the frontier some three hundred miles from tidewater, and the consequent shift of the center of population, called for a new institution, "not disturbing the old one in its possessions or functions, but leaving them unimpaired for the benefit of those for whom it is convenient." Again, Mr. Jefferson's own personal recollections of Devilsburg reminded him that the town was "eccentric in its position, exposed to all bilious diseases, as all the lower country is," and therefore it was by way of being progressively abandoned by all who could do so, "as that part of the country itself is in a considerable degree by its inhabitants."

On the whole, the project went better than one could have expected. The legislature of Virginia contemplated it with circumspection and diffidence, but, stimulated by the force of a considerable private subscription, rather gingerly endorsed it and made an initial appropriation of fifteen thousand dollars a year for its support. Mr. Jefferson made a felicitous choice of terms in describing his own relation to the new institution; he was the "father of the University of Virginia." He was its architect; he superintended its physical structure; he laid down its lines of organization and educational policy and directed the assembling of its faculty. These preliminaries occupied six years, and the cost of construction so far exceeded all estimates and expectations as to put Mr. Jefferson in impregnable character as a first-rate architect and also to arouse an immense amount of dissatisfaction which was promptly turned to account by those to whom, on other grounds, the project was distasteful.

Nearly all the professors were foreigners, the intention being "that its professors shall be of the first order in their respective lines, which can be procured on either side of the Atlantic." This objective view was held to imply a disparagement of sound Americanism. The university, moreover, had no official connection with organized Christianity and no chair of divinity, which gave unlimited range for the *odium theologicum* on the part of what Edmund Burke so well called "the dissidence of Dissent and the protestantism of the Protestant religion." The red rag thus deliberately unfolded was then as deliberately flourished in the face of sectarian ecclesiasticism by the appointment of Dr. Cooper to a professorship. No one could deny that Dr. Cooper was a man of first-rate ability, reputation, and character. But he had been prosecuted under the Sedition Act; his patriotism, good enough for Mr. Jefferson, good enough for James Madison, good enough for the university's Board of Visitors, had not been good enough to serve, in Dr. Johnson's phrase, as "the last refuge of a scoundrel." Besides, he was a friend of the arch heretic, Dr. Joseph Priestley, and might possibly, even probably, be a Unitarian! This was too much. All the hard, dogged, unintelligent inveteracy of official Protestantism promptly dug up the tomahawk and went on the warpath after Dr. Cooper, nor did it rest from its militant vindication of the true faith until the appointment had been canceled.

Mr. Jefferson wrote John Cartwright, the stout old British reformer, that there were "some novelties in the University of Virginia. . . . They will be founded in the rights of man." To the French philosopher, Destutt Tracy, he wrote that "this institution of my native State, the hobby of my old age, will be based on the illimitable freedom of the human mind to explore and expose every subject susceptible of its contemplation." In choosing a law professor, he wrote Madison, "we must be rigorously attentive to his political principles," in order that the student might assess "the honied Mansfieldism of Blackstone," under whose influence all the younger lawyers had already begun to "slide into toryism," not as a matter of logical conviction or intellectual persuasion, but through mere darkenings of counsel, supposing themselves all the time, indeed, "to be whigs, because they no longer know what whiggism or republicanism means!"

One can hardly wonder, therefore, that the university was not a commanding project with the legislature or the people and that appropriations sometimes stopped and at all times came hard. One wonders rather that it fared as well as it did, dedicated so explicitly to the satisfaction of nonexistent wants and to the promotion of purposes in which no one had any particular interest. Indulgence of this respectable old man and his phrases about the rights of man and freedom of the human mind, his preoccupation with a sterile nominalism, should be exemplary and to a degree punctilious, but obviously it could not be carried on forever. "The attempt ran foul of so many local interests, of so many personal views and so much ignorance, and I have been considered as so particularly its promoter, that I see evidently a great change of sentiment towards myself." Well, but if one will dance, one must pay the piper—it is only fair that one should pay. Mr. Jefferson was a distinguished man, an excellent man—a great man, if you like—but the fact remained that he had always been persistently on the side of some wholly impossible loyalty. He had always been against a hierarchy, against primogeniture and entail, against monopoly, against speculation, against every incentive, in short, which keeps alive the spirit of enterprise in the development of a great land of opportunity. Now, in the organization of the University of Virginia, he was proposing in a sense to institutionalize the spirit of his own life and of its heterodox philosophy and undertakings. Really, with the best will in the world and the utmost imaginable tolerance, what was one to do?

Yet the maintenance of the university was never too seriously threatened. "I can not doubt its having dissatisfied with myself a respectable minority, if not a majority, of the House of Delegates"; but even so, the indisposition toward Mr. Jefferson did not obscure the advantage of possessing his tradition. Certain traditions have great power of prepossession, even if they be not followed; indeed, much of the usefulness of a tradition is in the fact that it need only be possessed, not followed. In time the

University of Virginia would swing out of the shoals and back-
waters of obsolescence and into the current of a progressive national life. Meanwhile, and even afterward, the tradition of Mr.
Jefferson would have value; even his glossary of words and phrases
would have great value. Much could be done with them, even if
one were not always precisely clear about their meanings and
connotations. "The scope of words is wide," said Homer; "words
may tend this way or that way."

The first professor of Greek and Latin at the University of
Virginia was a very young Englishman by the name of George
Long. He served but a short time and then returned to take a
similar post in his own country. There was perhaps some significance, perhaps only coincidence, but at all events a singular and
felicitous fitness, in the fact that in his old age Mr. Long made
the translation of the *Meditations* of Marcus Aurelius that is
probably definitive. For many years those English readers who
knew no Greek and who yet have gained a satisfying view of
perhaps the most exquisite figure in human history have gained
it through the work of Mr. Long.

CHAPTER VIII

Advesperascit

I

WHEN he left the Presidency, Mr. Jefferson was about twenty thousand dollars in debt. His own Embargo Act had hit him hard, in common with all agrarian producers. He had accepted certain obligations of others, in addition to his own: some for his son-in-law, Martha's husband, who had sunk into despondency and inertness, and some for a friend as unfortunate as himself. Hence his later years were a continuous and unsuccessful struggle against insolvency. In a normal market, his property would have come to a total value of perhaps two hundred thousand dollars; enough to make him feel, by any kind of reasonable expectation, that his debts were not excessive, and that they were well secured —"not beyond the effect of some lopping of property," as he wrote Madison, "which would have been but little felt." But there is never a normal market for a forced sale. He even believed that in time he could have paid his debts out of income, "had crops and prices for several years been such as to maintain a steady competition of substantial bidders," and it is just possible that he might have done so. But by 1825 the screws had been put hard down on the agrarian; "a long succession of unfruitful years, long-continued low prices, oppressive tariffs levied on other branches (of industry) to maintain that of manufacturers, . . . calamitous fluctuations in the value of our circulating medium . . . had been long undermining the state of agriculture." This kind of thing was already an old story. Besides, the rich new lands of the West stood in desolating competition with the relatively poor, mismanaged, and largely exhausted lands of Virginia. Aside from use value, too, since the government permitted unlimited private ownership in these new lands and in whatever resources of minerals and timber they might be found to contain, they held out the lure of an incalculable speculative value. This also was an old story in the year 1825.

Mr. Jefferson had already sold his library. When the first Congressional Library was burned by the British in 1814, he offered his books to Congress at their own price, as the nucleus of a new collection. The Congress behaved a good deal better about this, on the whole, than one would expect. They wrangled a good deal. It was said that some of Mr. Jefferson's books were of an immoral and atheistical tendency. They had been told that his library contained one book at least, maybe more, by a man named John Locke and something by another man named Rousseau, who was thought to be a Frenchman. These were reputed to be subversive, perhaps specifically, perhaps only in a general way—they were under suspicion, at all events—and it would be a matter of evil example for the Congress to buy them and make them accessible. Furthermore, many of Mr. Jefferson's books were printed in foreign languages and therefore of no use whatever to the members of Congress. Still, for some reason, there was a good deal of public feeling in favor of the purchase; the newspapers had been very strong about it. So it was finally decided that if the library could be had at something under half price, it would probably be about the fair thing all round, and the purchase might be made. The Congress accordingly appraised the library at a little under twenty-four thousand dollars; Mr. Jefferson accepted the offer and never permitted himself to comment upon it. He threw in a catalogue and a classification for good measure gratis; and his classification remained in official use in the Library of Congress for seventy-five years.

This transaction was closed in 1815. Within the next ten years, things went into such desperate straits that in 1826—within two months of eighty-three, within six months of death, and with the responsibility of several dependents—Mr. Jefferson faced the prospect of being turned out of doors. He had only landed property, and everywhere in Virginia this had "lost the character of being a resource for debts." Buyers were few, at best; and those who might buy held off for a bottom price, knowing that the sale was forced. In these circumstances, he thought of putting a fair valuation on his property and disposing of it by lottery. This was a regular practice, "often resorted to before the Revolution to effect large sales, and still in constant use in every State for individual as well as corporation purposes." But the legislature of Virginia had taken over the licensing and regulation of lotteries, which made it necessary to move for the passage of a special act. There was no alternative, nothing else to do. "If it is permitted in my case," he wrote Madison, "my lands here alone, with the mills, etc., will pay everything and leave me Monticello and a farm, free. If refused, I must sell everything here, and perhaps considerably in Bedford, move thither with my family where I have not even a log hut to put my head into, and whether ground for burial, will depend on the depredations which, under the name of sales, shall have been committed on my property."

He accepted the bitter choice of appealing to the legislature. There were great searchings of heart about the propriety of his proposals. Lotteries were immoral, somewhat like games of chance with cards or dice. They were immoral because they offered something for nothing, which was really gambling, and gambling was wrong—wrong in a broad general sense, that is, and, admitting certain definite exceptions, like transactions in stocks and governmental securities and holding land for a rise. The legislature had grave doubts; the moral and religious sentiment of the state was very sensitive on the subject of lotteries, and this sentiment was probably sound. Its soundness or unsoundness was of little practical moment, however, for an unsound sentiment expresses itself at the polls as effectively as a sound one. Something should be done for Mr. Jefferson, no doubt. Perhaps he might accept a loan from the treasury of eighty thousand dollars, without interest, for the rest of his life. This could be managed; the proposer of this alternative might take it up tactfully with Mr. Jefferson and see how he felt about it.

It would not do. "In any case I wish nothing from the Treasury," Mr. Jefferson replied. He had always been paid the full wage of his various offices, and he could countenance no further claim on his behalf. "The pecuniary compensations I have received for my services from time to time, have been fully to my own satisfaction." Yet he had no false pride. When private persons voluntarily brought relief, he saw nothing against taking it. It was in the service of the great majority of his countrymen that he had been ruined, and when some of them came forward, in the only way they could, "to repay me, and save an old servant from being turned like a dog out of doors," he could find neither antipathy nor scruple against their "pure and unsolicited offering of love." But public money, "wrung from the taxpayer," who had no choice but to pay, was another matter, and he would have none of it. It was regrettable that the Virginia legislature saw reason to fear a compromising precedent in the proposed lottery, but he could not complain; the decision was theirs to abide by, and therefore it must be theirs to make. "I had hoped the length and character of my services might have prevented the fear in the Legislature of the indulgence asked being quoted as a precedent in future cases. But I find no fault with their adherence to a rule generally useful, although relaxable in some cases, under their discretion, of which they are the proper judges."

The interests that Mr. Jefferson had served all his life were too unorganized, immobile, and inattentive to do much for him. Their view of him was indistinct, as of one of a generation not their own. They knew in a vague way that he was supposed to have been more or less on their side, but they could hardly say how or to what extent. He had always been reputed rich, and his fellow producers, in so far as incessant preoccupation with the problems of labor and livelihood permitted them to think of him at all, still thought of him as rich; and even when his condition became known to them, what was every one's business was no one's. It was the "rich and well-born" who came to his rescue, and they were by no means out of character in doing so. The fact is interesting that while taking excellent care of their own advocates and servants, "the rich and well-born" are not often averse to doing the generous thing by a fallen enemy, if they are sure he has fallen for good and will not rise again. The moment the Eastern cities had the news that Mr. Jefferson was in straits, the mayor of New York picked up the first few thousand dollars he could lay his hands on at short notice and sent it on with the cordial assurance that there was plenty more where it came from. Philadelphia, where but a few years before people refused to speak to Mr. Jefferson on the street and turned corners to avoid a meeting with him, extemporized a similar emergency contribution, as did Baltimore and other cities. At this time, moreover, the lottery was finally sanctioned by the legislature after months of earnest lobbying; but the inflow of unsolicited gifts made it for the moment seem unnecessary, and it was never held.

Mr. Jefferson died in the belief that his debts were taken care of, and his family assured of a permanent home at Monticello. His last few weeks were therefore truly happy; as he said, his gratification "closed with a cloudless sun a long and serene day of life." But within six months most of his personal property was sold for debt, and all of it within a year. His lands were sold as soon as the depressed market would permit. His daughter and her family were turned out of their home; they received some assistance, but lived more or less poorly and precariously, getting on as best they might; and Monticello was alienated for a century, to serve as an object of idle sentiment and yet more idle curiosity to generations which its builder knew not, and which knew not him.

II

A dominant sense of form and order, a commanding instinct for measure, harmony, and balance, unfailingly maintained for fourscore years toward the primary facts of human life—toward discipline and training, toward love, parenthood, domesticity, art, science, religion, friendship, business, social and communal relations—will find its final triumph and vindication when confronting the great fact of death, "the great problem," Mr. Jefferson wrote Correa, "untried by the living, unreported by the dead." Looking back over his experience of life, he found it good; so good, so interesting and desirable, as to be well worth having over again—δὶς ἢ τρὶς τὰ καλά. "You ask," he wrote John Adams, "if I would agree to live my seventy, or rather seventy-three, years over again? To which I say, yea. I think with you, that it is a good world on the whole; that it has been framed on a principle of benevolence, and more pleasure than pain dealt out to us. There are indeed (who might say nay) gloomy and hypochondriac minds, inhabitants of diseased bodies, disgusted with the present and despairing of the future; always counting the worst will happen because it may happen. To these I say, How much pain have cost us the evils which have never happened! My temperament is sanguine. . . . My hopes indeed sometimes fail, but not oftener than the forebodings of the gloomy."

Yet though life had been good, though to relive it were desirable, in the appointed time of its relinquishment it was a thing to be relinquished willingly and with satisfaction. "Depart then satisfied," was the last great injunction that Marcus Aurelius laid upon himself, "for he also who releases thee is satisfied." In this forecast of departure there was none of the pain, the horror, and the ugliness of dying. Like a guest unexpectedly summoned from a banquet, one would rise quietly from one's place and go one's way without reluctance, glad of one's participation and in turn glad to go. "Our next meeting," Mr. Jefferson wrote Mrs. Adams, "must be in the country to which [the past years] have flown— a country for us not now very distant. For this journey we shall need neither gold nor silver in our purse, nor scrip nor coats nor staves. Nor is the provision for it more easy than the preparation has been kind. Nothing proves more than this, that the Being who presides over the world is essentially benevolent. Stealing from us one by one the faculties of enjoyment, searing our sensibilities, leading us like the horse in his mill, round and round the same beaten circle, . . . until, satiated and fatigued with this leaden iteration, we ask our own *congé*. I heard once a very old friend, who had troubled himself with neither poets nor philosophers, say the same thing in plain prose, that he was tired of pulling off his shoes and stockings at night, and putting them on again in the morning."

The last letter that Mr. Jefferson ever wrote was in acknowledgment of an invitation from the city of Washington to take part in a celebration of the fiftieth anniversary of the signing of the Declaration of Independence. In this, the wisdom which comes with death guided him into a singularly happy formulation, the clearest and most forceful that he ever made, of his lifelong contention "that the mass of mankind was not born with saddles on their backs, nor a favoured few booted and spurred, ready to ride them legitimately, by the grace of God." Then, almost at once, his last illness, which was rather a debility than an illness, came upon him. As he grew weaker, it became evident that his mind was being much revisited by events of half a century before. On the night of the third of July, he sat up in bed, went through the motions of writing, and said some words, only partly intelligible, about the Revolutionary Committee of Safety. He seemed to wish to live until the Fourth; he never spoke out plainly about it, but once or twice inquired whether it was yet the Fourth, and when told at last that it was, he appeared satisfied. He died painlessly at one o'clock in the afternoon, about five hours before his old friend and fellow, John Adams; it was the only time he ever took precedence of him, having been all his life "secondary to him in every situation" except this one.

After his death, his daughter Martha opened a paper that he had handed her two days before. It contained words which he never spoke—words which one does not speak—words of loving thankfulness for her devotion to him, declaring that the thought of parting from her was "the last pang of life," and promising to bear her love to the "two seraphs," her mother and her little sister, long shrouded in death, who now awaited him.

A

VIRO EXIMIO

EDGARDO SPEYER

HUNC LIBELLUM

PROBARI CUPIT

ALBERTUS IAIIUS NOCK

DATE DUE		
MAR 1 9 2002		
Dec 0 5 2003		